"No Sorrow like Our Sorrow"

"No Sorrow like Our Sorrow"

*Northern Protestant Ministers and
the Assassination of Lincoln*

DAVID B. CHESEBROUGH

The Kent State University Press

Kent, Ohio, and London, England

© 1994 by THE KENT STATE UNIVERSITY PRESS, Kent, Ohio 44242

All rights reserved

Library of Congress Catalog Card Number 93-31508

ISBN 0-87338-491-1

Manufactured in the United States of America

Library of Congress Cataloging–in–Publication Data

Chesebrough, David B., 1932–

   "No sorrow like our sorrow" : northern Protestant ministers and
the assassination of Lincoln / David B. Chesebrough.

      p.   cm.

   Includes bibliographical references and index.

   ISBN 0–87338–491–1 (cloth : alk. paper) ∞

   1. Lincoln, Abraham, 1809–1865—Assassination.   2. Sermons,
American—History and criticism.   I. Title.

E457.5.C48   1994

973.7'092—dc20   93-31508

                                                          CIP

British Library Cataloging-in-Publication data are available.

174403

For Terri
friend, encourager, wife

◆ ◆ ◆

Contents

Acknowledgments

No AUTHOR CAN claim solitary credit for a book. It is, therefore, important to acknowledge some of those who have been a part of the "group effort."

First on my list is the Kent State University Press. Beginning with director John T. Hubbell, the personnel of this Press has been a source of great helpfulness and support throughout the various stages of publication.

A special thanks is due to Professors Thomas Reed Turner and Ronald Rietveld, who read the manuscript and offered suggestions for its improvement. They, of course, bear no responsibilities for errors or weaknesses that may exist in the book.

During the time when the preparation of this work was in progress, I submitted portions and ideas from it to the *American Baptist Quarterly* and the *Lincoln Herald.* I am grateful to both journals for their suggestions and publication of articles related to this subject.

The staff of Milner Library at Illinois State University which has been so helpful to me on other projects, offered the same untiring service in the preparation of this book. I particularly want to thank Laura Gowdy in Special Collections and Carol Ruyle and Sharon Wetzel in Interlibrary Loans.

Finally, a big thank you to Sharon Hagan Foiles who typed the original manuscript and its various revisions. It is such a pleasure to work with Sharon; her competency is only surpassed by the delightful person that she is.

◆ ◆ ◆

Introduction

THOUGH OFTEN OVERLOOKED by many historians, sermons are important historical documents.[1] They are reflections of current thought, emotions, problems, issues, values, practices, prejudices, and beliefs. The more popular a preacher, the more likely it is that he or she mirrors the hopes and fears of a significant number of people. Paxton Hibben has written that Henry Ward Beecher, the most popular preacher in mid-nineteenth-century America, was "a barometer and record" of his times. "He was not in advance of his day," wrote Hibben, "but precisely abreast of his day." Indeed, one can trace the development of Northern thought on slavery by observing the evolution of Beecher's sermons on the same subject. In an 1845 sermon, Theodore Parker, one of the early and most vigorous antislavery clergy voices in the North, complained that his fellow ministers were not leading in the fight against slavery, that they were reflectors rather than shapers of public opinion.

> I am not inclined to attribute so much original power to the churches as some men do. I look upon them as indicators of public opinion, and not sources thereof—not the wind, but only the vane which shows which way it blows. Once the clergy were masters of the people, and the authors of public opinion to a great degree; now they are chiefly the servants of the people, and follow public opinion, and but seldom aspire to lead it, except in matters of their own craft, such as the technicalities of a sect, or the form of a ritual.[2]

Much has been written about the role of Southern preachers in legitimizing the institution of slavery and their promotion of secession and war. Though that role was considerable, it must be kept in mind that the Southern clergy was really enforcing and giving divine sanction to what was already in the Southern mind. Richard E. Beringer and his colleagues, after reflecting upon the vital role of Southern preachers in those years surrounding the war, observed: "But one should not presume that the clergy controlled or that they duped the people; if anything, they reflected rather than molded public opinion."[3]

The sermons considered in this volume cover the seven weeks following the assassination of President Abraham Lincoln on April 14, 1865. Most of the sermons were preached on one of four dates. The first date is April 16, Easter Sunday, two days after Booth fired the gun at Ford's Theater. The sermons preached on this Sunday are rather remarkable given the brief time the preachers had to prepare them. It was Good Friday night when Booth carried out his infamous deed; Lincoln died early the next morning. People heard of the assassination sometime on Saturday, and by this time most ministers had finished, or nearly completed, the preparation of their Easter sermons. Upon hearing the shocking news of what had happened the previous night, most of the preachers put aside their Easter sermons and prepared new ones that addressed the terrible tragedy that would be occupying the minds and hearts of their congregations. Their passion and adrenaline more than compensated for the lack of preparation time. As will be observed in this volume, some of those April 16 sermons were rhetorical masterpieces.

A second date upon which many of these sermons were delivered was April 19, the Wednesday that Lincoln's funeral services were conducted in Washington, D.C. April 23, the following Sunday, was a third date upon which many of these sermons were preached. A fourth and final date upon which several post-assassination sermons were delivered was June 1, a Thursday declared by President Andrew Johnson as the Day of National Humiliation, a day to remember and honor the slain Lincoln. In a sermon on June 1, in Pottstown, Pennsylvania, John C. Thompson remarked: "With this day perhaps will close the public honors to our fallen Chief."[4]

Because the time period covered by these sermons is limited to the seven weeks following the assassination, it is important to keep in mind that the preachers' emotions were heightened and heated during this period. Time had not yet had the opportunity to apply its cooling and leveling influences. But these sermons are extremely

TABLE I
Distribution of Sermons by Dates

Date	Number of sermons
April 16—Easter Sunday, two days after the assassination	102
April 19—Wednesday, the day of Lincoln's funeral services in Washington, D.C.	91
April 20—Thursday	4
April 21—Friday, the one-week anniversary of the assassination	1
April 23—the second Sunday following the assassination	58
May 3—Wednesday	1
May 4—Thursday, the day of Lincoln's burial in Springfield, Ill.	1
May 7—the fourth Sunday following the assassination	5
May 8—Monday	1
May 14—the fifth Sunday following the assassination	1
June 1—Thursday, Day of National Humiliation marking the end of the official mourning period for Lincoln	68

333 Total*

*The dates of seven sermons could not be determined.

valuable sources for depicting the emotions and thoughts that pervaded the North in the weeks immediately following Lincoln's murder.

During those days and weeks, attendance swelled to record numbers as people flocked to the churches seeking comfort, guidance, meaning, answers, perspective, or an adequate expression of their own grief. Newspapers throughout the northern portion of the nation reported overflowing attendance at most places of worship.

April 16, the day after Lincoln's death, was Easter Sunday, the day in the church year when attendance, under normal circumstances, reached its peak. When the assassination became an added factor, many church buildings could not hold the throngs wishing to attend. Hundreds, even a few thousand in some cases, had to be turned away at various churches. "Not since the days of '57 and '58, before the war, when religious revivals had swept the land, had the churches seen such outpourings of people as on this Sunday morning. 'Black Easter,' the people called it."[5] Some churches held their services on that Sunday in convention centers, meeting halls, opera houses, or any enclosure that would hold the enormous crowds. Maxwell P. Gaddis, pastor of the Sixth Street Methodist Church in Cincinnati, Ohio, arrived at his church on the evening of April 16 to discover thousands waiting to get into a building that could not hold a fourth of their number. The multitude followed Gaddis to Mozart Hall only to find the concert hall unavailable. Eventually, Pike's Opera House became the site of worship. Gaddis spoke to over four thousand people that evening at the Opera House, and still hundreds had to be turned away.[6] The people continued to crowd the churches on April 19 and 23. After that the numbers began to decrease but still ran far ahead of normal attendance figures. On Thursday, June 1, the Day of National Humiliation, once again many of the churches were filled and overflowing.

In preparing this work, I read and analyzed 340 sermons. After reading the first 100 sermons, I noticed that the same patterns began to emerge. The New England states (Connecticut, Maine, Massachusetts, New Hampshire, Rhode Island, Vermont) comprise a total of 96 sermons, or 28.2 percent of all the sermons observed. Midwestern states (Illinois, Indiana, Iowa, Kansas, Michigan, Nebraska, Ohio, Wisconsin) contribute 54 sermons for 15.9 percent of the total. Sermons from New York and Pennsylvania total 137 sermons for 40.3 percent, though several of the sermons from these two states are from their western parts, which, at that point in history, were more midwestern in nature than eastern. The three sermons from the Confederate states of Louisiana, Tennessee, and South Carolina are considered Northern sermons: those from Louisiana and Tennessee were delivered by Union chaplains, and the sermon from South Carolina was preached by a visiting Northern clergyman. Thirteen Protestant denominations are represented in these sermons. In some instances

TABLE 2
Distribution of Sermons by States

State	Number of sermons	Percentage of total
New York	86	25.3
Massachusetts	58	17.1
Pennsylvania	51	15.0
Ohio	19	5.6
New Jersey	19	5.6
Illinois	14	4.2
Maryland	12	3.5
District of Columbia	10	3.0
Connecticut	10	3.0
Maine	10	3.0
Michigan	7	2.1
New Hampshire	7	2.1
Indiana	6	1.8
Rhode Island	6	1.8
Vermont	5	1.5
California	4	1.2
Wisconsin	4	1.2
Missouri	3	.9
Iowa	2	.6
Delaware	1	.3
Kansas	1	.3
Kentucky	1	.3
Louisiana	1	.3
Nebraska	1	.3
South Carolina	1	.3
Tennessee	1	.3
	340	

the denomination of a minister could not be determined. Allowing for that, the numbers of preachers from each denomination are as follows: Presbyterian, 86; Congregationalists, 55; Episcopalians, 41; Methodists, 38; Baptists, 26; Unitarians, 26; Reformed Dutch, 13; Lutheran, 7; Universalist, 6; Swedenborgian, 3; Evangelical Reformed, 2; German Reformed, 1; and Christian, 1.

Two criteria were used in the selection of these sermons: they were Protestant and they were delivered by preachers who were Northern in orientation. Sermons were then chosen on availability. Catholic and Jewish sermons were excluded because there were so few available.[7] The denominational and geographic representation of sermons will not necessarily correspond to actual population demographics; for while thousands of post-assassination sermons were preached, most of them never found their way into print and, thus, have not survived. These sermons that remain are, for the most part, from those who pastored large urban churches and / or financially secure congregations. Only such congregations could afford to rush their ministers' sermons into print, and only pastors of such churches were able to draw the necessary attention that resulted in the publication of their discourses.

How was it that these sermons found their way into print? The pattern was almost always the same. Soon after the sermon was delivered, a delegation of men (always and only men) would either write to or visit the minister, telling him how impressive his sermon was and asking him to allow them the privilege of putting the discourse into print. After proper protestations of modesty and unworthiness, the preacher acceded to the request. The following is a fairly typical example of the process. On June 7, 1865, a written request signed by ten men was delivered to John C. Thompson, pastor of the Presbyterian church in Pottstown, Pennsylvania.

Rev. and Dear Sir: Being deeply impressed and highly delighted with your able and eloquent discourse of Thursday morning, commemorative of the virtues of our late illustrious and martyred chief magistrate, and feeling assured that by asking a copy of it for publication, we express the cordial wish of all who heard it, we the undersigned most respectfully solicit a copy of said discourse, that we may give it to the public at as early a day as possible.

On the same day, Thompson replied.

> Respected Sirs:—I comply with your request, not from a feeling that
> there is anything in the discourse really worthy of publication, but only
> from a desire to place on record my position towards, and estimation of
> one whom in the future it will be deemed an honor to have appreciated
> and sustained. Thanking you for your complimentary note . . . [8]

The preachers of these sermons chose ninety-seven different biblical texts, and there were some who chose no text at all. These texts
had their sources in thirty-two biblical books. Old Testament texts
outnumbered New Testament texts by almost a three-to-one ratio
(seventy-nine to twenty-eight). The most-often-used text (seventeen
times) was 2 Samuel 3:38—"Know ye not that there is a prince and
a great man fallen this day in Israel?" Other popular texts were:

> Thy glory, O Israel, is slain upon thy high places!
> How are the mighty fallen. (2 Samuel 1:19)

> And the victory that day was turned into mourning
> unto all the people. (2 Samuel 19:2)

> Be still and know that I am God; I will be exalted among
> the heathen, I will be exalted in the earth. (Psalm 46:10)

Most of the ministers chose a single text, using it either as a theme
to be elaborated upon or as a point of departure into other areas and
themes. A few ministers had multiple texts, sometimes choosing two
or occasionally three. Daniel Rice, pastor of the Second Presbyterian
Church in Lafayette, Indiana, however, listed nine separate texts,
eight from the Old Testament and one from the New Testament.[9]

Though the ministers were Christian, it is not surprising that in
most instances they turned to the Old Testament for their texts. It is
in the Old Testament that stories of warfare and slain rulers are
found. It is in the Old Testament that the concept of a "chosen people"—a group that is favored by God over all others—is located.
The God of the Old Testament—a God who became angry and administered severe justice, even vengeance, and who urged his chosen
people to become the instruments of that wrath—was the kind of
God most Northern Protestant preachers wanted to invoke after

Lincoln's assassination. New Testament passages that spoke of love, forgiveness, turning the other cheek, and walking the extra mile were not in accord with most preachers' moods and the points they wanted to stress in their sermons. As Robert Russell Booth, a Presbyterian minister from New York City, said in his April 23 sermon, "In such a juncture our Government needed an infusion of the Old Testament severity rather than the New Testament tenderness."[10]

No sermons were found that openly opposed Lincoln or the bulk of his policies. Several preachers thought Lincoln was guilty of being too gentle toward and too lenient with Southern "traitors," even suggesting that this was a reason that he was providentially taken. Even these preachers stressed that this may have been the only real flaw in the sixteenth president's character and political-military decisions. It is well known, however, that there were several Protestant preachers in the North who had been severely critical of Lincoln's character and policies throughout the preceding four years. But these preachers chose, in the post-assassination days, to either silence their criticisms of the assassinated president or to find matters of praise concerning the slain leader. It was exceedingly dangerous to do otherwise. One Northern minister was arrested for declaring that "If Johnson pursues the same course as Lincoln, he will meet the same fate." Only after this minister explained to the authorities that what he meant was that if Johnson continued Lincoln's policies of leniency toward the Rebels they would slay him too, was he released. Ministers were forced to weigh their words ever so carefully. Robert James Keeling delivered a sermon at Trinity Episcopal Church in Washington, D.C., on the evening of April 23 and said of the circumstances surrounding his sermon: "It was delivered at night, to an intensely crowded audience tumultuous with excitement, and under circumstances connected with my parochial position and southern birth, that called for all the prudence and preparation possible." On Sunday, April 16, an exchange minister, the Reverend Massey, of Bellingham, was supplying the pulpit of the Baptist church in the village of Medway, Massachusetts. Not once during the morning service did Massey mention the assassination. Immediately after the service, the congregation passed a resolution condemning the minister for his neglect and gave him fifteen minutes to leave town.[11]

In the post-assassination days, great anger, and even violence, was directed against those in the North who seemed to harbor any sympathies for the South or appeared to derive any satisfaction from the assassination. Rhetorician Charles Stewart has noted that "a study of twenty-one newspapers published during April, 1865, revealed incidents of eighty mobbings and arrests of persons who had used 'treasonable language' (any language that was deemed disrespectful to Lincoln)." It is Stewart's observation that these figures represent only a small proportion of the actual number of mobbings that took place.

> Although in most cases those accused of using treasonous language were run out of town or sentenced to a few months in prison, some actually met death at the hands of angry crowds. Dispatches from California told of several lynchings in that state; reports from St. Louis described an incident in which three men were seriously wounded and one killed; and the editor of a Democratic newspaper in Maryland, Joseph Shaw, was killed by a mob when he returned to his home after having been warned away a few days earlier. [12]

Newspapers that had opposed Lincoln were forced to moderate their stances following the assassination. Thomas Swaim, in a sermon at the Baptist Church of Flemington, New Jersey, on April 19, quoted from the *New York Daily News* of April 17. The *News,* which had been consistently critical of Lincoln, commented on the universal sorrow over Lincoln's death: "it has rarely happened that a people have been visited with such a cause for lamentation." Swaim, responding to the comment in the *News,* said: "If this forcible expression from the leading journal of the most persistent opposition to the administration of our late president be a fair index of the feeling of the party represented, then we justly declare that a whole nation is mourning." [13]

After reading a number of these sermons, I noticed five major themes that emerged. It is the purpose of this volume to demonstrate those five themes as developed by Northern Protestant preachers in response to Lincoln's assassination. Each theme has become a chapter in this volume. Chapter 1 deals with the predominant theme of grief, which the ministers expressed in haunting and poignant eloquence.

Chapter 2 deals with the character of Abraham Lincoln. The preachers, through their sermons, elevated the slain president to an almost saintlike status. They marveled at his accomplishments, singling out the Emancipation Proclamation as his greatest deed, though several ministers thought it necessary to explain why Lincoln delayed so long in issuing it. Lincoln's character traits that received special notice and praise from the preachers were his honesty, intelligence, wit, and common oneness with the people that made him a "representative man." Lincoln's gentleness drew high praise from some clergy and reservations from others, from those who were concerned that Lincoln may have been too gentle and forgiving in dealing with the country's enemies. Another matter of concern for many preachers was that though they perceived Lincoln to be a religious man in temperament, demeanor, and speech, he had never publicly confessed his faith or joined a church. Several preachers took time to either express their concerns about this matter or to offer an apology as to why Lincoln never took these steps. The one thing that seemed to bother many preachers the most concerning Lincoln's character was his attendance at a theater the night he was killed. Why was the good Lincoln to be found at such a questionable place? In their pain over this particular issue the preachers attempted to offer their explanations.

The theme of the Northern preachers seeking to answer the question as to who was really responsible for Lincoln's murder is developed in Chapter 3. John Wilkes Booth, most preachers judged, was of little importance in the assassination process. Ultimate responsibility must be laid upon the South, or what the preachers referred to as slavery. The words of the renowned rector of Holy Trinity Episcopal Church in Philadelphia, Phillips Brooks, were typical: "I charge this murder where it belongs, on Slavery."[4] In bitter terms the preachers attacked Southern character and enumerated previous alleged Southern atrocities that culminated in the assassination of the President.

The ministers could have responded to the assassination in one of two ways. They could have stressed love (even for enemies), forgiveness, understanding, and conciliation; or they could have emphasized rage, hatred, and revenge. Most preachers chose the second alternative. Charles J. Stewart, who has studied the post-assassination sermons in some detail, has written that "the reaction of the clergy was essentially the same as that of the general public."[5] Because, in the ministers' minds, the South was responsible for Lincoln's murder, as well as a host of other crimes, most of the Northern preachers demanded swift, harsh, and uncompromising justice upon the South, especially upon Confederate political and military leaders. This is the theme of Chapter 4. Quotations from many sermons demonstrate the preachers' demands for the most severe penalties, often death, for "Rebels" and "traitors," with Jefferson Davis and Robert E. Lee receiving special scorn and condemnation. But, at the same time, the preachers took time to justify how it was that men who represented a theology of love and forgiveness could be so vindictive in their attitudes and words.

In mid-nineteenth-century America, a basic theological premise held by many was that events were Providential, that they were ordained by God. Chapter 5 observes the Northern preachers stating that even such a tragedy as the assassination was within the parameters of the will of God; and, therefore, out of that which was seemingly evil, God would bring good. The preachers struggled to explain just what that "good" might be.

Chapter 6 is devoted to the sermons' final paragraphs. It is in the conclusion of a speech that an orator supposedly reaches his rhetorical heights, and by observing these sermon endings the reader will note how eloquent and gifted these mid-nineteenth-century preachers were. By reading these sermon endings, the reader may begin to understand what was truly the most important to a particular preacher.

In the conclusion of this work, these sermons, which cover only a seven-week period, are put into a broader perspective. How does what the preachers said from April 16, 1865, to June 1, 1865, compare and contrast to what they said in the years before and after this particular period of time? How does what these sermons proclaim correspond to what others have said and written on this subject?

The Appendix contains two complete sermons from this post-assassination period, and brief biographical sketches of the authors precede these sermons, along with an explanation as to why these two particular discourses were chosen. The Bibliography contains references to approximately 340 sermons from the period under study. In most cases, something about each sermon is cited. This bibliography will be a helpful source to others who wish to conduct further research in this field. Many libraries throughout the United States contain some of these sermons on microfilm or microfiche. Two libraries that have fine collections of original copies of many of these sermons are the Milner Library at Illinois State University in

Normal, Illinois; and the Illinois State Historical Library at Springfield, Illinois. The staffs at both of these libraries are most helpful to the researcher.

Because this is a volume about sermons, sermons will be referred to and quoted from often throughout this work. The mood, eloquence, and style of the times is best captured through the words of these mid-nineteenth-century preachers themselves.

1

• • •

A Nation Grieves

When was there ever a sorrow so universal
or a lamentation so profound?

—JOHN C. THOMPSON

TO READ THE post-assassination sermons from Northern preachers is to understand something of the overwhelming, painful, and pervasive grief that hung over the Northern populace when Abraham Lincoln was killed. More than any other theme, it was grief that dominated sermons emanating from Northern pulpits. On April 16, only two days after the tragedy at Ford's Theater, Edwin B. Webb, pastor of the Shawmut Congregational Church in Boston, described the nation's sorrow in haunting and poetic terms.

> Words express nothing. . . . An eclipse seems to have come upon the brilliancy of the flag,—a smile seems irrelevant and sacreligious. Even the fresh, green grass, just coming forth to meet the return of spring and the singing of the birds, seems to wear the shadows of twilight at noonday. The sun is less bright than before, and the very atmosphere seems to hold in it for the tearful eye a strange ethereal element of gloom. . . . It is manly to weep to-day.[1]

On that same day, Henry H. Northrop, a Baptist minister from Carthage, Illinois, noted that history had recorded many sad moments, "many mournful tragedies; but none can surpass that which in a moment has plunged a great people from fervent rejoicing into the deepest grief." Edward Everett Hale, a Unitarian from Boston, contrasted the glad Easter day with the nation's gloom. "The day of a nation's grief," he said, "is the day of the church's rejoicing." Nevertheless, it was the Easter message that made the present grief more bearable. Hale continued, "But for this resurrection, this immortality of which to-day is token and symbol, such grief were intolerable."² The preachers found numerous biblical texts to support their theme of grief. Some of the most often used were:

What aileth the people that they weep? (1 Samuel 11:5)

And the victory that day was turned into mourning unto all the people. (2 Samuel 19:2)

. . . all joy is darkened, the mirth of the land is gone. (Isaiah 24:11)

All ye that are about him, bemoan him; and all ye that know his name, say, How is the strong staff broken, and the beautiful rod? (Jeremiah 48:17)

The joy of our heart is ceased; our dance is turned into mourning. (Lamentations 5:15)

The preachers knew and understood the nation's sorrow because they themselves were personally experiencing it. On that Easter Sunday, A. P. Rogers, a Dutch Reformed pastor from New York City, shared his own feelings with his congregation. "I confess to you, my brethren, that I come to you with a heavy heart to-day. Never since that fearful blow which brought desolation to my own household in the first month of my ministry here have I come to this pulpit with such a lingering step, with such a burdened spirit. . . . I confess to you that I have shrunk from meeting you in this house of God to-day."³ Speaking to his congregation at the First Baptist Church of Philadelphia on April 19, the day of Lincoln's funeral service in the nation's capital, George Dana Boardman told his listeners: "I cannot, stricken countrymen, speak long to you to-day. I trusted, last Sunday, when I gave the announcement for this occasion, that, ere this, I should have regained sway over myself. But in preparing for this solemn hour I have felt the same indescribable stupefaction that I felt on the dreadful Saturday morning." And on April 23, Presbyterian Theodore L. Cuyler was still struggling with his own emotions. He told his New York City congregation that his words on that Sunday were extemporaneous, for throughout the past few days he could not "see to write under the shadow of this overwhelming sorrow." On that same Sunday, Rufus S. Sanborn, in the Universalist Church of Ripon, Wisconsin, shared his personal feelings upon hearing the news of the assassination. "Never before, in my experience," he recalled, "did I feel the weight of so great and terrible a grief; never came there such a blinding and staggering of faith in our common humanity."[4]

Because the preachers struggled with their personal griefs, they were able to empathize with and eloquently express the nation's grief. On April 19, Henry Lyman Morehouse, pastor of the First Baptist Church in East Saginaw, Michigan, described the nation's reaction upon hearing of Lincoln's murder.

> Over the wires the tidings came: "President Lincoln and Secretary Seward were assassinated last night." Business stopped; hearts throbbed almost audibly; knots of men congregated on the streets; telegraph offices were thronged by anxious faces; and all were incredulous that such a stupendous, nefarious transaction had occurred in America. Oh! what moments of suspense were those! The nation held its breath alternating between hope and fear. Again the wires click: "President Lincoln is dead." Then it was the darkness of midnight. It is midnight yet. Laughter ceased. Trembling lips, tearful eyes, saddened countenances, and suppressed tones, evinced the unspeakable emotions of the soul. The heart of the nation had been pierced and every member became numb. Commercial life, social life, everything was stagnant; and then the nation went into mourning—"a day of gloom and darkness." Flags everywhere hung at half mast; bells everywhere tolled their mournful sounds; the land was hung in black—its homes, its places of business, its public buildings, its houses of worship. The bonfires of exultation which the night before lighted up the streets of many of our cities, as if in anticipation of the terrible event had left their ashes and blackened embers, emblems of mourning and disappointment, to be in readiness for the general sorrow. America mourns as she never mourned before.[5]

Several Northern clergymen thought the national grief to be the greatest a nation had ever experienced. Leonard Swain, in the Central Congregational Church of Providence, Rhode Island, declared that "Never was there such a national sorrow since the world began." Morgan Dix, rector of Saint Paul's Chapel in New York City, echoed: "There has been, on this side of the world, no sorrow like our sorrow, so far as we can read back the history of the men who have dwelt here."[6]

The grief expressed by black preachers in the North was especially poignant. On Easter Sunday, Jacob Thomas, at the African Methodist Episcopal Zion Church in Troy, New York, lamented:

> We, as a people, feel more than all others that we are bereaved. We had learned to love Mr. Lincoln as we have never loved man before. We idolized his very name. We looked up to him as our saviour, our deliverer. His name was familiar with our children, and our prayers ascended to God in his behalf. He had taught us to love him. The interest he manifested in behalf of the oppressed, the weak and those who had none to help them, had won for him a large place in our heart. It was something so new to us to see such sentiments manifested by the chief magistrate of the United States that we could not help but love him.

On Wednesday of the same week, another black pastor, Wallace Shelton at the Zion Baptist Church in Cincinnati, commented that "had his assassins given us [black people] the choice to deliver him or ourselves to death, we would have said, take me; take father or mother, sister, brother; but do not take the life of the father of this people."[7]

The grief over the assassination was all the greater because it stood in such sharp contrast to the exultation Northerners had been experiencing in the days immediately preceding it. On April 3, the Confederate capital of Richmond had capitulated to Union troops. On April 9, Lee and his army had surrendered to General Grant at Appomattox Court House. Earlier in the day of April 14, special ceremonies marked the raising of the American flag over Fort Sumter after a four-year absence. For all practical purposes, the long and bloody war was over, and the Union was victorious. All over the North, church bells rang, guns boomed in celebration and salute, fireworks illuminated the night sky, and parades stepped forth in big cities and small hamlets. There was continuous rejoicing, celebration, and noise making. But the celebrations stopped—immediately and hauntingly—as the news of that dreadful event on the night of April 14 made its awful way across the nation. Within a few hours, gaiety turned to gloom and depression, laughter was transformed into mourning and tears, noisy celebrations became stupefied silence. The preachers experienced and noted the contrast. The

April 16 words of E. S. Atwood, a Congregationalist minister from Salem, Massachusetts, were echoed by ministers throughout the Northern states.

> We come into the house of God this morning, under a cloud so dense, so dark, so appalling, that, like children in the night, we know not which way to turn. A week ago, and these walls rang with jubilant strains of praise for the victories we had won, and for the foregleams of peace, that shone along the path,—but to day God gives us for beauty, ashes—for the oil of joy, mourning—for the garment of praise, the spirit of heaviness. In the very hour of our triumph, a blow as terrible as it was unforeseen comes with stunning force to remind us that the brightest morning may widen into the darkest day.[8]

When the ministers looked for historical parallels, the one most often mentioned was the assassination of the Dutch prince William of Orange. Along with many other preachers, Henry H. Northrop drew the analogy that "Never since the time when the bullet of Gerard closed the earthly career of the great-souled Christian, William, Prince of Orange . . . has a people been called upon to endure a shock so horrible, so intensely painful, as this mighty American nation within the past few days." Elias Nason, in a eulogy delivered before the New England Historic-Genealogical Society in Boston, also referred to the assassination of the Dutch leader. Lincoln, he said, was "instantaneously cut down, as the magnanimous Prince of Orange, in the prime and vigor of his manhood, just at the moment when the fruition of his hopes was about to be experienced;—in cold blood, mercilessly murdered by the impitiable hand of a dastardly minion of treason!"[9]

On June 1, John C. Thompson, in the Presbyterian Church of Pottstown, Pennsylvania, asked:

> When was there ever a sorrow so universal, or a lamentation so profound? When did lifeless King or Queen or Potentate draw after them such a mighty aggregate of love and sympathy and flowing tears, as that funeral pageant silently wending its way through the country's heart? The pulse of business stands still as the procession passes. Men of all shades and nationality press forward to do it honor. The very prisoners peering through their grated cells, reverently uncover their heads as the

procession passes. Four millions of swarthy freemen send up a wail of grief as for the death of their deliverer. And look all over the enlightened world if you would take in the aggregate of sympathy. Where was the death that had ever occurred which lowered the flags of Christendom to half-mast?[10]

The clergymen affirmed that the American people were experiencing something that was very personal in the death of Lincoln. The words of Elias Nason were typical.

It is, gentlemen, a profound personal grief we feel, as when a dear old father, a beloved mother, or a brother is torn relentlessly from our breast.

It is not mourning for some great national loss only that veils our faces in the shades of woe; it is lamentation for one who has been very near and very dear to us; for one who seemed to be of the immediate circle of our own familiar friends and acquaintances; for one who had so identified himself with our own views and feelings that he seemed to be an elementary part of our own being,—bone of our bone, blood of our blood; for one so entirely with us in sympathy, in genius, in love, in action, in aspiration, that he must ever bear the august appellation of the People's Own Beloved President. Even the little children looked upon him as their own kind-hearted ruler, and they now weep in the sweet simplicity of childhood over his sacred remains.

J. B. Wentworth, a Methodist from Buffalo, emphasized the personal family relationship that many felt with Abraham Lincoln. "Somehow," he affirmed, "we all felt that he was a brother and friend to us all. Unconsciously to ourselves, we felt a deep personal interest in him, and affection for him. His great soul had drawn us to him; and now we mourn for him as though a Father or a Brother had been taken away from us." Lincoln was referred to as "father" in many sermons. On April 19 in Boston, James Reed lamented: "We all feel to-day as if a father had been taken away from us." Charles Carroll Everett, in a sermon delivered at the Independent Congregational Church of Bangor, Maine, on April 16, mourned: "Our Father is dead. . . . He has fallen, because he was so great, and so good, and so incorruptible. He has fallen and we feel ourselves orphans." In remarks on April 19, Everett continued the father theme:

. . . he was only a simple hearted, a true hearted, a tender hearted man. This is why we loved him so, and why we so mourn for him to-day. He was so near to us, that he entered into our hearts. It would be strange to one who did not know the circumstances of the case, to hear how often the word "Father," has fallen from trembling lips these few last days. "I feel," says one, and another, and another, "as if I had lost my Father," or, "as I did when my Father died." Such is the common feeling and the common word.[11]

The mourning was great, the preachers attested, because of a deep love affair between Lincoln and the people: the people loved Lincoln and knew that Lincoln loved them. On April 19, at the First Presbyterian Church in Freeport, Illinois, the Reverend Isaac E. Carey spoke of this mutual love. "The nation loved him," Carey exclaimed, "loved him as it never loved another. He was the best and greatest, the greatest because the best, the most loving, the most lovable, the most brotherly, the most fatherly man of all our rulers. . . . How remarkable the affection of the people for this man!"[12]

This affection to Lincoln pervaded the North. John E. Todd, Congregationalist from Boston, affirmed: "There is in the heart of the people a profound grief arising from a sincere and very strong attachment to President Lincoln. And well he deserved our attachment." Methodist clergyman Gilbert Haven elaborated:

Never did a great people so universally recognize and repay such love in its ruler. Never did a ruler so love his people. Cromwell loved religion first; Wellington, duty; England was the second in their heart; her people, last. Napoleon loved himself, not France; Caesar, power, not Rome; Washington, the country more than its people. All the great leaders of the Revolution, all the great living leaders, reformatory, civil, and military, are devoted to the idea that controls them: this to liberty, that to union; this, America's glory, that, her destiny; this, philanthropy, that, piety; this, justice, that, honor; this, empire, that, prosperity. Not one of them can in a peculiar, profound, and personal sense be said to love the American people. That grace they want. Not that they do not love the nation; far from it. All have, all do; but it is a general, not a special regard; an affection that reveals itself in other forms than mere love. Not so with our great President. He held every one in his heart of hearts; he felt a deep and individual regard for each and all; he wept over the nation's dead boys at Gettysburg as heartily as over his own dead boy at Washington.

And J. B. Wentworth reminded his congregation that Lincoln "was full of all charitable emotions, of all loving and kindly affections. He loved everything human. His charity embraced all mankind."[13]

This love affair in the North between Lincoln and the people—or between Lincoln and the preachers—had not always been as universal as it was following the assassination. In the election of 1860, estimates are that most preachers in the North voted for Lincoln. Some, such as the famous Henry Ward Beecher, campaigned arduously and openly for the Springfield lawyer. However, in the same election, only three out of Springfield's twenty-six clergymen voted for Lincoln. Nine of the city's clergy did not vote at all. Lincoln could not understand the motives of his community's ministers. He noted that they claimed to be believers in the Bible and God-fearing Christians, yet they seemed not to care whether slavery was voted up or down. Lincoln commented that "God cares and humanity cares, and if they do not they surely have not read their Bible aright." The lack of support from the Springfield ministers was apparently more for theological reasons than political ones. They all knew that Lincoln did not belong to any of their churches, that he was not a regular attender, and that he had never, to their knowledge, made any kind of profession of faith. A few suspected that he might be an infidel. John G. Nicolay, a trusted Lincoln secretary, commented:

The opposition of the Springfield clergy to his election was chiefly due to remarks about them. One careless remark I remember was widely quoted. An eminent clergyman was delivering a series of doctrinal discourses which had attracted considerable local attention. Although Lincoln was frequently invited, he would not be induced to attend them. He remarked that he wouldn't trust Brother ——— to construe the statutes of Illinois and much less the laws of God; that people who knew him wouldn't trust his advice on an ordinary business transaction because they didn't consider him competent; hence he didn't see why they did so in the most important of all human affairs, the salvation of their souls. These remarks were quoted widely and misrepresented, to Lincoln's injury. In those days people were not so liberal as now and anyone who criticized a parson was considered a skeptic.[14]

After Lincoln assumed office, in the early years of the war, when the tide of battle was going against the Union, some of the clergy began to criticize the policies of the administration. On August 7, 1862, Henry Ward Beecher, who had campaigned on Lincoln's behalf in 1860 and would deliver an eloquent and mournful sermon after Lincoln's death, severely denounced not only Lincoln's policies, but his character as well.

> Certainly neither Mr. Lincoln nor his cabinet have proven leaders. Fear was stronger than Faith . . . And never was a time when men's prayers so fervently asked God for a leader! [Lincoln] has refused our petition! . . . not a spark of genius has he; not an element for leadership, not one particle of heroic enthusiasm . . . We must cease looking any more to Government; we must turn to ourselves. And the time may be here when the people will be called to act with a courage beyond all precedent. After . . . reverses have come and our rulers are fugitives from the proud Capitol, should they deem the task of maintaining the sanctity and integrity of the National Soil hopeless, then this Great People . . . may yet be called to take up the despairing work and carry it to victory.[15]

The one factor as to the policies of Lincoln in those early war years that Beecher, along with many other Northern clergy, condemned the most was the administration's failure to issue a clear statement on the emancipation of slavery. In a sermon on September 7, 1862, at the First Congregational Church of Leavenworth, Kansas, James D. Liggett asked why the war was not going well for the North. He was certain that the South was in the wrong and that God did not favor their cause. Why, then, was the Union defeated upon the field of battle? The reason, he replied, was because the Union had ignored the priorities of God. The North was fighting to preserve the Union first and then, maybe, to eradicate slavery. God's priorities were precisely the other way around. "Our President has said, and all his policy has been to preserve the national life and slavery too, if he can," complained Liggett. Not until the North made the abolition of slavery its first goal would God grant victory in war. "When the nation is fit for final victory," the preacher enjoined, "[God] will grant it; and it will be signal and complete."[16]

Lincoln's issuance of the Emancipation Proclamation on September 22, 1862, which would take effect on the following January 1, silenced this particular criticism from some Northern preachers who then used their pulpits to acknowledge the significance. On October 19, 1862, Israel E. Dwinell, at the South Side Church of Salem, Massachusetts, recognized the importance of the Emancipation Proclamation for the North. Early Union defeats, he emphasized, were due to the North's reluctance to emancipate the slaves. "The cause of the war is clearly slavery," he said, "and we tried for a long time . . . to fight the war, and save sin; and God would not suffer it. . . . Now we are openly and directly on the side of God; and now we may hope for his favor." The following month, Frederick G. Clark delivered a Thanksgiving sermon at the West Twenty-third Street Presbyterian Church of New York City wherein he echoed Dwinell and many other Northern clergy by declaring that the issuance of the Emancipation Proclamation meant that God was now clearly on the Union side. The next summer, on August 6, 1863, J. E. Rankin, before the United Congregational Churches in Lowell, Massachusetts, claimed that when the Proclamation was issued, God took the war into his own hands and began to administer military defeats upon the South.[17]

The Proclamation did not, however, bring about total support for Lincoln's policies nor assurances about the progress of the war. On April 30, 1863, Byron Sunderland, at the First Presbyterian Church of Washington, D.C., expressed deep pessimism as to when the war would end. Wearied by the continued bloodshed, Sunderland complained that "The day of peace is gone from us; God only knows when, or if ever, it may return to this generation."[18] The apprehensions of Sunderland were shared by many clergy and laity throughout the North.

It is important to recall that July and August of 1864—just nine months prior to the assassination—were some of Lincoln's darkest and most difficult days as far as Northern support for him and his policies were concerned, and one can only speculate that the Northern clergy reflected this lack of support. Lincoln had been renominated by the Republican party in June after a serious challenge by his treasury secretary, Salmon P. Chase, a challenge supported by the influential journalist Horace Greeley and some other leading Republican politicians. In late June, Grant was stalled in his attempt to take Richmond, and Sherman was bogged down as he marched toward Atlanta. The loss of Union military lives was staggering, and the criticism of administration policies increased accordingly. After another political rupture between Chase and Lincoln, Chase, as he had before, offered his resignation, and this time, to Chase's surprise, the President accepted it. The liberals of the Republican party were stunned. The truth was that Lincoln could please neither wing of his divided party. The liberals criticized him for not prosecuting the war with greater vigor, for being too lenient in his plans for Reconstruction, and for not pressing the issue of black suffrage; the conservatives accused the President of failure to actively pursue peace initiatives and of placing too much emphasis upon emancipation. Lincoln continued to steer a middle course and, therefore, attracted stinging blame from both the Left and the Right.

On July 4, 1864, Gilbert Haven, a Boston Methodist, delivered the sermon "Three Summers of War." He acknowledged the continuing carnage. "We have slowly waded," he confessed, "through the third summer of blood." He knew that many in the North had grown tired of the battle and were revulsed by the mounting military casualties. Seeking to encourage his listeners to maintain the course, he reminded them of the American Revolution. Those in the fight for independence also grew discouraged and were at times tempted to cease the struggle; nevertheless, they continued the battle and the consequences were well worth whatever the price that had to be paid. Haven reminded his audience of the progress already made during the civil strife. There had been military and moral victories. The Emancipation Proclamation had been issued. Citizens had gained a new awareness of and appreciation for the Union. The Fugitive Slave Law had been abolished. This was not the time to quit. Those who fought for independence faced much greater odds, far bigger obstacles, and more deplorable conditions. Therefore, Haven concluded: "If faithful to God, He will give us victory. . . . Slavery shall die. Our foes shall be made our footstool. . . . Let us be of good courage . . . knowing that there is in store for us a more abundant recompense."[19]

Another problem arose for Lincoln in July 1864 when Congress passed the Wade-Davis Bill, which challenged the President's role in

Reconstruction. When Lincoln pocket-vetoed the bill, many Congressional Republicans were furious. Sumner complained that he was "inconsolable" and issued caustic verbal attacks against Lincoln. Wade and Davis, the bill's sponsors, responded to Lincoln's veto with a searing manifesto directed against the President. The manifesto was so caustic and bitter in nature that many who generally agreed with the point it made refused to be associated with it. In response to this volley of verbal and printed Republican broadsides, Lincoln confided to Noah Brooks, "To be wounded in the house of one's friends is perhaps the most grievous affliction that can befall a man."

Friends and foe were certain that Lincoln could not be reelected. Throughout that long, hot summer, Confederate forces under Jubal Early had threatened Washington. On July 11, the rumble of cannon fire could be heard at the White House. On August 23, Lincoln penned a memorandum in which he expressed his own doubts about his chances of being returned to office and how he could best turn over the reins of government to his successor. On August 30, a group of disgruntled Republicans, including Greeley, Winter Davis, Benjamin Butler, William Cullen Bryant, and Chase, called for a new Republican convention to gather in Cincinnati on September 28 in order to choose another nominee for their party. Just the day before, August 29, the Democrats had officially nominated Gen. George McClellan and began almost immediately to smear Lincoln with, among other things, racist slurs. Lincoln experienced the lowest point of his political fortunes and popularity.

After McClellan's nomination, William D. Potts, a clergyman and physician from Newark, New Jersey, wrote a 127-page tract in which he bitterly criticized Lincoln, along with other Republican leaders, and urged the election of McClellan. Potts, a confessed and ardent Democrat, urged a return to "Union, Peace, and Prosperity," declaring:

> That, indeed, is a momentous work, and can only be accomplished by the absolute overthrow of Abolition power as represented by his Excellency, Abraham Lincoln & Co.
>
> How can that despotic power be overthrown?
> Only, But Surely,
> By A United Democracy,
> FOR THE SAKE OF OUR COUNTRY,

In the Use of Every Laudable Measure,
For the Election of
GENERAL GEORGE BRINTON MCCLELLAN
To the Highest Office
In the Gift
of
American Freemen!

Potts recognized that most Northern clergymen supported Lincoln, and his denunciations of them were almost as severe as his accusations against the President. "We have been taught," wrote Potts, "to respect the Clergy and credit their preaching. But we are compelled to fear that Satan has assumed the ministerial office, and occupies, unmolested, a large proportion of the pulpits, spreading enmity and destruction all around."[20] (A clergyman who was singled out for special verbal assaults by Potts was Henry Ward Beecher.)

A dramatic reversal in Lincoln's fortunes occurred on September 2 when Atlanta surrendered to Sherman. That single event commenced a startling change in the Northern perception of Lincoln. Later in the same month Philip Sheridan caught Jubal Early and, in October, soundly defeated him. Military triumphs brought political rewards to the President. Former critics Chase, Davis, and Greeley made peace with Lincoln and scurried to board his increasingly popular bandwagon. In October, state elections were conducted in Indiana, Ohio, and Pennsylvania. Union candidates won close victories in Pennsylvania and impressive victories in Indiana and Ohio. Lincoln's reelection seemed assured.

Preachers were also to be counted among those who came out in active support for the reelection of the President. On October 9, 1864, O. T. Lanphear, at the College Street Church in New Haven, Connecticut, delivered a sermon in which he urged the reelection of Lincoln as the surest way to realize peace. The minister denounced a vote for McClellan, the supposed "peace candidate." "The man who casts his vote in the election now pending, in favor of a peace not won by the conquests of our armies,"announced Lanphear, "does the rebel cause more service, if possible, than he would by joining the rebel army." And in early November, five days before the election, Methodist bishop Matthew Simpson, a close friend of the President, delivered his famous war speech in New York wherein he urged the reelection of Lincoln and the defeat of McClellan. The rousing, flag-waving, patriotic address, some two hours in length, concluded with these words:

> Your Fifty-fifth Regiment carried this flag (taking up a war-worn, shot-riddled flag, which was greeted with cheers); it has been at New Dern, and at South Mountain, and at Antietam. The blood of our brave boys is upon it; the bullets of rebels have gone through and through it; yet it is the same old flag, (most enthusiastic applause, the audience rising and giving three rousing cheers) our fathers followed that flag; we expect that our children and our children's children will follow it; there is nothing on earth like that old flag for beauty, (long and loud cheering) long may those stars shine! Just now there are clouds upon it, and mists gathering around it, but the stars are coming out, and others are joining them, and they grow brighter and brighter, and so may they shine till the last star in the heavens shall fall! (Great cheering and waving of handkershiefs and hurrahing.)[21]

On November 8, Lincoln triumphed over McClellan with 55 percent of the vote and a plurality of more than 400,000. In the electoral college, Lincoln's count was even more impressive, 212–21, whereby he carried every Northern state except Kentucky, Delaware, and New Jersey. After the election, Lincoln's fortunes continued to soar as news from the field of battle reported one impressive victory after another. On December 10, Sherman had completed his trek across Georgia and began shelling Savannah. Thomas crushed Hood in Tennessee. Savannah capitulated on December 21. The end of January 1865 saw Congress passing the Thirteenth Amendment, which abolished slavery as an institution in the United States. In February, Sherman sent his troops into South Carolina, wrecking havoc upon the state that led the secession movement. April witnessed the fall of Richmond and the surrender of Lee to Grant at Appomattox Court House. The northern portion of the nation was joyfully triumphant, and Lincoln was the Union hero.

The tragedy at Ford's Theater only served to elevate and enhance the image. Martyrdom, as it so often does, secured a place and reputation for the slain leader as nothing else could have done. Many of Lincoln's harshest critics mourned his death. It became perilous in the North to speak a word against the dead president. The love of the people for the sixteenth president was nearly universal, and the preachers eloquently expressed that powerful sentiment.

This love of a people for their president, mingled with overwhelming grief, gave birth to another emotion—intense anger. George Dana Boardman commented that his grief and "horrible stupefaction" was "succeeded by most poignant bitterness of soul." Rufus S. Sanborn after saying that "never before in my experience did I feel the weight of so great and terrible a grief," went on to explain that there was also "a corresponding burning indignation," an indignation that demanded "the foul wrong and insult shall be expiated." Sanborn continued: "I tell you that the people and the nation are at a white heat of righteous indignation against this dastardly act which has lacerated millions of souls, as well as the national feelings, and now it is the time for traitors to beware! and take full warning, for the day of reckoning is come, and the great, tortured and bleeding heart of the people will no longer bear the insult borne."[22]

A few preachers, taking note of the anger that their grieving counterparts were expressing, offered words of caution. Henry H. Northrop urged: "Let us be Christians even in our wrath. Let us in all things be consistent with the religion of that meek and holy Jesus who cried out upon the cross; 'Father, forgive them, they know not what they do!' " John E. Todd was even more specific in his warning.

> There is another feeling which naturally succeeds the emotions of horror and grief; it is rage. I would not say a word to inflame the passions and exasperation which are already filling the public mind. I would rather say that which may soothe excited feelings. It is time for every man to lay upon himself a strong control. It is easy at such a time to be ungenerous and unjust. Let us discountenance all violence and passion. . . . Let us not jump hastily to the conclusion that the perpetrators of this vile deed were in the employ or the counsels of the enemy.[23]

As later chapters will demonstrate, the words of caution and warning as expressed by Northrop and Todd were exercises in verbal futility. Most Northern clergymen became primary instruments in fanning the fires of sectional discord and passionate rage, a rage that would demand harsh reprisals upon the South, especially upon its leaders, for a large catalog of traitorous acts, the assassination being only the culmination of a long list of atrocities.

2

· · ·

The Character of Abraham Lincoln

There is something greater than greatness itself.
—JOSEPH P. THOMPSON

NORTHERN PREACHERS WERE effusive in their praise of Lincoln's character, in some instances elevating him to an almost superhuman status. Edward Searing, a Congregationalist from Milton, Wisconsin, proclaimed that Lincoln was "one of the most faultless examples of true manhood ever prominently exhibited to the world. . . . while he possessed all virtues he was free from all vices." George Dana Boardman, pastor of the First Baptist Church in Philadelphia, announced that Lincoln "was absolutely incorruptible. . . . that never trod the earth a more sympathetic, unselfish, large-hearted, forgiving man than he." On April 19, Charles Carroll Everett compared the traits of Lincoln's character with the eight beatitudes enumerated by Jesus (Matthew 5:1–12). A more realistic, yet noble, ascription was pronounced by Seth Sweetser, pastor of the Central (Congregational) Church in Worcester, Massachusetts, when he said that Lincoln's "mistakes were as few and as venial as could reasonably be expected from a short-sighted mortal."[1]

The preachers were nearly unanimous in proclaiming that Lincoln was a truly great man. Abram N. Littlejohn, from New York City, preached that "If he was not great, then, by some strange fortune, it fell to his lot to achieve results hitherto deemed possible only to the highest order of faculty. If he was not great, history will have its most startling wonder to record." Littlejohn than went on to list the tests of greatness and demonstrate how Lincoln more than met these tests.[2] And on April 30 in the Broadway Tabernacle Congregational Church in New York City, Joseph P. Thompson exclaimed that "great" was an inadequate word to describe the martyred president. Lincoln was "something greater than greatness itself" Thompson said.

Not greatness but grandeur is the fitting epithet for the life and character of Abraham Lincoln; not greatness of endowment nor of achieve-
ment, but grandeur of soul. Grand in his simplicity and kindliness;
grand in his wisdom of resolve and his integrity of purpose; grand in his
trust in principle and in the principles he made his trust; grand in his
devotion to truth, to duty, and to right; grand in his consecration to his
country and to God, he rises above the great in genius and in renown,
into that foremost rank of moral heroes, of whom the world was not
worthy.[3]

Phillips Brooks remarked on April 23, while the body of Lincoln
was lying in state in the city, that there was "an essential connection between Lincoln's character and his violent and bloody death."
Lincoln's character "was the character of an American under the discipline of freedom." But, asserted Brooks, "there was another American character which had been developed under the influence of
slavery." After contrasting what he perceived as the enobling character of freedom, exemplified at its very best in Abraham Lincoln,
and the debasing character of slavery, Brooks asserted: "It was inevitable in the nature of things that two such natures living here together should be set violently against each other." Therefore, Brooks
exclaimed, "I charge this murder where it belongs, on Slavery. I bid
you to remember where the charge belongs . . . to give it to the
history of these times, that all times to come may hate and dread the
sin that killed our noblest President." Slavery, accused Brooks,
killed "the gentlest, kindest, most indulgent man that ever ruled a
State!" On April 16, Alonzo H. Quint, in the North Congregational
Church of New Bedford, Massachusetts, contrasted the traits of
Lincoln with those of the greatest Confederate leaders. The confederates may have outdistanced Lincoln in certain skills, according to
Quint, but Lincoln far surpassed them all when it came to character.
Lincoln "had not the scholarly culture of a Davis," Quint said, "but
he never perjured himself; nor the refinement of Lee, but he never
turned traitor; not the eloquence of Stephens, but he never lied."[4]
    In order to adequately portray Lincoln's character as well as his
accomplishments, several preachers included in their sermons brief
biographical sketches of the slain leader. These sketches, some of
them running six pages in length, enable the reader to perceive how
Lincoln was viewed from a short-term perspective and what his

contemporaries thought were the important aspects of his life. These sketches include some materials and information not found in several full-length biographies.[5]

Thomas Mears Eddy, a Presbyterian from Waukegan, Illinois, affirmed that there were "four grand landmarks of principle" that governed the decisions and policies of President Lincoln: an insoluble Union, a government of the people, the right of all men to freedom, and religious dependence.[6] These same four principles can be found dispersed throughout other Northern sermons.

There were many Lincoln accomplishments to which the preachers pointed. The saving of the Union, leadership in war, and his ability to unite the people in an effort to subdue rebellion were successes to which the Northern clergy referred again and again. However, towering about all other accomplishments, the preachers praised Lincoln the most for his part in the freeing of the slaves, specifically for his writing and issuing of the Emancipation Proclamation. Gilbert Haven declared that because of the Proclamation, Lincoln will "stand forth in all coming time. To him was decreed the greatest honor history has conferred on man." Samuel C. Baldridge, in a sermon delivered at the Presbyterian Church of Friendsville, Illinois, declared that "the crowning glory of [Lincoln's] life, and of this age, is the part he was permitted to take in the destruction of the system of human slavery in this land." Sidney Dean, in a eulogy delivered at the City Hall in Providence before the governor and other state and municiple authorities, affirmed that by the Emancipation Proclamation, Abraham Lincoln "made himself immortal. . . . Wherever in coming ages, liberty is known and honored, the Emancipation Proclamation of President Lincoln will be cited in proof of his heroic devotion to the rights of man." E. S. Atwood, from Salem, Massachusetts, proclaimed: "Let Abraham Lincoln be known to posterity by no other name than that of the Great Emancipator, and his fame is secure. No other man ever dared so much in such a cause." Thomas E. Bliss, pastor of the Union Church in Memphis, echoed the thought of many Northern preachers when he declared that the Emancipation Proclamation was that deed which clearly brought God to the Union side in the war. "From that hour," Bliss said, "it seems as though the frown of the Almighty in a great measure passed away. The mighty God of battles now went forth with our hosts to victory."[7]

The ministers were well aware that Lincoln had been very cautious in issuing the Proclamation, that it was midway through the war before it was issued. Several ministers had been instrumental in pressuring and persuading the President to make such a statement. Even after his death, some were critical of Lincoln's delay. Alonzo H. Quint spoke for many of his fellow pastors when he declared: "I think he was too cautious. And this illustrates one want in him, I suppose. He did not strike out boldly when the people wanted to be led." Quint did conceed, however, that once Lincoln "had decided, no power could move him a hair's breadth."[8]

Most preachers, though perhaps wishing that Lincoln had issued the Proclamation at an earlier date, nevertheless, defended his hesitency. Amory D. Mayo, on April 19, at the Church of the Redeemer in Cincinnati, emphasized that the people had to be educated before the Emancipation Proclamation could be effective.

> Why did he wait so long, almost two years, before he struck the decisive blow at slavery which has gained us the victory of arms while it has saved us a free Republic? Because the people, even in January, 1863, were hardly prepared for so great a challenge. Consider how you regarded slavery ten years, five years ago! It was a great divinity, against which we all dreaded to speak. We may have feared and hated it, but we kept ourselves respectful in its haughty presence. I believe the Emancipation Proclamation came not one day too late. Two years ago the children in our streets were throwing stones at colored women. He waited till slavery had taught the people its hideous nature by sending affliction into myriads of homes, and bringing the nation to death's door. So, when he did speak, a black cloud seemed to lift; and from that day our armies never lost a mile of territory really gained, and pressed on to final victory.

George L. Chaney, from Boston, declared that the real cause for Lincoln's delay on the Proclamation was found in his respect for the Constitution.

> The real cause of this delay, however, was his respect for the Constitution. He was scrupulously true to his oath to support that. He spoke of himself, in homely phrase, as of one who had engaged to do a job, and who felt morally obliged to do it well, according to the terms of the agreement, viz., the Constitution; and history will declare that there

never was a President who took more conscientious pains to be faithful to constitutional government.

And the Reverend Elbert S. Porter, from New York City, said that Lincoln was only able to issue the Proclamation when he could do it as a war measure. "When, however, foreign intervention became imminent," Porter declared, "the President issued as a war measure the proclamation of freedom to the slaves. . . . It was believed by the President to be necessary for the preservation of the Union."[9]

The preachers spoke much about the various traits that marked Lincoln's character. They could do this, the clerics said, because Lincoln was so transparent. There was no pretension, nothing hypocritical or deceptive about him. Joshua T. Tucker, on June 1, at the First Parish (Congregational) Church in Holliston, Massachusetts, uttered what many other preachers were saying, when he stated:

> Within the whole range of my historical reading, I know of no public character more thoroughly transparent, more readily understood than that of our late President. From the first advent of Mr. Lincoln on the political stage, until the curtain dropped so suddenly, he carried his heart (so to speak) pinned upon his sleeve, where everyone could see it, just as it was from day to day. He had no concealments.[10]

This openness, the lack of "concealments," was all a part of Lincoln's honesty, a trait the preachers called attention to again and again in their post-assassination sermons. Tucker declared that the people "felt that there was, at the head of the government, a thoroughly honest man." Pliny H. White, acting pastor of the Congregational Church in Coventry, Vermont, stated that even Lincoln's "bitterest enemies never dared to call in question his personal or political honesty." In a similar vein, the Buffalo Methodist J. B. Wentworth asserted that Lincoln's honesty "was a trait in character which everybody beheld and admired. His enemies never called it in question." Lincoln's honesty was not "of that ordinary type. . . . It was a grand and rugged honesty, befitting his great and manly soul." Charles Hammond, after remarking that Lincoln's "inflexible integrity" was his "crowning glory . . . as a ruler," complained that this quality was lacking in most politicians prior to Lincoln. Before the war, Hammond accused, "no man was elected to office by unsought suffrages except in the rarest instances." Lincoln, however, was different, trumpeted Hammond, he was a leader of "sterling honesty." Gilbert Haven emphasized that honesty was "the foundation" of Lincoln's character. The martyred president was marked by an "absence of selfishness," Haven declared, and "only one president before him seemed almost utterly free from it."

> Jefferson talked indifference, but was a ceaseless schemer and mover of political wires. . . . Adams, Franklin, Jackson, Clay, were men of great parts, but a sense of their necessity to the movements of the nation gave to their strength the weakness of men. Their personality was to them an essential element in the events of their age. Not so with Washington and Lincoln.[11]

Because the people sensed Lincoln's honesty, they trusted him. The Reverend Henry A. Nelson, in an address delivered at the Presbyterian Church of Springfield, Illinois, on May 7, the Sunday following Lincoln's burial, asked: "And which of all her heroes or sages, not even excepting that first and greatest, has this nation more deliberately and more fully trusted?" Charles Hammond declared that it was because of Lincoln's honesty; that "the people gave their unwavering confidence, and by that confidence he became strong in spite of the politicians. His presence in the seats of power, at the close of the venal administration of his predecessor, caused a dismay like that, when the money-changers were driven from the temple." Jeremiah E. Rankin summarized what most of the Northern preachers were saying about the honesty that characterized Lincoln's life and administration.

> It is a rich inheritance for the American people to have the memory of one public man in modern times who has achieved such greatness as his, without a stain upon his personal character. There are men who have risen faster than he,—men of eminent intellectual ability, who have had their eye upon the presidential chair, who have schemed and intrigued and contrived until they have succeeded in sitting there; and others who have failed, and died disappointed. But Abraham Lincoln attained the position which he occupied while living, and which he will occupy in history, by the strictest integrity, by old-fashioned, downright honesty.

"Honest old Abe," inelegant as is the phrase, was no unmeaning sobriquet. It was written all over him,—in gait and feature and dress.[12]

Another quality in Lincoln that many preachers appreciated was his intellect. Drawing special attention to the "independence" and "serenity" of Lincoln's mind, Samuel C. Baldridge proclaimed that "the first feature of [Lincoln's] greatness . . . was the power and comprehensiveness of his mind. . . . He had the eye to pierce through the maze and confusion of our affairs, and see what was to be done." Isaac E. Carey, from Freeport, Illinois, remarked that "The intellect of Mr. Lincoln was undoubtedly of a very high order. . . . I believe that very few men among our statesmen have been more nobly endowed in this respect than was our lamented President." In an extemporaneous address on April 23, Theodore L. Cuyler said that God gave Lincoln "a clear and vigorous head and a most marvelous sagacity. . . . a sagacity that never made a serious mistake." As to mental qualities, Cuyler emphasized that Lincoln "was a man who has no superiors in the American annals." Continuing, Cuyler compared the late President to other greats in American history.

> The backwoodsman of Illinois did not lay claim to Hamilton's imperial intellect, yet Hamilton never read events more sagaciously. He did not claim John Jay's profound wisdom, yet Jay never decided more wisely. He did not pretend to Daniel Webster's massive and magnificent oratory; but Webster never put more truth into a portable form for the common people.[13]

The preachers highlighted different aspects of Lincoln's intellect that they felt made his mind especially unique. Phillips Brooks declared that it was a rare combination of goodness and intelligence, heart and mind.

> It is the great boon of such characters as Mr. Lincoln's, that they reunite what God has joined together and man has put asunder. . . . Not one of all the multitudes who stood and looked up to him for direction with such a loving and implicit trust can tell you to-day whether the wise judgment that he gave came most from a strong head or a sound heart. . . . There are men as good as he, but they do bad things. There

are men as intelligent as he, but they do foolish things. In him goodness and intelligence combined and made their best result of wisdom.

Joseph P. Thompson, from the Broadway Tabernacle Church (Congregational) in New York City, said that Lincoln's "mental processes were characterized by originality, clearness, comprehensiveness, sagacity, logical fitness, acuman and strength." At Lincoln's burial service, Bishop Matthew Simpson declared: "If you ask on what mental characteristic his greatness rested, I answer, on a quick and ready perception of facts; on a memory unusually tenacious and retentive; and on a logical turn of mind, which followed sternly and unwaveringly every link in the chain of thought on every subject which he was called to investigate." Simpson continued:

> I think there have been minds more broad in their character, more comprehensive in their scope, but I doubt if ever there has been a man who could follow step by step, with more logical power, the points which he desired to illustrate. He gained this power by the close study of geometry, and by a determination to perceive the truth in all its relations and simplicity, and, when found, to utter it.

George Dana Boardman asserted that it was the comprehensiveness of Lincoln's mind that made him great. "He was not a man lustrously brilliant in any one direction," Boardman said. "No one faculty of brain markedly towered over another. But he was none the less great in that his greatness was so rounded, having less the transient dazzle of the meteor than the steady quiet sparkle of the fixed star." Lincoln's well-rounded intellect, according to Boardman, was the reason he "so rarely made mistakes." He was guided by "a system of well-nigh infallible instincts, by which he knew what he ought to do, and when to do it, and how to do it."[4]

Several preachers equated Lincoln's intellect with what they labeled as "common sense." L. M. Glover, pastor of the First Presbyterian Church in Jacksonville, Illinois, stated that Lincoln's mind "was somewhat rough, but it was massive. . . . The University did nothing for it, and it remained to the last essentially a piece of nature's work. . . . We cannot speak of it as profound; we cannot attribute to it genius; strong common sense was its predominating quality." In a similar vein, George Putnam from Boston remarked:

"It was not genius, inspiration, brilliancy: no man ever used those words in connection with his name. There was in him, the shrewdest common sense, a deep sagacity, intuitive and almost infallible, though not rapid or flashing." Morris C. Sutphen preferred the word "wisdom" to describe Lincoln's mental faculties.

> President Lincoln was not, in the ordinary acceptation of the phrase, a man of learning. He made no pretension to high literary accomplishments. Nor was he an expert in the dark sinuosities of diplomacy. Neither has he been regarded as specially proficient in statesmanship, or deeply versed in constitutional law. But if he had read little, he had thought much. If he possessed small learning, he possessed great wisdom.[15]

Though the preachers saw Lincoln as moral, wise, great, and accomplished, they did not perceive him as dour or lacking in wit. Several preachers remarked about the sense of humor that was an important part of the slain president's character. Theodore Cuyler declared that "Lincoln's humor was as natural to him as breathing. It was a happy gift. It kept his temper sweet, and lubricated his mind, that might otherwise have been worn into sullenness or into despondency by the tremendous friction of care and overwhelming anxieties." Others also spoke of Lincoln's natural gift of humor that enabled him to endure the strains and pressures of his heavy responsibilities. Denis Wortman, at the First Reformed Dutch Church in Schenectady, New York, on April 16, exclaimed:

> He had a vein of humor which marked him from all other men in his position, and lost him, perhaps, the reputation of official dignity; and yet this very humor, which in most important emergencies could not refrain from making the witty repartee or telling the pointed anecdote (always to the point), undoubtedly helped him to endure those fatigues and cares under which he would otherwise long since have sunken."[16]

Similarly, Joshua T. Tucker commented on Lincoln's humor as being "as natural as his pulse. It never could have welled up so sweetly and richly from a despot's breast. It was not levity. It betokened no indifference to his country's woes. It was often coupled with a seriousness too deep for tears. But for this escape-valve for his overworked, wearied, aching sensibilities and energies, he used to say that he should die." Andrew L. Stone, a Congregationalist from Boston, said that humor was an integral part of everything Lincoln was and did.

> This quaint, ever-ready humor was the soft cushion upon which the great burdens of his public cares impinged, covering and shielding his nerves from laceration. It saved him half the wear and tear of his official work. It kept his friends, and conciliated those who differed from him. He could convince with a smile, refute with a jest, turn the flank of heavy reasoning with this agile lightness of wit and conquer kind feeling, if not persuasion,—generally both.[17]

Joseph P. Thompson, along with several other preachers, linked the martyred president's humor with his capacity for storytelling.

> Mr. Lincoln's logic was pointed with wit, and his ethical reasoning was often set home by a pithy story. The reputation of a story-teller and a jester was turned by his opponents to his disparagement; but his stories were philosophy in parables, and his jests were morals. If sometimes they smacked of humble life, this was due not to his tastes but to his early associations. His wit was always used with point and purpose; for the boy who committed all Esop's fables to memory had learned too well the use of story and parable to forego that keen weapon in political argument.

And Gilbert Haven compared Lincoln's sense of humor to that of other renowned historical figures.

> A merry twinkle ever sat in his eyes. Ever when saddest with sorrow, a ray of this sunlight played on their salt drops. Napoleon, Luther, Socrates, Cicero, Caesar, Wesley, Franklin, Webster, many great men, were of this nature. A jest-book attributed to Cicero was current in Rome long after his death. Caesar was ever pointing his speech with these glittering specialties. Napoleon was full of mirth and jokes, even on the night before Waterloo. Their bon-mots were as brilliant as their battles. Lincoln, next to Franklin, if next, was the most famous jester of America. Each of these ever used a witty story to point an argument; and many was the laughable word uttered by the great diplomat of the Revolution, that did the people of that sad hour good like a medicine.[18]

Yet another quality the preachers saw in Lincoln was that he was a representative man, a man of the people, like the people, and at one with the people. At Lincoln's burial service, Bishop Simpson noted that one of the great traits of Lincoln's character "was his identification with the heart of the great people, understanding their feeling because he was one of them, and connected with them in their movements and life." Simpson went on to say that Lincoln's "simple" education, the fact that "he read few books," his identity with "the working masses," his home "in the growing West" all contributed to making Lincoln a man of the people, a truly representative man. This theme was emphasized again and again in the post-assassination sermons of the Northern preachers. On April 16, George Hepworth, a Unitarian from Boston, declared:

> If you should look this broad continent over to find a man who came from the people, who knew their wants and their troubles by experience; who had been educated only in the schools of the people; who possessed their confidence; who was proud of his ability to do them good; who had been led neither by scholarship nor ambition to a forgetfulness of their exact condition: in other words, if you should search this nation through to find a man who should be a true type of the America of to-day, you could not discover one so fit for the purpose as Abraham Lincoln.[19]

One of the few qualities that drew mixed reviews from the preachers was Lincoln's gentleness, his kindly disposition. The preachers were unanimous in their recognition of his gentle spirit. The words of Theodore Cuyler are typical of those spoken all over the nation in recognition of Lincoln's gentleness.

> Beneath that manly head He gave him a woman's heart. Did you ever hear that our Father Abraham ever spoke a harsh word to one of his children? Did you ever see his now dead hands stained with cruelty? With almost unlimited power entrusted to him, did he ever play "the tyrant"? He loved everybody, and wanted everybody to love him. . . . This plain homespun kind-voiced President was so near to every one of us—so like our own relative that we were wont to call him "Uncle Abe" and "Father Abraham." There was no disrespect in this; but rather a respect so deep and honest that it could afford to be familiar.

William Adams, like many of his counterparts, compared this quality to something more often found in women.

> He was the mildest and most inoffensive of men. Called by Providence to solemn and painful duty, he was always inclined to leniency. He was most tender-hearted, as gentle, by nature, as a woman. I do not recall a word of his which was intended to insult, goad, taunt, or exasperate any man; not one act which looked like unnecessary severity, bearing any resemblance to cruelty. Many acts of kindness and generosity are reported of him; for he was benignant, honest, and thoroughly conscientious. [20]

Nevertheless, there were several Northern preachers who proclaimed that Lincoln's virtue of gentleness may also have been his greatest fault. Henry J. Fox, from New York City, attested that whenever Lincoln "erred, it has been on the side of mercy." A similar thought was expressed by Henry W. Foote when he complained "that we have felt at times that he erred on the side of gentleness." And John E. Todd decided that Lincoln's "faults, for grave faults he undoubtedly had, were principally those of over-leniency and generosity," while E. S. Atwood said that Lincoln's "greatest fault" was "a heart too large and kindly—too sanguine in its trust of human nature." [21]

Several preachers proclaimed that the guilelessness and gentleness of Lincoln's spirit made it difficult for him to perceive a different kind of spirit in others, and thus he was unable to administer stern justice upon those who deserved it, most especially upon Confederate traitors. Robert Lowry proclaimed that Lincoln "was so free from bitter vindictiveness, so prone to lenient dealing even with enemies, that even the just infliction of punishment on the worst of traitors, might have been too hard a task for a nature so generous and charitable." Thomas Mears Eddy, in a sermon delivered in Waukegan, Illinois, on April 19, said that an "unsuspecting and pure" Lincoln "could not credit unmixed guilt in others, and with difficulty could he bring himself to suffer condign punishment to be inflicted." Cephas B. Crane feared that Lincoln "would subordinate his executive function to his personal sympathies; . . . would forget that God has placed the sword of retributive justice in his hands to be used; . . . would feel that the traitors had suffered enough already, and needed no further punishment; . . . would even pardon Davis and Stephens and Johnson and Lee if they should come into his power."[22]

However, not all Northern clergymen shared the idea that Lincoln erred on the side of kindness and leniency. J. D. Fulton, on April 19 at Tremont (Baptist) Temple in Boston, questioned the accusations that Lincoln was too lenient. "If he erred in leniency," Fulton asked, "did he not prove himself ready to be just, in condemning men who evidenced that they were ready to trifle with the imperilled interests of the country?" Others went on to say that Northern citizens should seek to remember and emulate the gentle spirit of Lincoln. Henry W. Foote urged: "Let not the shock of our bereavement cause us to forget the Christian spirit which breathed six weeks ago in that Inaugurel. 'With malice towards none, with charity for all.' " And Rufus Ellis, a Unitarian from Boston, implored:

> We shall have lost our noble leader indeed, if we lose his spirit, the wise and considerate mind, the excellent judgment, the tender, humane heart, that were in him; if, with all the wrongs, cruel wrongs, foul wrongs, that we have suffered as a nation, we forget that we are a Christian nation, and proceed to demand, and that, too, in the name of our gentle sufferer, measures of severity which he would never have sanctioned; so taking advantage of his dying, to thwart one of the high aims of his living.[23]

But voices from Northern pulpits that joined Ellis in a plea to follow the gentle example of Lincoln were in a distinct minority.

The preachers had much to say about the spiritual qualities, the religious dimensions of Lincoln's life. The Reverend Phineas Densmore Gurley, who had been a close friend of the Lincoln during his years in Washington, summed up those spiritual qualities in his funeral sermon delivered at the White House on April 19. After commenting on several of Lincoln's qualities, Gurley continued:

> But more sublime than any or all of these, more holy and influential, more beautiful and strong and sustaining, was his abiding confidence in God, and in the final triumph of truth and righteousness, through him, and for his sake. This was his noblest virtue, his grandest principle; the

secret, alike of his strength, his patience, and his success. This, it seems to me, after being near him steadily, and with him often, for more than four years, is the principle by which, more than by any other, he being dead yet speaketh. Yes, by his steady, enduring confidence in God, and in the complete, ultimate success of the cause of God, which is the cause of humanity, more than in any other way, does he now speak to us, and to the nation he loved and served so well.[24]

The many other ministers who knew Lincoln less well, or not at all, also felt constrained to say something about the President's trust in, dependence upon, and faithfulness to Almighty God. Hiram Sears stressed that "We have not had a President since the days of Washington who, in his public walks, seemed to have a better appreciation of this particular Scripture than himself: 'In all thy ways acknowledge Him, and He shall direct thy paths.' " Matthew Simpson remarked: "As a ruler, I doubt if any President has ever shown such trust in God, or in public documents so frequently referred to Divine aid." And Gordon Hall commented: "That he was a diligent student of the scriptures we know. That he committed his ways to God in prayer, and loved the Savior, he testified. That he rested his hope on the Great Redeemer, we believe, and that he has been called up higher,—his warfare accomplished,—the crown of the faithful bestowed upon him by the Prince of glory."[25]

Yet for several ministers there was a certain uneasiness about Lincoln's religious commitment. Because the late president had never made a public declaration of his faith, and because he had never officially joined a church, there was some expressed uncertainty about his spiritual status. Samuel C. Baldridge lamented, "It is to be bitterly regretted that he did not make a public profession of that faith in the Lord Jesus Christ, which he often confessed in private to his more intimate friends. But we will dwell with gratitude, for a moment, upon the intimations we have of his piety." Theodore L. Cuyler raised the same issue. "What was the degree of our President's heart-faith in Jesus Christ is known only to the Omniscient. He never made any public confession of his faith in the Redeemer. This I regret from my inmost heart." And Joseph P. Thompson went as far to comment that "It is said upon good authority, that had he lived he would have made a public profession of his faith in Christ." Henry A. Nelson, in a sermon delivered in Springfield, Illinois, noted that Lincoln's "name had never been enrolled on your list of communicants, and that he had never here been known as a professor of religion." However, Nelson brushed these observances aside, and along with most ministers pointed to the abundant evidence of the President's personal faith.

> But that he was an honest believer in not only theoretical, but experimental Christianity, is generally understood; and, without making more or less of the explicit professions of recent conversion which have been publicly reported of him, I may say that during the last two or three years, if not ever since his elevation to office, his published language and his public deportment have increasingly, and very decidedly impressed us as altogether becoming to a Christian. We believe that spiritual Christianity was an experience, a life, with him. So is our deep sorrow assuaged, not only by our thankful memories of his noble and useful career, and the great blessings to our country and to mankind, of which God made him the instrument but by the precious hope that he was a child of God, and an heir, through grace in Christ Jesus, of the bliss of Heaven.[26]

To assure their listeners that Lincoln was a true believer, several ministers thought it necessary to point to a specific time of conversion of the President. Albert S. Hunt, a Methodist from New York City, recited an incident that was offered as evidence of Lincoln's personal faith. It seems that shortly after Lincoln returned to Washington after delivering the address at Gettysburg, someone asked him if he loved Jesus. Hunt related that Lincoln, with tears in his eyes, replied: "When I left my home in Springfield to come to Washington, though I felt my responsibility and asked my neighbors to pray for me, I was not a Christian. When my dear boy, Willie, was taken from me, I still was not a Christian, but when I stood on the field of Gettysburg and looked upon the graves of its heroes, I gave myself to God, and now I can say that I do love Jesus." Henry H. Northrop, in a sermon delivered at Carthage, Illinois, on April 16, referred to a slightly altered version of this same event and said, "According to his own confession, Abraham Lincoln was a Christian."[27]

This account—or some version of it—of Lincoln's conversion was recited in many of the post-assassination sermons. Baptist, Methodist, Presbyterian, Congregational, Episcopal, and Dutch Reformed ministers told the story in their attempts to Christianize the assassinated Lincoln. Though the story had obviously made the rounds of various clergy circles and had been printed in religious periodicals, there remains serious doubts as to its authenticity (though I discovered only one sermon that called the conversion story into question). William J. Potter, a Unitarian from New Bedford, Massachusetts, asserted on June 1: "I do not credit the account, recently published, of an interview had with him by some Western clergyman, in which phrases are put into the president's mouth that sound very much like the exclamations heard in an excited meeting of revivalists." Other preachers supported Robert Lowry's anecdotal contention that Lincoln was most truly a Christian.

A clergyman in New York, having business with the President, sought an interview early in the morning. Being detained in the waiting-room longer than seemed to be indispensable at that time of day, he inquired the reason of the President's non-appearance. He was answered, that this hour was employed by the President in the reading of the Scriptures and prayer, and no interruption would be permitted until these sacred exercises had closed.

I am told that, a few months ago, a lady, visiting the Presidential mansion, was invited to a seat in the family carriage. In the course of the ride, the conversation turned on the subject of religion. The President was deeply interested, and begged the visitor to describe, as clearly as possible, what was that peculiar state of mind in which one might know himself to be a Christian. She repeated to him the simple story of the cross; and explained, that when a poor sinner, conscious that he could not save himself, looked to Jesus, and saw in his death a full atonement for the sinner's sins, and believed that Christ's death was accepted as a substitute for the sinner's death, he felt himself to have been delivered from Divine wrath, and to be "at peace with God through our Lord Jesus Christ." The President replied, in a tone of satisfaction, "That is just the way I feel."[28]

Most preachers, however, seemed content to acknowledge that though Lincoln was not a professed Christian, he was certainly a practicing one. Joseph A. Seiss, pastor of St. John's Lutheran Church in Philadelphia, made the point that

Though not, so far as I am informed, a professed Christian, at least not in all particulars, he was a man of decided religious turn of mind, who lived and acted in the light and influence of a practical faith. It was from religious persuasions that all his ideas were shapen, and according to which he honestly sought to settle his judgment and direct his cause, whether in matters of private life or of public policy.[29]

A matter that seemed to concern the preachers even more than the fact that Lincoln never publicly professed his faith or joined a church was the concern that he was killed in a theater. Robert Lowry referred to it as "a question which will disturb every Christian mind. . . . We would have had it otherwise. Pulpits will speak of it." And speak of it they did. Baptist, Presbyterian, Methodist, Episcopal, Lutheran, Congregational, Reformed, Evangelical, and other denominational pulpits acknowledged, with some embarrassment, Lincoln's presence at a theater and struggled to explain and apologize for it. George D. Boardman exclaimed: "I could have wished, indeed, that since he must fall, he had fallen elsewhere. . . . It is the solitary cloud that flecked the expanse of his public career." Andrew L. Stone lamented, "We feel . . . we could have wished . . . a different scene for the last hour of his health and consciousness on earth. . . . Yes, it would have been better." J. D. Fulton acknowledged, "We remember, with sorrow, the place of his death. . . . He was shot in a theater. It was a poor place to die in. It would not be selected by any of you as the spot from which you would desire to proceed to the bar of God." Morris C. Sutphen proclaimed, "my heart bleeds most at the thought that he should have received the fatal blow within the walls of a theater." L. M. Glover summarized the thoughts of many:

I think it my duty, however, to say that in common with many others, I have a regret that, if he was to fall by the hand of an assassin, the event had not occurred elsewhere, in the street, in the council chamber, in the national mansion, or even in the sanctuary of God. And yet my regret does not take the form of expression adopted by some, that being in the theatre he was out of God's jurisdiction and forfeited the divine protection, but that regret is this, that besides the general impropriety of the indulgence for one whose example gives law, and especially while public affairs were so troubled, the fact should have been made by "wicked hands" to serve as the link of destiny, and seized upon as the fatal condition of such universal down-casting and grief. And yet in all this painful matter there is nothing which a gracious God cannot or which a generous people will not forgive. [30]

Obviously, many preachers did not approve of theatergoing and found it incongruous that Abraham Lincoln—the truly good man, the devout soul, the one of "inflexible integrity"—should have been found in such a place. Several of the clergy remarked that Lincoln was at Ford's Theater not because he wanted to be there but that he went out of a sense of duty. Thomas Laurie, at the South Evangelical Church in West Roxbury, Massachusetts, commented: "It is a relief to know that our beloved President went with reluctance to the fatal spot." Similarly, George Duffield complained, "Would that he had fallen elsewhere than at the very gates of Hell—in the theater, to which through persuasion, he so reluctantly went." Robert Lowry's rationalization for the President's attendance at the theater was typical.

It cannot be said that the President went to the theatre because he loved to be there. He was not, in the common acceptation of the term, a theatre-goer. It is known that he went with great reluctance. He was in no state of mind to enjoy a scene like that. But the newspapers had announced that the President and General Grant would be there on that evening. The people thronged the house to do honor to the great men who had saved the country. General Grant, who had no time to waste in amusements, left Washington in the evening train, to superintend the removal of his family to Philadelphia. The President knew that the people would be disappointed, if they saw neither of the faces that they delighted to honor. Weary as he was, he decided to go. He went, not to see a comedy, but to gratify the people. . . . For the people he gave up his life on the night of that fatal Friday.

There is another consideration. In all the countries of Christendom, the rulers are expected to visit the theatre as an act of state. We may deplore the custom, but it is nevertheless, universal. It is an observance that stretches back through long generations. There is a supposed necessity for it. It is only there that the Executive can receive the formal acclaims of all classes of citizens. . . . From a religious stand-point, we cannot approve of it. But we must not confound the act of the President,

prompted by high considerations of state, with the visit of a private citizen, moved thereunto by the low desire of a mere selfish gratification.[31]

Most of the preachers seemed to assume that their congregations
knew why the theater was such a den of iniquity. Undoubtedly, they
had preached on the subject several times before. However, there
were those who took the occasion of Lincoln's death to elaborate on
the evils of the theater. E. J. Goodspeed, pastor of the Second Baptist Church in Chicago, called theaters "royal roads to perdition" and
that in them "men are trained for villainy or nurtured in vice."
Goodspeed noted that there were only a few exceptions of people
trained in the theater "who would be considered suitable companions
for our children, or visitors in our homes. There is a taint upon them
which we should shun like the plague." John Wilkes Booth, Goodspeed reminded, was trained in the theater. "Familiar with tragedies
where the dagger and poison played important parts, intoxicated by
a vain ambition which the theater fosters, he was ripe for any crime
which might be suggested." Goodspeed concluded his comments on
the theater with a moral lesson. "One thought has been driven
deeply," he exclaimed. "Go not to any place where you would not
wish to be found by death. . . . I dismiss the point with the expression of a renewed determination to give no encouragement henceforth to theaters."[32]

Thomas Laurie also noted that Booth had been educated in the
theater.

How could he commit so amazing a crime in so theatrical a way! That
one word "theatrical" explains it all. No other could express such com-
mingled wickedness and insensibility. That stupendous crime was the
fitting fruit of an education that, passing by the ordinary manifestations
of depravity as too commonplace, brings the soul into contact, and holds
it in communion, with all that is most intensely exciting in human
crime. An education that, making the heart familiar with the foulest and
most bloody deeds, bends the whole energy not to be good, but to put
on its seeming. It has nothing to do with goodness, save to ape its attitudes and steal its words. It teaches a man to pass by genuine piety as
beneath regard, and heaps its praises on the clever counterfeit of its most
impassioned manifestations.

Laurie went on to comment that the theater trains one "to counterfeit and win applause by the perfection of counterfeiting." Drawing the lesson, Laurie asked "which we shall choose for our children—the education of the theater or of the church: of the book of plays, or the book of God?" Laurie then inquired if Lincoln's attendance at the theater would influence and draw others to attend such a place. Because of the disasterous consequences Lincoln suffered, Laurie thought the lesson would serve as a deterrence to theatergoing.[33] But Frederick Starr, Jr., in a sermon that was delivered on April 16 in the First Presbyterian Church of Penn Yan, New York, said that Lincoln, by attending the theater, "gave his countenance to a class of individuals, who are perhaps beyond any others . . . the most depraved, vicious and unprincipled in society; and gave his influence and presence, to fill the coffers of those who are the most useless members of the whole community, in contributing anything to the well-being, the prosperity, or the property of the nation." Starr lamented that Lincoln had never been instructed as to the evils of the theater, and "had its moral influence and the evil of the example been pointed out to him, that noble, honest, benevolent man would not have yielded to any urgency, or invitation to attend that place."[34]

In assessing the character of Abraham Lincoln, the preachers compared and contrasted him to many historical figures. The three names that drew the most attention from Northern pulpits were Moses, the Hebrew lawgiver; William I, Prince of Orange, leader of the revolt against Spanish rule and the Catholic religion in sixteenth-century Netherlands; and George Washington, the first and the most revered American president.

The biblical figure to whom Lincoln was most compared was Moses. Charles Lowe, from Massachusetts, but speaking at the Unitarian Church on Archdale Street in Charleston, South Carolina, on April 23, drew analogies between the two figures at several points during his sermon.

> He stands before us, and will so stand in history, as the Moses of this Israel of ours. The medium and the willing instrument of God, he has led us through the wanderings of the wilderness for four long years. "Meek," but, like his great prototype, not with the meekness of imbecility, but of reliance on a power that was not his own; yearning, like him, for the deliverance of the people he was appointed to lead; standing

firm in his purpose when they, in moments of discouragement, sighed after the flesh-pots they had left behind,—the parallel became complete when, at last, after the final act of the struggle was consummated, and after, in the rebel capital (the goal of his efforts), he was able to declare the rebellion substantially at an end, and the wanderings over; "with his eye not dim, nor his natural force abated," he was called to die. It was like Moses upon Mount Nebo, where he was permitted to see, but not himself to enter, the Promised Land.

But to the people it is given to enter in, rejoicing after their weary wanderings, and without one lost tribe. The promised land of peace and Union, and freedom for all, and prosperity restored.[35]

Scores of preachers drew the comparisons of Moses and Lincoln leading their people to the Promised Land, but, themselves, not allowed to enter. Henry Ward Beecher proclaimed: "Again a great leader of the people has passed through toil, sorrow, battle, and war, and come near to the promised land of peace, into which he might not pass over. . . . he looked upon it as Moses looked upon the promised land." On April 19 at the Church of the Covenant (Episcopal) in Philadelphia, Clement M. Butler emphasized that Lincoln "was our Moses who had only just taken us over the blood-red sea of rebellion . . . and we expected that he would lead us across the desert into the promised land. . . . On the very day of his death our great leader had looked upon it from his Pisgah of observation, and had rejoiced at the goodly heritage upon which his people were about to enter." Samuel K. Lothrop, a Unitarian from Boston, echoed a similar thought. "Like Moses on the banks of the Jordan, [Lincoln] saw this peace in near prospect, and felt that the object of all his noble efforts, his days and nights of anxious thought and painful solicitude, was just within his grasp. But, like Moses, he was not permitted to enter into that peace, to attain personally that object." However, noted Alonzo H. Quint, both Moses and Lincoln completed their tasks. Quint asked about Lincoln: "Because thus cut off was his life unfinished? Who shall say that of Moses? With us as with the Hebrew, our leader's life was a completed epic. The result was not to be enjoyed by him, but his work was done."[36]

Henry Ward Beecher pointed out that to the freedmen Lincoln was Moses in a very special sense, and thus their grief at his death was uniquely poignant. "There will be wailing in places which no ministers shall be able to reach," declared Beecher. "When, in hovel and in cot, in wood and in wilderness, in the field throughout the South, the dusky children, who looked upon him as that Moses whom God sent before them to lead them out of the land of bondage, learn that he has fallen, who shall comfort them?" Joseph A. Seiss devoted an entire sermon to comparing Moses with Abraham Lincoln. As he brought the sermon to a conclusion, he left his congregation with a practical application. "We may not, indeed, be Moseses or Lincolns," remarked Seiss, "but like both of them, we can be ourselves; and by being honestly our true selves in humble things, we know not what high spheres we yet may be raised. . . . And both the histories of the men whose names I have associated in these remarks, preach and illustrate the same hopefulness."[37]

Several preachers drew parallels between Lincoln and the martyred sixteenth-century Dutch hero William I, Prince of Orange. In his sermon on April 16, James M. Manning, pastor of Old South Congregational Church in Boston, compared the two patriots.

> We had traced a resemblance, often, between our beloved President and the great Prince of Orange,—called William the Silent. The same devotion to country, the same trust in a Divine Providence, the same cautious and persevering wisdom, the same tender regard for the people who confided in them. Oh, could not the parallel have been left imperfect? Must it be carried on to the bitter end? We loved to think that they were alike in their patriotism; but—poor, blinded mortals!—we did not foresee the dreadful event that was to make them so much alike in their death! Both slain with wife and friends around them, in the moment of social freedom and unconcern, by the assassin who long had been waiting for his chance to strike.

Theodore Cuyler also discovered surprising similarities in the deaths of William and Lincoln and in their respective murderers, Gérard and Booth.

> No one can read the narrative of the murder of the deliverer of Holland, without being amazed at the coincidence between the crime of Balthazar Gérard and the crime of the brutal Booth. One could almost believe that the American miscreant had learned his horrible part from the Burgundian fanatic. The lofty and magnanimous character of the two illustrious

victims—the same cowardly assault upon both when unarmed and un-
protected—the same weapon employed—the fact that both the victims
were attended by their wives—the method of attemped escape—all
these furnish a resemblance that is as startling as if drawn from the realm
of a horrible fiction. The crimes were not more coincident than the characters of those who figured in these two foremost assassinations of modern history.

William the Silent was a noble representative of Protestant heroism,
Protestant faith, and Protestant liberty. Gerard was the fiendish embod-
iment of all that was crafty, bigoted, and revengeful in Spanish Popery.
Abraham Lincoln was the representative of American Republicanism in
its most pure and primitive type. In Booth, the butcher, was incarnated
the diabolical spirit of Southern slavery. He is a specimen of the pupils
which the "peculiar institution" has graduated for half a century.[38]

Goodspeed observed yet another parallel in the two violent
deaths. "As our deceased Chiefton treated the assassin kindly but an
hour before the fatal wound was given, recognizing him with a ge-
nial smile, William of Orange received into his bed-chamber and
supplied with money the ruffian who, a few hours after, shot his
benefactor with the weapon purchased by that money." A. P. Rogers,
from New York City, found hope and encouragement in comparing
the two assassinations and their consequences. "It was a darker day
for the Netherlands," he said, "when William of Orange fell by the
assassin's hand than for our country now, and yet how nobly that
little republic weathered that terrible storm which broke her strong
staff and her beautiful rod. So we need not despair of our republic.
Our fathers' God is ours!"[39]

In the mid-nineteenth century George Washington was rated by
most Americans, North and South, as the greatest American who
ever lived. It was natural, then, for the Northern preachers, in their
eulogies of Lincoln, to draw comparisons between the first and sixteenth presidents.[40] Some of the Northern clergy agreed with Joshua
T. Tucker, who exclaimed, "Our annals are enriched with another
rare model for youthful study and imitation, second only to that of
the Father of our nation, in all the catalogue of our public men." Seth
Sweetser questioned: "If the statue of George Washington fills, by
unanimous consent, the first niche in the Pantheon of illustrious wor-
thies, will not that of Abraham Lincoln fill the second?" Hiram Sears

called Lincoln "the second Father of his Country, and the great moral hero of the nineteenth century." Denis Wortman said, "I believe, my friends, that since the days of George Washington, we have not had a purer statesman, a wiser, a nobler, a more Christian man at the head of this government."[41]

Most preachers were not content to place Lincoln second to Washington, instead judging him to be the equal of the first president. Sidney Dean said of the martyred Lincoln, "He is interwoven into our nation's history, as no man living or dead can be, with the exception of George Washington. He was the first Saviour of his country; Abraham Lincoln was the second and his equal." Joel F. Bingham, at the Westminster Church in Buffalo, announced on May 7 that George Washington, previously "unopposed" and "uncompared," must "now henceforth . . . divide his glory" with Abraham Lincoln. William R. Williams, pastor of Amity (Baptist) Church in New York City, spoke of Washington as the "Founder" of the country and Lincoln as its "Restorer." John G. Butler, pastor of St. Paul's Lutheran Church in Washington, D.C., declared on April 16 that "In all future history [Lincoln's] name will stand beside that of Washington. If he was the father of his country, under God, Abraham Lincoln was its saviour." Similarly, Amory D. Mayo stated: "Washington was Father of his Country; our country owes to him her independent life. Abraham Lincoln was the Father of the American people: first under him was there one free people of the United States. Together in sainted memory will these men abide." Henry B. Smith, from Union Theological Seminary in New York City, said that "the names of Lincoln and Washington will be linked in the nation's memory, and embalmed in the nation's heart. Different as they were in their training and character, they were both equally the vessels of Omnipotence; God chose them to do an unequalled work, not only for this land, but also for mankind."[42]

There were a few preachers who went so far as to proclaim that Lincoln was even greater than Washington. Rollin H. Neale, a Baptist pastor from Boston, hinted at a possible Lincoln superiority when he said, "There will be hereafter as now, and through all time, and amid all controversies, a unanimity of profound respect for the honesty, the moral integrity, the lofty patriotism the well balanced mind, and the administrative ability of Abraham Lincoln, not surpassed, if even equalled, by that which is paid to the memory of

Washington." Wisconsin Congregationalist Edward Searing declared without reservation that Abraham Lincoln was greater than George Washington.

> I confidently declare that he was greater than Washington, as a man, and did a much greater work. I say this in all soberness from a calm judgment of the simple facts. I would not dim by so much as one ray the splendor of Washington's just fame, but as the nation that Lincoln saved is greater than the nation that Washington founded, so surely must justice declare the defender superior to the founder. Washington obtained independence for some colonies, and that only with the aid of France. Washington fought on the defensive against foes who crossed an ocean to assail him, and whose councils were divided by faction.
>
> Lincoln preserved the integrity of the world's greatest nation against twelve millions of foes on its own soil. Washington neglected to destroy in the bud, the iniquitous cause that, in full bloom, produced the rebellion which Lincoln quelled. Washington belonged to one of "the first families of Virginia." Lincoln, of obscure and humble origin, destroyed many of the last families of that traitorous and degenerate state.
>
> As his main work, Washington for three millions of men secured independence. As an incident in his work, Lincoln to four millions gave freedom. Washington's work was great, Lincoln's gigantic. Finally, Washington gave to the country his faithful services. Lincoln added to these his life. Intellectually, I believe Lincoln to have been much superior to Washington—superior as a speaker, as a writer and as a clear-headed original thinker. There is equality only in purity of life, singleness and purity of motive, and in unyielding and trustful tenacity of effort. [43]

3

• • •

Responsibility for the Assassination

Whence came this blow?
—SAMUEL T. SPEAR

ON SUNDAY, APRIL 23, 1865, nine days after Lincoln's assassination, Samuel Thayer Spear, a Presbyterian cleric from Brooklyn, asked from his pulpit, "Whence came this blow?" It was a question that preachers all over the North were posing. Who was responsible for the assassination of Abraham Lincoln? Of course, John Wilkes Booth pulled the trigger. Sidney Dean referred to Booth as a "second Judas" who, "worse than his namesake, went out from the presence of the chief priests and counsellors of treason and himself committed the murder."[1]

As Dean implied, however, the preachers viewed Booth as only a small cog in the mechanism of the assassination. It is somewhat surprising how few of the preachers even mentioned Booth's name. Leonard Swain emphasized that "the individual perpetrator is nothing. The nation scarcely cares who he is, or what he is. He is the mere instrument, the hand which held the pistol." Wilbur F. Paddock, rector of St. Andrew's Church in Philadelphia, stressed that Booth was only "the tool. . . . he was not the inspirer . . . not the soul of this murder. There were others much more guilty than he." E. J. Goodspeed announced who those other guilty people were: "I believe the wretch who foully slew our magnanimous, incorruptible and idolized Chief Magistrate was spurred and prompted to his plot, and aided in its execution by the Confederacy . . . baffled in its attempt to take a nation's life, fiendishly sought to take its constituted head."[2]

In their assigning of blame for the assassination, most of the preachers in the North agreed with Goodspeed. It was the Confederacy, the South, slavery that was ultimately responsible for the murder of Abraham Lincoln. Chester Forrester Dunham has written,

"The Northern Clergy were virtually a unit in the belief that slavery was the impelling cause of the assassination, that the perpetrators were representatives or tools of Southern officials." Albert G. Palmer expressed the sentiments of most Northern preachers when he declared that "Yes, it was treason, it was the Rebellion, it was the internal wickedness of slavery that sped the ball . . . for the life of Abraham Lincoln. . . . Abraham Lincoln was brutally murdered at the instigation and under the cognizance of the Confederacy."[3]

Charges similar to those of Palmer's echoed and thundered from numerous Northern pulpits. From Michigan, Henry Lyman Morehouse proclaimed that "the taint of this assassination [will] cleave to the people of the South wherever they go. . . . the hour of the triumph of evil is the hour of its disaster. . . . Southern 'chivalry' has earned for itself the title of barbarism; Southern civilization—the boasted paragon of perfection—has shown itself to be a whited sepulchre full of corruption within." Alfred S. Patton, at the Tabernacle Baptist Church in Utica, New York, declared that some in the South had been conspirators of the assassination and had applauded the finished act.

> The bloody act of this assassin is of one nature with all the barbarous acts previously committed by savage traitors, and we know that in the South no later than December 1st, 1864, money was called for to be devoted to this very object,—the names of Lincoln and Johnson, and Seward being given as the selected victims of assassination. Nor was this infamous proposition rebuked by the Southern people, but rather approved. . . . Tell me not that the leading men of the South disapprove these acts. Tell me not that they mourn for the death of Lincoln—it is what they have wished for, and as their barbarous spirit led them to applaud the cowardly Brooks, so, in their secret souls, they to-day approve the miscreant murderer Booth.

When Patton had this sermon printed, he added a footnote to explain his charges. "Soon after Mr. Lincoln's reelection the following appeared first in *The Selma Dispatch* and was copied unrebuked into other Rebel organs":

> One Million Dollars Wanted, to Have Peace by the 1st of March.—If the citizens of the Southern Confederacy will furnish me with the cash,

or good securities for the sum of one million dollars, I will cause the lives of Abraham Lincoln, William H. Seward, and Andrew Johnson to be taken by the 1st of March next. This will give us peace, and satisfy the world that cruel tyrants cannot live in a "land of liberty." If this is not accomplished, nothing will be claimed beyond the sum of fifty thousand dollars, in advance, which is supposed to be necessary to reach and slaughter the three villains.

I will give, myself, one thousand dollars toward this patriotic purpose. Every one wishing to contribute will address box X, Cahawba, Ala. December 1, 1864.[4]

Others also declared that the South was rejoicing over the death of Lincoln. E. S. Atwood accused:

Before high heaven, I charge the leaders of the Rebellion, and their aiders and abettors, North and South, with this foul and most unnatural crime. The bells will clash merrily in the remnant of the Confederacy, and the blood-thirsty crowd will shout themselves hoarse with savage joy, when the tidings reach them, of their deliberate vengeance accomplished. The pious hypocrite who heads them, will stay long enough in his flight to dictate an order for Te-Deums to be sung in the churches. The boasted chivalry, the scum and refuse of humanity, will gloat large-eyed and eager-eared, over the details of the dying agonies of the great and good and wise President whom God has taken to himself.

Alonzo H. Quint, whose sermons were especially bitter toward the South declared that in the South "there will be rejoicing!" because of Lincoln's murder.

In the heart of the arch rebel and his traitorous crew; among the slave drivers and the slave sellers; among the makers of coffles, and the foragers of fetters, and the traders in whips. . . . Among the despots and the tyrants; the oppressors and their sycophants; the robbers and plunderers of men; the hypocrits who will offer pretended sympathy, with deceit in their heart. . . . There will be jubilee in hell.[5]

Northern preachers called upon the South to disavow and condemn the assassination, but they claimed to see no evidence that such a disavowal was taking place. On June 1 Joshua T. Tucker, in the

First Parish Church of Holliston, Massachusetts, called on the South to "wash its hands of the crimson stain. Has it been done? Not a beginning." Morgan Dix, on April 19 at St. Paul's Church in New York City, demanded:

> The judgment is set, and the books are opened; Christian civilization waits attentively to hear them speak. There is but one thing to do, if they would stand in this audit. To denounce the act, to join in the common cry against the outrage done to God, to man, to Christ, to the age; to disclaim any responsibility for it; to shrink back from the bloody actors in that murder; to say, we, too, are Christians, civilized beings, men; we abhor as much as you can a deed like this; charge it not on us; it is the work of desperadoes for whom we are not accountable: think not of us as though we would excuse or defend a crime fit only for a barbarous zone, and from which, with the enlightened world, and as acceptors of the principles of Christianity, we equally with yourselves revolt in disgust and horror. Such must be their answer, if their claims be true . . . I tremble lest it should be otherwise, lest we shall hear some quite different voice, perhaps a brutal cry of approval.[6]

To add credence to their charges of widespread Southern responsibility for Lincoln's death, the Northern preachers pointed to other unconscionable acts they claimed were committed by Southerners. Prior to the assassination, most, but not all, Northern preachers were hesitant to speak about the rumored and alleged Southern atrocities. The murder of Lincoln removed the hesitancy. In those days after April 14, Northern sermon after Northern sermon charged the South with the most inhumane deeds. According to the preachers, the assassination of Lincoln was only the most recent in a continuing series of atrocities. The words of Andrew L. Stone, Congregationalist from Boston, are fairly typical of such charges. The spirit that killed Lincoln, Stone charged,

> is the same spirit that has been deaf for generations to the groans and sighs of the bondman; the same that struck with parricidal hand at the breast of the country's life; the same that opened the murderous thunders of war in Charleston harbor, and has kept them resonant over the land through four wasteful, tragic years; the same that sent hired incendiaries to fire the mansions in our Northern cities, when women and babes as

well as men slept in unsuspecting security; the same that laid in wait for
the President elect, with murderous intent, when he first left his Western home for the Capitol; the same that advertised for bids upon his
head, through the consenting press of the South; the same that administered keepers' discipline in Libby Prison and Castle Thunder, for a step
or gesture amiss, with bullet and bayonet; that made grim Famine Jailer
at Belle Isle and Andersonville, over tens of thousands, to whom death
only brought release. This black, consummate crime is only the ripe
fruit of that system of barbarism which has struck its roots so deep, and
had such stalwart growth in this continent.

On May 7, Joel F. Bingham, at the Westminster Presbyterian
Church at Buffalo, summarized what he perceived to be the foul
methods and strategies of the South.

Look, now for a moment, at the Southern methods of prosecuting their
public and civilized warfare, so-called, which the late climax of crime has
powerfully illuminated. In Virginia, arsenic was thrown into the wells,
where national armies were likely to pass; and the inhabitants of the
country whom these armies had spared life and property, were employed
to bring into the national camps and sell to these soldiers poisoned pies
and fruit. Sheridan himself, early in the summer of 1864, barely escaped
from a fatal dose, received in a similar way. . . . [There was] the wholesale massacres of hundreds and thousands of national troops after surrender, of wounded national soldiers, on the field of battle and in the
power of the enemy, purposely left to welter and languish for days, without attendance or so much as the service of a drop of water for their
terrible thirst; of unnecessary and cruel amputation, by rebel surgeons,
with the double purpose, openly avowed, to punish and disable, of
hospitals purposely set on fire, with sick and wasted national soldiers
left, by scores, to roast and consume in a burning building. . . . The
world will read . . . how great and peaceful cities far remote from
the armies in conflict, were secretly set on fire . . . of the attempted destruction of moving railroad trains, filled with unarmed men, women
and children . . . and of the cruelest ocean piracies on record. . . . But
the blackest page . . . will be . . . the horrors of the rebel prisons
which . . . [were] pits of torture, where a deliberate, systematic, long
protracted process of freezing, infection and starvation was coolly and
unrelentingly carried forward upon tens of thousands of men taken in

open battle. . . . Our posterity will turn pale as they read the record. Mankind will execrate the story with everlasting curses, and confess that this alone were enough to consign the exploded slave-holders rebellion to the blackest abyss of human infamy.[7]

George Duffield, from Detroit, added to the list of so-called Southern atrocities. "There is strong circumstantial evidence to prove," he asserted, "that the death of President Harrison, and of President Taylor, was secured by poison, administered slowly, in pursuance of a plan and purpose that no Northern man should ever be President of the United States." Duffield went on to accuse certain Southerners of an "abortive attempt to poison President Buchanan." Evidence would one day be brought forth, Duffield assured, to prove the South used germ warfare during the civil conflict that brought various diseases to citizens of Northern cities.[8]

In what may be the most vitriolic of all Northern sermons toward the South, Alonzo H. Quint, on the Sunday afternoon of April 16, declared that the assassination of the President had revealed the true Southern character, a character about which he and many others had been deceived.

It was long the feeling that a Southern Gentleman was the perfection of humanity. He was a noble, generous man, above mean and petty acts. He was no Yankee, to love a dollar. A kind of patriarchal protector, in his lordly mansion, to the attached and happy servants who could not take care of themselves. Rather passionate, but that was the natural fault of high toned feeling. His honor was proverbial. His hospitality was boundless. In government, he took the offices,—not for money, but because he was educated to statesmanship. At northern watering places, of a summer, he was feted and petted,—the generous, chivalric, Southerner. He had a right to look down on "northern mudsills" and "greasy mechanics."

It took time to find out that this was a delusion. That he was, with exceptions of course, revengeful, treacherous, murderous. That he was a liar and a cheat. That he loved money dearly, and wrung it out of the tears of his bondmen. That his lordly mansion was, nine times in ten, unfit for a sty for northern pigs. That his slaves were chained, and whipped, and branded. That his statesmanship was mere craft, to get salaries on the one hand, and, on the other to enable him to get and keep more negroes. That he was lazy, and selfish, and often stupidly ignorant. That his hospitality always wanted pay for the wayfarer's dinner, except when his ruling principle, vanity, prevented.

It took time to learn this. It did, me. I had known some honorable Southerners, so far as a slave holder can be honorable; and I thought they were samples. But I saw the reality, in Southern lands.

But we had not really felt all this, even after this war, plotted by perjurers and felons, and carried on by barbarians. And so, to impress it upon our minds, we have had this last, this crowning evidence, of what Southern Chivalry is. It is to assassinate an unarmed man.[9]

Many Northern preachers were harsh in the judgment of Southern character. Boston Congregationalist Edward N. Kirk declared that "arrogance, treason, perjury, breach of trust, brow-beating, cruelty, assassination; these are the epithets history will apply to their conduct." Marvin R. Vincent, a Presbyterian from Troy, New York, contrasted what he perceived as some basic differences between North and South. Northerners, he claimed, have been for "order, the government of reason and not of passion, fair and open discussion, patriotism, loyalty, devotion to the morals rather than the politics of government." Southerners, on the other hand, were those "representing treason, disloyalty, impatience of control, passion, disregard of the principle of majority rule, oppression of the weak, deeper degradation of the degraded, its principles represented by factious demagogues who would rather 'rule in hell than serve in Heaven.' " Vincent claimed that "No distinction was ever clearer." Henry J. Fox drew these conclusions from the assassination of Lincoln:

That the wicked leaders of this rebellion are capable of such a crime against the nation and against God, as such a conspiracy involves, it seems to me needs no proof. The men who could deliberately fire upon the nation's flag as it floated over Sumter, when they knew that that first shot would involve the death of countless thousands; who could, with wicked and deliberate intent, starve the thousands of prisoners, who, by the misfortunes of war, were so unhappy as to fall into their hands; who were capable of plotting the destruction of this city, with its helpless women and children, by a sudden midnight conflagration, and who have been overtaken and detected in other infamies, were capable of planning and taking the necessary means to execute this crime, than which history does not present another so truly appalling.[10]

Preachers all over the North proclaimed that the Southerners had inflicted the greatest damage upon themselves. Henry J. Fox proclaimed that "The [Southerners] have struck down the hand that was lifted oftener and more lovingly than that of any other man, to shield, protect and befriend them. . . . They have silenced the voice which would have proclaimed their pardon in stronger, sweeter strains than ever fell under like provocations from human lips." D. T. Carnahan preached that Lincoln was the South's "best friend, disposed to extend to them greater leniency and a fuller pardon than they could expect." And Charles Carroll Everett said, "The rebels have lost more in Lincoln than we have lost. He was their wisest friend. I fancy that President Johnson will not be more lenient than the man that they have slain." S. C. Baldridge also surmised that "Well might the rebels say that 'the death of Mr. Lincoln, just now, was the heaviest blow the South had yet suffered.' Verily, they have killed the man of mercy, with their own suicidal hand, in the very hour when they needed most of his vast and unimpassioned mind and boundless magnanimity." James Reed said, "The saying is in everybody's mouth, that those, on whose behalf this villany was done, have lost thereby their best friend."[11]

Southern preachers were well aware of the accusations their Northern counterparts were making against the South, and they used their pulpits to respond to the charges. On April 23, with the fleeing Confederate President Jefferson Davis in attendance, the Reverend George M. Everhart, rector of St. Peter's Episcopal Church in Charlotte, North Carolina, called Lincoln's assassination

a blot on American civilization, which in this nineteenth century of the Christian era is doubly deep in infamy. It is the tapping of a fountain of blood, which, unchecked, will burst forth and flow onward through the South as well as the North, and bear on its gory bosom a reign of terror like unto which that in the days of Robespierre would fade into insignificance. . . . This event, unjustifiable at any time, but occuring just now, renders it obligatory upon every Christian to set his face against it—to express his abhorance of a deed fraught with consequences to society everywhere, and more especially to Southern society.[12]

A fairly typical Southern pulpit response was delivered by J. Lansing Burrows at the First Baptist Church of Richmond on June 1, the day set aside by President Johnson for humiliation and mourning in remembrance of the slain Lincoln. Stung by Northern imputations of Southern atrocities, Burrows countered with charges of Northern atrocities.

> The blackest crimes of the horrible war through which we have just passed, have found and yet find justification from some who claim to be personally upright and even pious. Robbery and arson and massacre and rape; cruelty to prisoners and faithlessness to solemn oaths; the spoiling of unarmed citizens and defenceless women; the wanton destruction of household goods and agricultural implements, of growing crops and stored grain; the whole black catalogue of outrages perpetrated by maddened armies, which authority and discipline are often too weak to restrain, and which are condemned alike by the law of nations and the law of God—we sometimes hear palliated and defended.

Responding to claims that Southerners took pleasure in the murder of Lincoln, Burrows said: "We have no feelings but those of horror and indignation and grief in contemplating this deed of infamy. . . . that we should justify his assassination, or express or feel any emotion but horror and detestation and grief for such crime—that be far from us Christians and honest men." Lincoln's death, he claimed, was a tragedy for the South.

> We may further lament on our own account the sudden death of Mr. Lincoln. We have reason to do so. We believe he was disposed to be generous and liberal in his measures for the reconstruction of the government. No harsh or vengeful or malignant thoughts toward our people seemed to find place in his heart, in arranging for the settlement of the great controversy. He would, I doubt not, as leniently and benevolently as possible, have exerted his great influence and authority. His death is, therefore, a calamity to us for which we mourn.[13]

Burrows protested that to accuse the South of complicity in Lincoln's death was a gross sin. "To treat as criminal one who asserts his innocence, and against whom no crime has been proven, under the impulses of prejudice or passion or fanaticism; to condemn and punish such as though they were confessed and convicted offenders, is a crime against humanity and a sin against God," he preached.

> Condemning the innocent is a vice that bears toward malignity. It evinces a readiness, an eagerness, to believe evil concerning another. It has its origin in evil surmisings, suspicions, jealousies and cruelty. It is ready to believe the worst; to look upon the blackest side of human conduct. Its basis is a malevolent spirit, and, therefore, God abhors it. It hounded the martyrs to the dungeon, the scaffold and the stake. It dragged the Son of God to Calvary, and murdered him there.

Burrows went on to quote from several Northern religious periodicals in which "the people of these Southern States, as a whole, are pertinaciously and fiercely condemned and denounced as responsible and guilty of the vile deed." He then asked about the meaning of these Northern charges. Responding to his own question, he said: "They mean that the Southern people, as a body, are responsible for the murder of President Lincoln, and should be, without mercy, punished for it. . . . Without a tittle of evidence; against our solemn pleas of 'Not Guilty,' we are condemned and judged as murderers." Impassioned, he continued, "Oh! my brethren, it is hard to bear injustice meekly, to endure unfounded and unreasonable reproaches, humbly and unresistingly, and yet this is the spirit of which our Lord set us a glorious example, and which he requires of His disciples: 'I say unto you resist not evil.' 'Overcome evil with good.' "[14]

There were, however, a few Northern preachers who were not willing to place all of the blame for Lincoln's assassination upon the South. Marvin R. Vincent declared that "Northern men with Southern principles" wear skirts that "are not clear of the President's blood." Alfred S. Patton spoke of "men here in the North who are not guiltless in relation to this assassination. Show me one who, with tongue or pen—while our noble President was working with unfaltering energy to put down this rebellion—did nothing to help him, but dared to style that tender-hearted and generous man a tyrant, and you show me one on whose conscience, to-day, rests the blood of Abraham Lincoln." Responsibility for Lincoln's murder was placed upon "the disloyal press both North and South," which, some claimed, educated Booth for his nefarious deed, and upon the Copperheads. The Southern people in their hatred of Lincoln, J. B. Wentworth proclaimed,

> have been wonderfully aided by a class of journalists and politicians at the North, well and truly known as copperheads. Do we not remember how these villains have continually charged him with violating the Constitution, called him despot, and accused him of having designs upon the liberties of people? . . . That this base and causeless malignity manifested towards him by Northern men, encouraged and intensified Southern hatred of his person and character, can not for a moment be doubted. And who shall say that copperheads, North, are not as responsible for his murder, as rebels, South?

Marvin R. Vincent declared that there was "nothing in the letter or spirit of the Constitution which should prevent such men as Vallandigham" from being silenced and "put beyond the possibility of doing further mischief." And there were even a few Northern pulpits that placed at least part of the blame for Lincoln's murder upon the radical Republicans, suggesting that they held views that were similar to those of Southern leaders and Northern Copperheads and thus they aided in the assassination of the President.[15] But such a point of view would seem to stretch the mind beyond the point of credulity and only a very few preachers made such a connection.

Taking as his text Acts 23:5, "Thou shalt not speak evil of the Ruler of thy people," William R. Gordon, pastor of the Reformed Protestant Dutch Church in Schraalenberg, New Jersey, devoted an entire sermon to the idea that Lincoln was killed because of the sin of reviling, "treating a person with vile epithets of language, cursing him, wishing him harm, and loading his character with reproaches and railing accusation." He then asserted that "reviling the President of the United States, is a crime against God, and against the government."

> When any party succeeds in placing its men in power, it is the duty of all to cease opposition, and make the best of it. . . . It is the duty, inseparable from moral order, of every man to refrain from speaking evil of the Ruler of his people. . . . Had all our Northern people acted according to this obvious duty, I believe Mr. Lincoln would not have met a

violent death. . . . Let, then, the sins of the reviling tongue be checked, and the dangers from the spirit of treason will be evaded.[16]

A rationale similar to Gordon's expressed by J. P. Daily claimed that the assassination had its roots in "speaking evil of political opponents, and especially of those in authority, though wide spread and of long standing, is the poison source of many of the bitter streams that reach all classes and all parties of our people, spreading blastine and mildew over all our social, political and moral interests." On April 23, in the First Congregational Church of Oakland, California, George Mooar put the question of responsibility in an even wider perspective, declaring that the attitudes and deeds of the assassins were the sins of everyone.

> If you were to converse with these assassins, it is not improbable they might even win your sympathies. It would be found that they were influenced by no worse feelings or motive than the men who profess to abhor them; nay, it might be found that they were ruled by the same sinful motives which actuate ourselves. Covetousness, or love of notoriety, or personal resentment may have prompted the deed. These motives look bad when we see them seeking the lives of men so eminent and so kindly as Abraham Lincoln and William H. Seward; but Oh! how many times have we given way to precisely these motives in our own life? In how many millions of our countrymen are the same sins working to will and to do?[17]

Most Northern preachers, however, were not willing to think or speak of a wider responsibility for the assassination. The great majority placed the blame upon the leaders of the South, the elite of the South, the slaveholders of the South, or the South as a whole as being the motivator and instigator of Lincoln's murder. Therefore, the South, they determined, must be brought to a certain and harsh justice. It was not time to consider nor pursue leniency and mercy.

4

• • •

The Demand for Justice

We have lost all sentiment of clemency.

—ROBERT LOWRY

PRIOR TO LINCOLN'S assassination, the Northern preachers had been divided as to how the South, most especially its leaders, should be treated after the war. Many wanted stern judgment and appropriate punishments; others spoke of the need for mercy, forgiveness, and conciliation; and several took no strong positions at all on the matter. The assassination seemingly altered the degree of division by bringing about a more homogeneous attitude among Northern preachers, an attitude that demanded swift, harsh, and certain justice.

Robert Lowry, an Episcopalian from New York City, spoke of the unity the assassination had brought to the North. "See the effect on the people of this dastard blow," he said. "We are melted down into unity. . . . We have lost all sentiment of clemency." A number of preachers spoke of this change in attitude. Samuel C. Baldridge, of the Presbyterian Church of Friendsville, Illinois, commented that "The current of a credulous sympathy was beginning to flow towards the ruined Traitors. Since they had not succeeded in destroying the government, we were falling into the absurdity of pitying them for their want of success and their misfortunes. This murder, perpetrated in their behalf, and by their inspiration, has violently checked the tide." Morgan Dix spoke of the change the assassination had wrought in his own personal attitudes. Prior to April 14, he believed the Southern civilization was based upon "the principles of Christianity and that the moral condition of the people is not below that of the rest of civilized mankind." For Dix, Lincoln's murder changed that charitable point of view. "But now," he charged, "the thing is to be determined—the truth is to be made plain—in the red and bloody light of this cruel and bloody outrage." Denis Wortman also preached of the change in Northern sentiments: "For one, I doubt very much whether we shall, whether we can be so lenient as we had hoped to be. It was in the heart of the President, it was in the heart of all this great people, to forgive as no executors of justice ever forgave before. . . . But upon our unwilling hearts we bear the pressure of a certain necessity for judgment."[1]

Indeed, the assassination did bring about a widespread change in the attitudes of many Northern clergymen; a change from conciliation to punishment, from clemency to a demand for stern justice. This change was epitomized in the words of Seth Sweetser on April 23 at the Central Congregational Church of Worcester, Massachusetts.

> Treason and rebellion and barbarity have done their worst. . . . It is right that justice should have its course upon desperate and incorrigible criminals. . . . Let us pray that Government may be sustained in its duty, in its whole, severe duty, true to the demands of justice, without abjuring the sentiments of humanity; that punishment may be righteously meted out to whomsoever deserves it, according to the spirit of law and the demands of right.[2]

Many preachers expressed their concern about the growing laxity they had perceived in the North and their hope that one positive consequence of the assassination would be a stronger sense of the need for and the rightness of a retributive justice. "Justice and judgment—are the foundation of every throne, and of every government," Congregationalist Edwin B. Webb preached. "[It was a] tremendous mistake and folly and sin, for the people of a great nation to think that they can neglect or violate the laws of God with impunity. . . . There has been a miserable, morbid, bastard philanthropy. . . . We are weak in our sense of justice." New York City Presbyterian William Adams, along with many other preachers, blamed the nation's laxity upon a popular but mistaken "rose-water religion." "There is too much of this mawkish sentimentalism abroad; this milky, rose-water religion, which," he said, "beginning with a denial of future punishment, and arguing for universal salvation against the explicit assertion of the Scriptures . . . would dispense with all the severities of justice, and resolve all government, human and Divine, into an aromatic essence."[3]

R. S. Cushman complained that "mistaken views of Christian mercy has poisoned and demoralized so many minds and hearts among us." However, reminded William Ives Budington from New York City, Lincoln's death "checks that unreasonable, and . . . unchristian charity, which ignores the guilt of sin, and denies the necessity of punishment." Another minster from New York City, the Lutheran J. E. Rockwell, preached, "And may it not be that God has permitted this great crime . . . to awaken us to a sense of justice and to a full exaction of the penalty of God's law upon those who have planned and accomplished the horrible scenes of the past four years?" Alfred S. Patton could not understand why nor how some Northerners could still be conciliatory towards the South. "A few northern men I know," he claimed, "are still begging mercy for these heartless traitors. Nor can we account for their course, except by supposing that either they are blind adherents of perverted systems of morals and politics, or else, being in sympathy with treason, they have themselves a wholesome fear of justice."[4]

Few Northern preachers failed to use their pulpits to ask for severe retribution against those whom they perceived as "wicked and traitorous rebels." Mercy and forgiveness were in short supply. The Reverend S. D. Burchard declared, "If I were the President I would show no mercy to traitors and rebels and assassins at the expense of justice. I would see to it that the majesty of law was vindicated and the government sustained, if it required a whole hecatomb of human victims." Jeremiah E. Rankin emphatically charged that "the leading spirits in the South ought not to be forgiven by this people. God does not intend it shall be forgiven. And yet who will say that this was not the tendency of public sentiment before the death of the late President?"[5]

Many Northern preachers demanded the death penalty. Warren Randolph, on April 16, at the Harvard Street Baptist Church in Boston, singled out Jefferson Davis, Robert E. Lee, and John C. Breckenridge for special attention and said that "nothing but the gibbet can ever give to them their just deserts [sic]." Randolph continued his argument: "Where is the man, I would like to know, who would hesitate to hang Wilkes Booth, if he could be found? . . . He has slain but one, while the infamous Richmond trio, more than any others, have been the means of slaying thousands, aye, perhaps a million." Marvin R. Vincent called upon the government to hang the leading traitors and added, "I would their gibbet were so high that every man North and South might see it from his housetop, and learn as he looks that treason is not safe for the perpetrator." Jeremiah Rankin reminded his audience that if John C. Calhoun had only been hung, Jefferson Davis and others would have taken warning. "But," he lamented, "treason was permitted to make its nest in the very Cabinet, to utter its words of defiance upon the floor of the Senate, and then to depart unquestioned, and unchallenged." Presbyterian Samuel T. Spear suggested gradations of punishment.

> I . . . would divide the responsible leaders and prime authors of the rebellion into three classes, according to the grade of their guilt. The first of which and the smallest—of which Jefferson Davis is a conspicuous example—I would hang by the neck until they are dead! The second class of which, and a larger class, I would expel from the country, and send them forth as fugitives over the face of the earth. The third of which, and still a larger class, I would dispossess of all political power, denying to them the right to vote, and making them ineligible to any office of profit or trust under the government of the United States.[6]

On Easter Sunday at the Baldwin Congregational Church in Boston, Daniel C. Eddy demanded retribution. "It is plain," he said, "that the leaders in this rebellion must be executed or banished. The Union is not safe if they are allowed to stay here. . . . The sooner the screws are put on, the better for the nation and the better for humanity." That same day Alonzo H. Quint, in a caustic and bitter attack upon the South, demanded exile, confiscation, or hanging for various members of the Confederacy. In his advocation of exile, he demanded,

> Let the land be cleansed of persistent sullen rebels and households. Say to Southern Chivalry, Go; for this our lines are open. Carry your perjuries to other shores; England is a good place for you. This land is sick of your presence. You are a stench in the nostrils of honest men. Go, Virginian descendents of transplanted convicts. Go, you who have lived by oppression and robbery. Never return. Your heritage is gone. Return, and the rope awaits your first step upon our shores. . . . The men who have caused this war,—leave them landless and penniless, to do what they have despised us for doing, earn an honest living by the sweat of the

face. . . . Let the land be cleansed. Let the sword and the scaffold do their righteous work. Let treason die, that the country may live. . . . let Southern Chivalry be destroyed, root and branch, twig and leaf.[7]

In their demand for justice, most preachers were careful to make a distinction between the guilty leaders and the innocent, misled masses of the South. Typical was Methodist bishop Matthew Simpson's oration at Lincoln's burial in Springfield:

> Let every man who was a senator or representative in Congress, and who aided in beginning this rebellion . . . be brought to speedy and certain judgment. Let every officer educated at public expense . . . who turned his sword against the vitals of his country, be doomed to a traitor's death. . . . But to the deluded masses we will extend the arms of forgiveness. We will take them to our hearts, and walk with them side by side, as we go forward to work out a glorious destiny.

The Reverend Leonard Swain drew a similar distinction. "Let the leaders of the rebellion, or a suitable number of them, be tried, sentenced, and executed for treason, as by the laws of the land ordered and provided; then justice, having had its place, and the majesty of the law having been honored, mercy may have its exercise, and the people of the rebellious States be forgiven."[8]

The two Confederate leaders most often mentioned by the Northern preachers and often linked together as deserving of harsh punishment were Jefferson Davis and Robert E. Lee.

> Let us hear no more praising of the statesmanship of Davis, or the generalship of Lee, and declaring that we shall yet live as a people to be proud of their skill, their prowess, their military genius, or of anything whatever that pertains to them. . . . Let them go to their own place in history, and stand side by side with Benedict Arnold, and with Judas Iscariot, from whose example nothing is to be drawn but warning, and whose names are never to be used except as a synonym for all ignominy and reproach.[9]

Joshua T. Tucker accused Jefferson Davis of being an "accomplice" in the murder of Lincoln. He claimed that "evidence is in the hands of our government which will prove him to have been an accomplice before the fact, in this plot of damnable guilt." Samuel Spear, on the other hand, affirmed that "Jefferson Davis, the head of the rebel Confederacy, has not personally assassinated the President, I am aware—perhaps he had no direct connection with this atrocious murder—yet, by his authority, by his agents, with his knowledge and approbation, thousands of our soldiers have been literally starved to death in rebel prisons." Davis, therefore, Spear declared, deserved to be hanged.[10]

The attacks on Robert E. Lee by the Northern preachers were not as numerous as those leveled against Davis, but the preachers who did speak about Lee demanded strong judgment upon the Confederate general.

> General Lee may be a Christian gentleman—some say he is—yet he is a traitor to his country, who richly deserves to be hung for his crimes. Libby Prison and Belle Isle were directly under his eye at Richmond; he knew how our prisoners were treated in those dens of death as well as elsewhere; he was, too, the man of great influence in the Confederate government; and when and where did General Lee ever lift his voice, or do a solitary thing to mitigate these outrageous enormities? I am speaking in plain way. My soul is stirred within me.

The Reverend Justin D. Fulton exclaimed, "We cannot bear to hear such men as Robert E. Lee, Judge Campbell, and others praised. The blood of our starved brothers, in different rebel prisons, cries out against them. . . . It is no honor to be a rebel, and to have bravely fought. Fighting in support of crime is murder."[11]

The preachers were aware of a certain sympathy for Lee in the North and spoke to counteract any feelings of magnanimity for the general. Edwin B. Webb complained, "I cannot understand, the policy which allows General Lee to commend his captured army for 'devotion to country,' and 'duty faithfully performed' . . . to pardon them is a violation of my instincts, as it is of the laws of the land, and the laws of God." J. B. Wentworth was particularly vehement in his denunciations of Lee.

> Some good people have professed a degree of sympathy for General Lee, and expressed a hope that he at least might be exempted from punish-

ment. Can they tell why? Has he not been as great a traitor as the worst of them? Was he not bound to the government by the most sacred obligations,—having been educated at public expense, and honored and trusted by the government all his days? Was he not, at the outbreak of Rebellion, an officer in our army, and sworn to uphold the Constitution and laws of the country? And has he not been the chief support and stay of confederate Treason for more than two years past? Why, then, should he be excepted? Is it because he has displayed great skill and abilities as a military chieftain?—All the worse for him, and for the country he had sworn to defend. The greater his talents, the greater his guilt.[12]

Wentworth's condemnation of Alexander Stephens was equally strong. The fact that Stephens was late in declaring for secession only made him that much more "a despicable traitor."

Some have thought Stephens to be a proper subject of executive pardon. For myself, I must say that my hatred of his treason is hightened by my contempt for his cowardice and hypocrisy. Though he disapproved of secession, he had not the courage to hold to his convictions and breast the tide of fire-eating phrensy. Against the dictates of his own judgment and conscience, he yielded to the clamors of the mob. . . . A more despicable traitor than he is not to be found in the whole South. He ought to be hung for his meanness and perfidy—if for nothing else.

Richard Eddy put together his own list of noteworthy Southern traitors and warned against any speech that would praise them.

I regard him as a corrupter of our public morals, an enemy to our good, an unsafe and ruinous teacher of our young who couples the names of Davis, Stephens, Stonewall Jackson, and Robert E. Lee, or any of the associates with anything that can appeal to American pride and honor. Let them have place with Haman of old, with Benedict Arnold of modern times, whose example offers nothing but warning, whose names are synonymous for all ignominy and baseness. Let their names, as "the name of the wicked," rot.[13]

The preachers realized there was a need to justify such harsh and seemingly unforgiving sentiments. How was it that men who were supposed to represent a theology of love, compassion, and forgiveness could be so judgmental and condemning in spirit? John Chester recognized and addressed the issue.

> I am well aware of the cry that may be raised at ministers of the Gospel advocating such sentiments; but just so was it raised years ago, when ministers of the Gospel undertook to denounce slavery and the complicity of this Government with it as sin against God and man. This country has lived to see that they were right, and only to regret that it did not sooner heed the warning. So now the time will come as surely as there is a righteous God, when, if this people let this sin of rebellion go unpunished, they will repent it in sackcloth and ashes.

Henry B. Smith from New York City stressed that there were "some crimes that a nation cannot forgive."

> If there is a crime, there must be a penalty. It is wrong to the innocent to let the guilty escape. . . . If these leaders live it must not be in this land; those that plotted and fought to destroy their country must henceforth be without a country; and through dishonored lives, with the mark of Cain upon them, go down to unhonored graves. . . . Their names must be forever named with those of Cataline and Nero, and we will teach our children, and they theirs, to carry them down through all coming time as the dread symbols of an unequalled perfidy and an unpardoned crime against humanity itself.

J. B. Wentworth proclaimed that punishment of traitors was imperative to the perpetuation of society.

> To pardon their crime would be treason to civil justice; to remit their penalty, would be a gross outrage on public law; to let them go free, would be to give license to every species of disorder, and to unsettle the very foundations of political society. . . . It is necessary that these great villains should be executed according to law, in order to impress upon the public consciousness the idea that Justice is the basis of the state."[14]

The preachers insisted that their demands for justice had their origins in the highest of motives. The nation had a responsibility to carry out unwanted and unpleasant duties. On the day of Lincoln's funeral, Clement M. Butler declared: "Brethren, we must prepare ourselves for stern duties. While merciful and magnanimous to the misguided and the penitent, we must hew this Agag of unrelenting murder to pieces before the Lord." He then spoke of administering such duties in the right spirit. "Not—God forbid!—in a spirit of revenge, not in unholy zeal for a holy cause," he emphasized, "but in calm and indignant sorrow that such a duty devolve upon us, should this work be done." On April 23, Henry E. Butler echoed a similar theme and referred to the same biblical example. "There is a danger," he announced, "lest revenge, a passion always bad, should mingle with righteous indignation. America's spirit should be that of Samuel when he hewed the guilty Agag in pieces, sad, serious, determined, God-like."[5]

The administration of justice was, after all, a divinely appointed task. One New York City minister claimed that the cry for justice "is the Spirit of a just God which kindles a holy indignation in the human mind against crimes, whether committed against nations, communities, classes or individuals." Another warned that the failure to punish was sinful. "It is our perogative to punish," Henry J. Fox said. "Not to do this is weakness and a sin against society and against God." The Reverend E. S. Johnston insisted that because vengeance is of God we must not impede it. "To us as a Government he has entrusted the executions of his punishments on the guilty. It is neither wise nor safe for us to arrest the vengeance which does not belong to us, but to God." To those who wondered why vengeance could not be left to God to administer, one pastor responded:

> But how does he do it?—No longer does he open the windows of Heaven and sweep away wickedness with a deluge. . . . Vengeance upon wickedness is taken through human instrumentality. . . . it is the duty of Government to do it. . . . Paul declares that the civil power "is a minister of God, a revenger to execute wrath upon him that doeth evil." And woe to that Government that fails to do the mission of God.[16]

Not only was justice a God-ordained task, it was also imperative for the maintaining of effective government and an orderly society. George Duffield declared that Lincoln's murder exemplified "the horrible malignity of human corruption" and thus demonstrated the necessity of government to be able "to restrain and punish . . . by every consideration of fidelity to God, and respect for its own safety and prosperity." Robert Russell Booth devoted an entire sermon to reconciling the Bible's call for personal forgiveness on one hand and its emphasis on public justice on the other.

> There is a law of public justice, which must transcend altogether the dictates of personal and private forgiveness. . . . we are not authorized to bring these personal sentiments, which we cherish as individuals, into the administration of public affairs. . . . Unrestrained mercy to criminals is always cruelty to the innocent. It is necessary for us to make rebellion perilous and odious for all time to come. We cannot afford . . . to invite by our leniency a new assault upon our union and liberty.

Joel F. Bingham, at the Westminster Church of Buffalo, thought he detected a lesson from history. "It has most commonly been the gentlest of governments," he said, "and the most generous of rulers, that have fallen by treason and murder." He pointed to Julius Caesar, Henry IV of France, Philip II of Spain, and William of Orange as examples of his lesson. Looking at the United States, Bingham stated that "the danger which chiefly threatens us lies not in the direction of severity, but in that of leniency."[17]

John Chester echoed many Northern preachers in warning that justice must be administered through law and proper governmental institutions and authorities. "Refrain from all acts that would take the law into your own hands. . . . If it is important that [justice] should be executed, it is equally important that it should be executed by the lawfully constituted authorities." Chester continued, "Next to rebellion there is nothing worse than mob law. It is anarchy, and anarchy is the sister spirit of rebellion." Charles S. Robinson, too, asked for the law to take its course.

> the law of the land should now take its course in relation to all the aiders and abettors of this infamous rebellion. . . . Tired of war, longing for quiet, eager for trade, sickened with bloodshed, we were ready to say, let the criminals be pardoned, let all the penalties of the law be remitted. The next act in our national history was, in all likelihood, to be a general amnesty proclamation. . . . [But now] murder is done at the capital. . . . Hence, there is no revenge in the popular heart today, but only retribution. . . . let the majesty of the law be vindicated upon them as traitors.[18]

According to the Northern preachers, the terrible wickedness of the South demanded stern penalties. Alonzo H. Quint spoke of the so-called "Southern Gentleman" who was thought to be "the perfection of humanity," when in fact he was "revengeful, trecherous, murderous. . . . a liar and a cheat. . . . lazy and selfish, and often stupidly ignorant." The assassination of Lincoln was the "crowning evidence, of what Southern Chivalry is." Passionately, Quint informed his Northern listeners what this revelation of the real Southern spirit told them.

> It tells you, you have always been too lenient. You were too kind. You have played at war. Barbarians respect only force. You have not treated them rightly. In the very beginning, when Baltimore fired on our troops, you should have made a street a mile wide through Baltimore. When they hung men in Tennessee, you should have hung men in Louisiana. When they shot McCook, you should have shot Buckner. When they burnt Chambersburg, you should have burned Huntsville. When they shot black prisoners at Pillow, you should have shot white prisoners in South Carolina. That is hard? It is war. War is not play; it is not for women; it is not a lullaby for your children. It tells you to be the instrument in God's hand of cleansing the land of its pollution.

Frederick Starr, Jr., referred to the execution of John Brown and the nation's haste to impose justice on him. But he could not understand "the long delay of just and legal retribution on those who deliberately, avowedly, insultingly, plotted against the nation's peace and life, and inaugurated a bloody war."[19]

It is important to note, however, that this call for stern and uncompromising justice was not unanimous among Northern preachers. There were those who pleaded with and asked their fellow Northerners to forget and forgive, to repudiate vengeance and vindictiveness, to moderate their passions and pronouncements, to demonstrate mercy and work for reconciliation. One of the few times in his ministry that he did not represent the popular point of view, Henry Ward Beecher called for leniency toward and reconciliation with the South. However, still, as Chester Forrester Dunham has written, "The conciliatory attitude of Dr. Beecher represented only a minority of Northern Clergy. The vast majority shared the opposite

views." Similarly, E. J. Goodspeed appealed to his listeners to rise
above the spirit of revenge.

> The idea of vengeance should be carefully excluded from every mind,
> and the spirit of revenge from all hearts. We may cry to God for justice,
> we may appeal to our magistrates for justice, but remembering that we
> too are sinners, that fortuitous events gave us birth in the North and
> determined our creed, that our late lamented President, in the spirit of
> Jesus, counselled moderation and clemency, let us show the deeds of
> mercy, and push on the car of civilization to new elevations of humanity
> and Christ-like love. Let us not push it back into the old ruts of retal-
> iation, persecution and barbarism.[20]

Washington Gladden, "Father of the Social Gospel," was also a
part of that conciliatory minority. At an April 19 memorial service
for Abraham Lincoln, he reminded his audience:

> This assassination seems to have awakened in the breasts of all people a
> disposition to use stern and severe measures to the end that such an act
> may not be repeated. My belief is that stern and severe measures, instead
> of preventing the repetition of such acts, will have a tendency to multiply
> them. . . . It is easy enough at such times to gain applause by falling in
> with the popular current. A man has only to shout, "Hang them! Crush
> them! Exterminate them!" and the ceiling will resound with cries of ap-
> proval; but that applause is not worth having. Rather should the reason,
> the calm, unprejudiced reason, be appealed to; rather should these in-
> stinctive feelings be rigidly challenged and held in check.

Commenting upon the reception of that sermon, Gladden, perhaps
with resignation and certainly with sadness, said that "of the few
hundreds who listened, a score may have been convinced; but a voice
like this affected the raging of the populace about as much as the
chirping of the swallows on the telegraph pole affects the motion of
the Twentieth Century Limited."[21]

To read the vast majority of sermons from Northern pulpits in
those few weeks following the assassination of Abraham Lincoln is to
become aware of how angry, bitter, and vengeful the passions were
that gripped the North. Though the preachers were only reflecting
the sentiments of the general populace, they legitimatized and ex-

asperated those sentiments by anointing them with divine approval. Much has been said and written about the significant role of Southern preachers in perpetuating sectional differences and animosities for several decades following the war.[22] Though less attention has been given to the role of Northern preachers after the war, they, too, played an important part in widening the gap and promoting bitter differences between the two sections of the nation. For some months after the assassination, the accusations and passions of the Northern preachers were more vitriolic and condemning than those of their Southern counterparts. The overall role of the Northern clerics in stirring the troubled waters of the sectional pot was, however, much shorter lived than that of the Southern clergy who continued their stirring well into the twentieth century. The bitter passions resounding from Northern pulpits for stern judgments against the South began to moderate shortly after the impeachment of Andrew Johnson in the spring of 1868. Before another decade had passed, the pain of Lincoln's murder had significantly subsided and the preachers' calls for retributive justice against the South were largely forgotten.

5

◆ ◆ ◆

The Assassination
as an Act of Providence

It is not chance; it is not accident; it is the Lord.
—THOMAS LAURIE

MOST PREACHERS IN the mid–nineteenth century perceived events, whether individual or national, as providential. God had his hands on his creation. He led nations into war, bringing victories and administering defeats. Thus, most Northern preachers insisted that even such an abhorent deed as President Lincoln's murder somehow fell under the purview of God. On April 23, Seth Sweetser reminded his congregation that "Events are God's teachers." He then asked, "Shall we say, that the hand of the assassin, which struck at so noble a life, did it for any fault of his? or shall we say, that God permitted for a greater good to us, to our country, to posterity, that the sword, with a sharper edge than ever, should cut to the very core of our hearts?" From Brooklyn, Presbyterian Samuel T. Spear declared that "Providence has permitted what seems to us an untimely fall. I cannot explain it—I shall not try." "Yet," he said, "I am comforted by the thought that God has made no mistake. . . . He has permitted this great apparent calamity for some wise reason. . . . On earth we may never see this reason; yet the Lord knows and this should suffice us."[1]

On April 19, at the South Evangelical Church in West Roxbury, Massachusetts, Thomas Laurie offered, "I cannot point you to all the reasons for such an event, for I know them not any more than you; but we can together enjoy the consoling thought—it is not chance; it is not accident; 'It is the Lord; let him do what seemeth him good.' " George Mooar asked: "And would it not be a curse to think that all these things were happening, just as men throw dice, that there was no Hand of a personal God on the secret springs, ordering events, and bringing good out of evil?" Because the assassination was an act of Providence, George Duffield noted, we must accept it and learn the lesson God wished to teach.

What can we say, while weeping in the amazement and bewilderment of our grief, but that God hath done it? His hand arrested not the arm of the assassin. No angel messenger was dispatched to avert the fatal shot. Known to Omniscience was the plot of hellish treason, and the instruments of its accomplishment. Yet His providence, which could have easily prevented the fatal result, averted it not. . . . A holy and righteous God allowed it for His own wise and holy ends. What remains for us, and what can we else do, than to accept it as of His ordering, and humbly, prayerfully, and penitently improve the lesson, which the infinite wisdom and adorable sovereignty of Him who doeth His will in the armies of Heaven and among the inhabitants of the earth, designs to teach us by this overwhelming calamity?[2]

At Lincoln's funeral service in Washington, D.C., on April 19, Phineas D. Gurley stated that "Through and beyond all second causes, let us look and see the sovereign permissive agency of the great First Cause." He went on to echo what preachers all over the North were saying. Because God was in control, there was promise and hope that he would "bring light out of darkness, and good out of evil."

In the light of a clearer day, we may yet see that the wrath which planned and perpetuated the death of the President was overruled by Him, whose judgments are unsearchable and His ways past finding out, for the highest welfare of all those interests which are so dear to the Christian patriot and philanthropist, and for which a loyal people have made such an unexampled sacrifice of treasure and blood. Let us not be faithless, but believing.[3]

Some preachers, while admitting that Lincoln's murder was providential, attempted to make a distinction between an act that was caused by God and one that was permitted by God. The assassination, these preachers declared, happened under the second category, the permissive will of God. "The Lord . . . has permitted this shocking deed. But let us remember that He has not caused it. He is the cause of no evil whatsoever."[4]

What, then, was God doing and teaching through this tragic but providential event? There were those who confessed they did not know and doubted that such divine purposes could be ascertained.

Henry H. Northrop admitted, "I cannot see into His providences, I know not why he has permitted this thing, why the land is afflicted with such monsters as his murderer." L. M. Glover told his listeners that he was "incapable of reading the lesson at the present. I know not what the Great Ruler of the Universe means by it. . . . And is it not presumptuous in any man to stand forth at once with his divining rod and declare, as with certainty, the interpretation of the thing?" In a similar vein, Charles Hammond remarked, "we venture at the outset, that human speculation is utterly unable to scan the purposes of Divine Providence in such a calamity as this. And yet, from the day of Mr. Lincoln's death, there have not been wanting those, who have presumed upon their ability to penetrate so profound a mystery."[5]

In the providential interpretation of events, hope always remained. One of the great purposes of God, most preachers assured, was to bring ultimate good out of what appeared to be a temporary evil. Lincoln's assassination was no exception. "Not only did the death of the President, at this time and in this manner, enter into God's plan for the administration of affairs on earth, but He will overrule it for good, for greater good than could have been secured by his continued life." William Ives Buddington stated, "God needed the blood of martyrs, in their day, to corroborate and sanctify His Gospel! God needed, likewise, the blood of Abraham Lincoln! We can already see that it is doing what his life and his best services were powerless to accomplish." In Philadelphia, Morris C. Sutphen declared: "It is his province and prerogative to bring good out of evil; and how often has he turned the gloominess of his people into gladness." And Henry Lyman Morehouse assured his parishioners that "We believe God has permitted it that the power of evil arrayed against us may be the more quickly and effectually crushed."[6]

Though these Northerners preached that Lincoln's assassination may have been providential, a tragic event from which God would bring good, they wanted it known that this did not excuse the assassins. Thomas Laurie declared that the murder of Lincoln was an act of God; but not wanting to excuse his murderers, he reminded his congregation that though Providence was the first cause, "second causes [were] better supplied by villains than by honest men." Several preachers saw in the assassination a signal from God that Abraham Lincoln's work on earth had been completed. As God took

Moses and Jesus when their tasks were completed, so God took Lincoln. Cyrus A. Bartol, a Unitarian from Boston, reasoned that God "would not have permitted [Lincoln's] life to be taken, had he not done his work. He has finished it, how well and nobly." Bartol's fellow Bostonian James Reed expressed a similar sentiment: "Certain it is that our President would never have been taken away, if he had not finished his appointed work." In the Presbyterian Church of Pottstown, Pennsylvania, John C. Thompson assured that "That stroke which startled the nation did not alter the purposes of Jehovah. Abraham Lincoln lived until his work was accomplished." A Baptist cleric from Boston, J. D. Fulton, declared, "He died because his work was done. . . . The purpose which God had to accomplish through his instrumentality had been fulfilled." Chandler Robbins instructed that Lincoln had "died in a good time for himself; in a moment of joy, in an hour of hope and triumph, in the midst of peaceful and generous thoughts, while offering grateful aspirations to God, and devising acts of forgiveness and magnanimity towards man."[7]

The war was nearly over. Lincoln had successfully guided the nation through the crisis. Ahead lay the task and turmoil of Reconstruction. Perhaps, suggested several preachers, Lincoln did not possess the qualities for this new national emphasis. Perhaps he was too lenient, too compassionate, and too forgiving for the coming difficult days. Thus, Robert Lowry proclaimed, "Let us look for the good hand of our God in this calamitous visitation. The tender heart that has been laid low by violence, may have shrunk from the stern duties of the coming time." Isaac E. Carey, a Presbyterian clergyman from Freeport, Illinois, said that Lincoln "had fulfilled the purpose for which God had raised him up, and he passed off the stage because some different instrument was needed for the full accomplishment of the Divine purpose in the affairs of our nation." From Detroit, George Duffield announced:

Unquestionably, there was reason to fear, that treason would be dealt with too leniently, in the flush and joy of our victories, and triumph over rebellion. Perhaps our venerated President, fraught with benignity and mercy, and prompted, by his kindness of heart, to use the pardoning prerogative too freely, may not have been the man for the keen and necessary work of punishing treason, as it deserves, with the full penalty of the law. God has removed him in the hour of his triumph, and left this work to be performed by other hands.[8]

Warren H. Cudworth, from Boston, stated, "God may have seen that a sterner hand than his was needed to hold the helm of state during the next four years of reckoning and reconstruction." That "sterner hand," the preachers declared with varying degrees of confidence, was the new president, Andrew Johnson. From Waukegan, Illinois, Thomas Mears Eddy said: "When treason slew Abraham Lincoln, it slew the pardoning power, and by its own act placed authority in the hands of one of sterner mold and fiery soul—one deeply wronged by its atrocities." E. S. Atwood, from Salem, Massachusetts, continuing the theme that Tennesseean Johnson had been wronged by the South, said that the Rebels' "maniac and fiendish act has lifted into power a man who had felt the cords of rebellion tightening on his own neck; who has been stripped of his property and driven from his home, by the men with whom he is now to make terms." W. S. Studley, from Boston, emphasized that "In dealing with traitors, Andrew Johnson's little finger will be thicker than Abraham Lincoln's loins. If the OLD president chastised them with whips, the NEW president will chastise them with scorpions."[9]

To support their contention that the new president would deal sternly with the South, the preachers quoted from recent speeches Johnson had delivered as vice-president. Studley quoted from a Johnson discourse delivered a month before the assassination to the United States Senate. "Show me the man who makes war on the government, and fires on its vessels, and I will show you a traitor. And, if I were President of the United States, I would have all such arrested, and when tried and convicted, by the eternal God, I would have them hung." Commenting upon Johnson's remarks, Studley exclaimed: "There is hope, therefore, in the bright beams of this Easter sun! Our new ruler knows how to deal with traitors!" Robert Russell Booth also quoted from a recent Johnson speech, one delivered to the Illinois delegation shortly after the assassination of Lincoln.

The American people must be taught, if they do not already feel, that treason is a crime, and must be punished; that the Government will not always bear with its enemies; that it is strong, not only to protect, but also to punish. . . . With other and inferior offenses our people are familiar, but in our peaceful history, treason has been almost unknown. The people must understand that it is the blackest of crimes, and will surely be punished.

Booth reacted to Johnson's words, saying, "These are brave words, and the nation is stronger to-day than ever before, because they were uttered with the clear emphasis of one in authority."[10]

Not all Northern preachers were unreservedly enthusiastic about a Johnson presidency. A few preachers referred to a very recent incident that had happened on Lincoln's inauguration day, March 4, 1865, an incident that caused some to have serious reservations about the character of Johnson and his capacity to rule. The then vice-president was publicly intoxicated on that day. The preachers who mentioned that incident were not pleased with Johnson's behavior on that special day, but most were willing to overlook it as a one-time moral mistake and not a permanent character deficiency. The following are examples of the preachers' perspectives on this point.

Confidence is indeed a plant of slow growth, and, like affection, must be won before it can be bestowed. It can not be denied that our confidence in his fitness, even for the subordinate place to which he was elected, was seriously impaired by his drunkenness on the 4th of March, and that it requires some effort to confide in his fitness for the higher office to which he was not elected. But the charity which "covers the multitude of sins," will not hesitate to regard with leniency that single shameful act, of which he has already repented, and against the repetition of which he has solemnly pledged himself. His previous career as a man and a statesman, furnishes such a guarantee of his honesty, patriotism, and ability, as justifies the sure expectation that he will show himself equal to the responsibilities of his new position. Nor are there wanting some special reasons for giving him our entire confidence. . . . While Abraham Lincoln was the choice of the people, Andrew Johnson was the choice of God. God is wiser than we are. *Pliny H. White*

In regard to the newly inaugurated President, let me speak kindly, yet candidly. There is no need of concealing the painful distrust with which the public mind has been filled since the unfortunate transaction that occurred at his inauguration into the Vice-Presidency. All right feeling men experienced a deep mortification then, and consequently a certain want of confidence now. There are considerations, however, which tend greatly to relieve this public distrust. . . . He is too much of a man for the American people to cast him off for a single error. Indeed, my friends, even though there should prove to be no extenuating circumstances, I shall not be surprised, if from that very scene of his self-disgrace shall come a clearly visible good. But for that event he might come to his present position with too great self-reliance . . . we will not greet him with frowns, and insinuations, and fears. . . . We will rally round him as our President. *Denis Wortman*

I cannot cease speaking without commending to your prayers and confidence him who is called so suddenly to the Chief Magistracy of the land. I feel compelled to do this, because of the unfortunate impression made upon the country by Mr. Johnson at the late inauguration. With a haste as unreasonable as it is uncharitable, he has been condemned, as if an act proved a habit. . . . It may have been, nay, we are bound to believe it was an accident, pure and simple—proof only of an enfeebled body, and of an anxiety, in spite of sickness, to discharge a public duty. . . . Let us give him our confidence, and pray for him, as we did for his lamented predecessor. *William Ives Budington*[11]

With this single reservation, which even the few preachers who raised the issue were willing to overlook and forgive, the Northern preachers, as nearly one voice, called upon their congregations to pray for and support the new president of the United States.

We must now address ourselves to the duties of the hour. It is ours to strengthen the arm of the Executive, to encircle him with our sympathies, our confidence, and our prayers. *John G. Butler*

Let every loyal soul rise up and stand to-day like a wall of strength by Andrew Johnson, now, by the Providence of God, President of this Republic, regenerated and renewed by the sacrifice of bloody war. By this event we are shown that no one man is great enough to do this mighty work before us, neither is any one man indispensable. *Amory D. Mayo*

Under another leader, we are to be conducted into the promised land. We are to give him our allegiance, and with an earnest cooperation, encourage and strengthen his heart. He will need all the support of our prayers, and the guiding hand of God. *Seth Sweetser*

The prayers of God's people made President Lincoln what he was to the nation. It is not beyond the power of prayer to make President Johnson even more of a blessing to us in the days that are to come. *A. P. Rogers*

We will rally round this man. He, when generals said Nashville could not be held, sent the citizens into the trenches, and held it, and kept the flag flying. He will defend the flag as well now, and will man the ramparts with faithful men. The kindly heart is gone; the avenger has come. *Alonzo H. Quint*

And with great hope, several of the Northern clergy joined with Congregationalist Edwin B. Webb from Boston and challenged the new chief executive.

And do you make crime odious; disfranchise every man who has held office in the rebel government, and every commissioned officer in the rebel army; make the halter certain to the intelligent and influential, who are guilty of perjury and treason, and so make yourself a terror to him that doeth evil, and a praise to him that doeth good,—and we will stand by you, Andrew Johnson.[12]

The preachers' hopes for and support of President Johnson were short lived. Within a year's time, most Northern preachers turned against Johnson with vehemence, using the power and authority of the pulpit to discredit him. As far as most Northern preachers were concerned, Andrew Johnson proved to be much too lenient in his policies toward the South. Paul C. Brownlow, in an article that describes the tactics used by Northern preachers in their attacks upon Johnson, has written, "Northern Protestant clergymen supported President Andrew Johnson in 1865, but during 1866–1867 they repudiated him primarily because he had forsaken Radicalism in favor of a moderation which they believed would ruin the country."[13] Those preachers who had confidently proclaimed that Providence took the life of Abraham Lincoln so that he could be replaced by the sterner hand of Andrew Johnson were found wrong in their attempts to decipher the ways of the Almighty.

There were, however, other reasons as to why the omnipotent and omniscient God may have dealt with Abraham Lincoln and America as he did. Henry Ward Beecher affirmed that Lincoln's influence would be greater than ever before.

Even he who now sleeps has, by this event, been clothed with new influence. Dead, he speaks to men who now willingly hear what before they refused to listen to. Now, his simple and weighty words will be gathered like those of Washington, and your children and your children's children shall be taught to ponder the simplicity and deep wisdom of utterances which, in their time, passed, in the party heat, as idle words. Men will receive a new impulse of patriotism for his sake, and will guard with zeal the whole country which he loved so well: I swear you, on the altar of his memory, to be more faithful to the country for which he has perished. Men will, as they follow his hearse, swear a new hatred to that slavery against which he warred, and which in vanquishing him has made him a martyr and a conqueror: I swear you, by the memory of this martyr, to hate slavery with an unappeasable hatred. Men will admire and imitate his unmoved firmness, his inflexible conscience for the right; and yet his gentleness, as tender as a woman's, his moderation of spirit, which not all the heat of party could inflame, nor all the jars and disturbances of this country shake out of its place: I swear you to an emulation of his justice, his moderation and his mercy.

Other clergy saw the assassination as a tragedy that united the loyal portion of the nation. "One thing is clear: even now the American people are united as they were never united before." James Eells declared that "our common feeling of loss and outrage will tend, more than any arguments and appeals could have done, to bring all classes of our people together and cement them by the impulses it will arouse in all alike." Unitarian James Freeman Clarke emphasized that "This crime will unite the whole North to make thorough work with the rebellion, and put it down where it can never stir itself again."[14]

Yet another positive consequence of Lincoln's murder, the clergy believed, was that it awakened the country to the cruelty of the slave system. In New York City, William R. Williams, the pastor of Amity (Baptist) Church, noted that in the later months of the war the North was at last beginning to learn about the barbarism of the slave system, and Northern indignation was being awakened. Yet, continued Williams, the Union needed "a more malign outbreak, and a more distinguished sacrifice, to have its holy wrath aroused and intensified into a deadly and uncompromising decision against all further tolerance of the system." Warren H. Cudworth discovered a similar providential purpose. "Finally," he declared, "God has again providentially lifted the veil that apologists for slavery—Northern and Southern—have drawn over its hideous features, and shown us just what spirit it is of." Because Lincoln's death was the ultimate exposure of the decadence of slavery, the foul deed would hasten slavery's demise.

> The bullet-shot and the knife-stab, that evening delivered, have effectually nailed to the mast of the ship of state the banner of Emancipation—of universal—unconditional—uncompensated and unrepealable enfranchisement. . . . These men of the South have themselves driven, with their own violent hands, the nails that fasten it in place. Who, North or South, has power to draw the nails so driven?[15]

A great number of preachers agreed with Thomas M. Hopkins when he suggested that Lincoln was providentially taken because the American people were beginning to idolize him. "God cannot tolerate idols," asserted Hopkins. "This nation was on the point of worshipping Mr. Lincoln. . . . We knew not how much we loved him until he was gone. This fact alone shows us that there was danger of his occupying too great a space in our hearts." Baptist George Dana Boardman also asked, "Was not the President's death necessary to the nation's life? Were we not leaning on an arm of flesh forgetful of the ever loving God?"[16]

Many preachers thought that through Lincoln's assassination God was punishing the people of the North for their sins. Henry E. Niles gave expression to this conviction: "O! what a wicked nation ours must be when to the catalogue of her martyred sons, must be added this illustrious name, fallen in the sacrifice for popular sins!" A similar theme expressed by the preachers was that God used the assassination to humble the North. Richard Duane of St. John's (Episcopal) Church in Providence remarked that Northerners "were in danger of being exalted beyond measure by [their] successes." He continued, "Already we were uttering the old words of pride and self-sufficiency, for which God has rebuked us so fearfully." Henry W. Bellows asked, "May we not have needed this loss to sober our hearts in the midst of our national triumph, lest in the excess of our joy and pride we should overstep the bounds of that prudence and the limits of that earnest seriousness which our affairs demand?"

Yet another gain the preachers saw arising from the assassination was that the North had learned about the importance of administering stern justice, a lesson many had seemingly forgotten and certainly neglected.

> In such a juncture our Government needed an infusion of the Old Testament severity rather than the New Testament tenderness, and it seems clear that God has intended, by this sudden and appalling calamity, to bring to our remembrance those truths of distributive justice which stand out so clearly in His dealings with Israel of old, and which do indeed underlie the whole framework of Gospel salvation.[17]

On April 16 at the First Presbyterian Church of Brooklyn, Charles S. Robinson attested as to "the power of martyrdom in fixing great principles."

> We, therefore, have stood for the rights of men, the truth of the Gospel, the principles of humanity, the integrity of the Union, the power of Christian people to govern themselves, the indefeasible equality of all the creatures of God in natural conditions of existence, no matter what may be the color of their skin. So the nations of the world have looked upon us, and held us responsible. We were the enemies of all class-systems, castes, and aristocracies. We were the champions of manhood in all that was noble, of womanhood in all that was pure. This has been, and still is, our cause. And what I call you to learn now is, that this cause is safe. A martyr's blood has sealed the covenant we are making with posterity.

And on the same day, at the First Baptist Church in Philadelphia George Dana Boardman was triumphant in exclaiming that out of Lincoln's death the greatness of the nation would rise to new and greater heights.

> The richly kerneled and tasselled stalk springs from the death of the solitary seed. Even so, the nation's triumph and greatness may spring from Abraham Lincoln's death. Had he been permitted to live till the term of his great office had expired, and, afterwards, in a green old age, to die amidst the tranquilities of his Illinois home, he would still have been the glorious nobleman that God crowned him in his birth; but he might

have abided alone, fructifying into no national harvest. We should still have revered him, as we revere all of God's great ones; but no nation would have been born of him. But when, beneath the sufferance of an inscrutable Providence, the assassin's bullet laid him low, the glorious seed died, that it might no longer abide alone, but bring forth much fruit. Even here, in the cause of Liberty, as in the cause of the Church, it shall be found that the blood of the martyrs is the seed of the Republic. Take courage, then, my countrymen: for even now I see springing from the tear-wet bier of Abraham Lincoln the green and tender blades which foretell the birth of an emancipated, united, triumphant, trans-figured, immortal Republic. Even so, Father! For thus it seemed good in Thy sight![18]

This concept of providential faith was not confined to conservative Christianity or to those still clinging to vestiges of a Puritan theology. Unitarian as well as Congregational ministers were attempting to place Lincoln's assassination in some kind of providential scheme. Lincoln himself, who was not a church member or a publicly professed Christian, was a strong believer in Providence. An example is found on the day of his second inaugural, when he feared, as did others, that an attempt would be made upon his life; when Edwin Stanton offered to provide special protection for the President, Lincoln replied, "Stanton it is useless. If it is the will of Providence that I should die by the hand of an assassin, it must be so."[19]

In the spring of 1865, a belief in Providence seemed to be essential to both clergy and laity as they sought to make some kind of sense out of their loss and grief. Only a belief in God, who ordained the affairs of men, the world, and history, could bring any meaning or comfort in the midst of such tragedy. On this the preachers were nearly unanimous. Whether they were Baptists, Presbyterians, Episcopalians, or Unitarians, whether conservative or liberal, Old Side or New Side, the clergy dealt with their own and the nation's grief by believing in and looking for the directing hand of God. Only this made their burden bearable. Only this brought order to what was otherwise meaningless chaos.

Where the preachers differed was in their interpretation of what God was trying to teach and do through Lincoln's murder. As has been noted, some proclaimed that such a purpose could not be discerned by mortal minds. One could only believe that there was a purpose, even though that purpose could not be known. Other preachers, however, were not so timid and proclaimed with some assurance that they knew what God was doing and why. Most proclaimed that good would arise out of temporary evil; such were the ways of God and, thus, there was always hope. Others were certain that God had taken Lincoln because the work to which he was called had been completed, or because Lincoln would have been too lenient to effectively deal with the problems of Reconstruction and a sterner Andrew Johnson was needed at the nation's helm. Some preachers talked about the expansion of Lincoln's influence through his death; the uniting of the North in the postwar era; the awakening of the nation to the cruelty of the slave system; the danger of idolizing Lincoln; the punishment of Northern sins; the need for humility; the alerting of the North as to the importance of administering stern and certain justice upon the South; the fact that the example of martyrdom instills great principles within a people; and the belief that Lincoln's death would contribute to the coming millennium.

But on one of those perceived divine purposes the preachers—and there were many of them—were wrong: believing and declaring that the death of Lincoln would bring in a sterner administration. Nothing could have been a greater contradiction to what actually took place. As to the other purposes, many of which to one degree or another did happen, certain questions arise. Did these events come about as a result of Lincoln's assassination, or did they come about in spite of his death? Would such events have happened anyway? Were such events truly good and beneficial in nature? Finally, however these questions are answered, were these events ordained and directed by a providential hand?

For the most part, contemporary clergy would not answer these questions with the certainty or the assurances with which most nineteenth-century preachers answered them. Contemporaries, if they hold to some kind of providential faith, would most likely tend to agree with J. L. Janeway, who held that though the assassination could be viewed within the bounds of Providence, he hesitated to proclaim what that specifically meant. "I feel incompetent to interpret God's providence," he said. "I prefer humbly to watch and wait the end, when God himself shall make plain what is now so dark and mysterious."[20]

6

• • •

Sermon Conclusions

Hero, Martyr, Friend, Farewell!

—MATTHEW SIMPSON

THERE CAN BE no great rhetoric if the conclusion of a discourse is weak and uninspiring. Most of the preachers who composed their sermons as a response to the assassination of President Lincoln understood and practiced this cardinal rule of oratory. As they drew their sermons to a close they reached the summit of their oratorical and homiletical skills. Their concluding sentences and paragraphs are dramatic, moving, eloquent, and well crafted. They make a profound impact upon those who can only read the words; and one can only speculate as to the effect these words had upon those who heard them in a time of great emotional upheaval. By sharing some of those concluding paragraphs, contemporaries may in some limited way recapture the highly charged feelings and tensions of those spring days in 1865, as well as come to appreciate how highly skilled these preachers were in the employment of their craft.

Many, perhaps most, of the concluding paragraphs are the preachers' final attempts to eulogize the martyred President. On Sunday, April 23, at the Holy Trinity Church of Philadelphia, as the body of Lincoln lay in state, the revered Episcopalian rector Phillips Brooks drew to a close what some think is his greatest sermon by likening Lincoln to a shepherd who faithfully fed his flock.

> The Shepherd of the People! that old name that the best rulers ever craved. What ruler ever won it like this dead President of ours? He fed us faithfully and truly. He fed us with counsel when we were in doubt, with inspiration when we sometimes faltered, with caution when we would be rash, with calm, clear, trustful cheerfulness through many an hour when our hearts were dark. He fed hungry souls all over the country with sympathy and consolation. He spread before the whole land

feasts of great duty and devotion and patriotism, on which the land grew strong. He fed us with solemn, solid truths. He taught us the sacredness of government, the wickedness of treason. He made our souls glad and vigorous with the love of liberty that was in him. He showed us how to love truth and yet be charitable—how to hate wrong and all oppression, and yet not treasure one personal injury or insult. He fed all his people, from the highest to the lowest, from the most privileged down to the most enslaved. Best of all, he fed us with a reverent and genuine religion. He spread before us the love and fear of God just in that shape in which we need them most, and out of his faithful service of a higher Master who of us has not taken and eaten and grown strong? "He fed them with a faithful and true heart." Yes, till the last. For at the last, behold him standing with hand reached out to feed the South with mercy and the North with charity, and the whole land with peace, when the Lord who had sent him called him and his work was done![1]

On the same day, Henry Ward Beecher's conclusion spoke eloquently of Lincoln's body being returned to the soil of Illinois.

Four years ago, O Illinois, we took from your midst an untried man, and from among the people; we return him to you a mighty conqueror. Not thine any more, but the nation's; not ours, but the world's. Give him place, ye prairies! In the midst of this great Continent his dust shall rest, a sacred treasure to myriads who shall make pilgrimage to that shrine to kindle anew their zeal and patriotism. Ye winds, that move over the mighty places of the West, chant his requiem! Ye people, behold a martyr, whose blood, as so many articulate words, pleads for fidelity, for law, for liberty![2]

After making several comparisons between George Washington and Abraham Lincoln, on May 7 Joel F. Bingham finally elevated Lincoln to "the best who shall rise among us."

Finally, WASHINGTON lived for his country, and died as a great and good man would wish to die, who had no more sacrifices to make for his fellow men. The life of the just departed LINCOLN, after having wrought out the painful salvation of the Republic, has been offered, a bloody sacrifice, upon the altar of human freedom and the happiness of his fellow countrymen. He has taken the last degree of glory, and set above his undying name the martyr's crown. The best who shall arise among us, in the future, may imitate, but none can surpass him. Further than his, human effort and human glory cannot go.[3]

The Reverend John E. Todd brought his sermon to a close by noting that Lincoln "fell in the very height of glory."

For President Lincoln himself, perhaps there was no better time to pass away. . . . It may be that he could not, in a hundred years, have found a moment in which to fall so lamented, or leave behind him such a memory. Henceforth a humble tomb in the capital of Illinois will divide with Mount Vernon the homage and pilgrimages of our countrymen. Perhaps if these mighty dead, the leaders in the two wars for freedom, are permitted to revisit their resting-places, the murdered President will experience the greater joy, in finding not only his head-stone worn with the kisses of his own race, but the sods of his grave sprinkled with the tears of eyes that used to weep in the house of bondage.
God bless the memory of Abraham Lincoln!
God bless the President!
God in his mercy bless and save these United States of America![4]

June 1, 1865, the Day of National Humiliation, was set aside by President Andrew Johnson to revere the memory of Lincoln. On that day, John C. Thompson mentioned that this observance might be the last of "public honors" for Lincoln but that individual hearts and minds will pay him homage for many years to come.

With this day perhaps will close the public honors to our "fallen Chief," but individual hearts will do him honor, and private tongues will continue to speak his worth; and oft in coming years, when the peaceful waters of the Potomac shall have cleansed the gore-sodden soil which lines its banks; and when nature shall have kindly covered up, with her luxuriant robe of harvest the battle-scarred and blackened bosom of the earth; unnumbered pilgrim feet shall wend their way to the great man's tomb, and bitter tears will fall upon the sacred soil where the Chieftain sleeps![5]

On April 16, John Chester, in a sermon delivered at his church, the Capitol Hill Presbyterian Church in Washington, D.C., concluded with words of eloquence and pathos to the sleeping President.

Lay there quietly in thy last sleep, oh beloved dust!! Around thy body the sentinels this day keep watch, but around thy memory our hearts shall keep guard in this generation, and then commit the sacred trust to our children's children.

Sleep there calmly. Thou under whose Administration a race has broken its shackles and risen from its degradation. Over thy bier this day, that race is shedding more heartfelt tears than ever before moistened the couch of an earthly ruler.

Sleep there, environed by all the glory of thy nation's fame. Thou, who enteredst the Presidential chair in the time of thy nation's trial, and left it not until thine eyes beheld its triumph. The lovers of freedom throughout the world respect thy worth.

Sleep there, eloquent even in death. "Though being dead, thou yet speaketh." "Thy blood crieth unto God from the ground for vengeance." The assassin's weapon only deprived thy body of life; thou still livest, enshrined in our hearts, and nations yet unborn shall rise up and call thee blessed.[6]

A personal and touching sermon conclusion was delivered by Lincoln's close friend Bishop Matthew Simpson at the burial in Springfield on May 4. Simpson used his final paragraph to bid farewell.

Chieftain! farewell! The nation mourns thee. Mothers shall teach thy name to their lisping children. The youth of our land shall emulate thy virtues. Statesmen shall study thy record and learn lessons of wisdom. Mute though thy lips be, yet they still speak. Hushed is thy voice, but its echoes of liberty are ringing through the world, and the sons of bondage listen with joy. Prisoned thou art in death, and yet thou art marching abroad, and chains and manacles are bursting at thy touch. Thou didst fall not for thyself. The assassin had no hate for thee. Our hearts were aimed at, our national life was sought. We crown thee as our martyr—and humanity enthrones thee as her triumphant son. Hero, Martyr, Friend, Farewell![7]

On April 19, Charles Carroll Everett ended his sermon by urging his listeners not to give way to "cowardly thoughts of despair."

I heard a little girl, surprised that the robin was singing its old song, exclaim, "I thought that the birds would sing sad, now that Abraham

Lincoln is dead!" But, no, the birds sing as of old. The spring flowers will open their delicate buds as sweetly as if he were here to welcome them. Nature is unchanged. Principle is unchanged, Providence is unchanged.

Let us, then, not dishonor the memory of Lincoln by cowardly thoughts of despair. We will leave our hearts in his grave. We will give our confidence, though we cannot yet give the same love, to those that come after him. Nay, we will gather here a fresh confidence. We will strengthen our hearts by a fresh purpose of devotion to his cause and ours. And, though as we go away, our eyes are dim with tears, these shall not blind us to the promise of the future.—Rather shall its brightness, shining through our tears, make them radiant with its glory.[8]

Bringing a rather lengthy sermon to a close, Joseph A. Seiss issued a challenge to his listeners. Much of the sermon had been devoted to a comparison of the lives and contributions of Moses and Lincoln, and Seiss concluded by inviting his congregation to emulate the example and inspiration of these two notable figures.

We may be humble, feeble, and unnoticed in the great crowd of men; but we are each God's workmanship. He has put each of us here for a purpose; and we each must some day answer to Him for the manner in which we have fashioned our lives, and fulfilled our mission.

We may not have nations to lead, or to organize to new ideas, or to guide and keep in the hours of trial; but we each have spheres of importance in which to operate, and little gardens which we ourselves alone can cultivate, and webs of little deeds to weave, in which our highest life is to be found.

We may not, indeed, be Moseses or Lincolns, but, like both of them, we can be ourselves; and by being honestly our true selves in humble things, we know not to what high spheres we yet may be raised. We have the highest authority for it, that faithfulness in that which is least, is faithfulness also in much. We know by whom, and to whom, it was said, "Well done, good and faithful servant; thou hast been faithful over a few things, I will make thee ruler over many things." And both the histories of the men whose names I have associated in these remarks, preach and illustrate the same hopefulness.

Lives of great men all remind us
    We can make our lives sublime,
And, departing, leave behind us
Footprints on the sands of time—

Footprints that perhaps another,
    Sailing o'er life's solemn main
A forlorn and shipwrecked brother,
    Seeing, shall take heart again.

Let us then be up and doing,
    With a heart for any fate;
Still achieving, still pursuing,
    Learn to labor and to wait.[9]

Universalist Rufus S. Sanborn drew his sermon together by noting that there were significant personal, national, and universal lessons to be gleaned from Lincoln's death.

I am not angry—I breathe no spirit of revenge—I harbor no hatred against men, but I feel strong and clear for the right—clearer, stronger and calmer than ever before; and I have registered the determination, as thousands of others have done the past week, that I will live for the right, labor for the just, and resist the oppressive, in all right and honorable ways, so long as I live. The elevation of the masses, and the emancipation of the world from all kinds of oppression, this is mine, this is yours, and my country's mission, which is written and declared in the irresistible and sublime logic of passing events. The peoples' President is murdered! but the peoples' cause lives, and will live and grow purer and grander the longer it lives! Hear it, tyrants, all over the world; hear it ye who would live on the toil and sweat of the many; hear it ye short sighted powers of evil: ye cannot assassinate a righteous cause! You may battle for the wrong, and thousands may die in the contest, but all that is pure, and holy, and just, and true, belongs to the eternal and imperishable; these cannot die! for it is written, "surely the wrath of man shall praise Thee; the remainder of wrath shalt Thou restrain." Now I see the cloud folds of this great national bereavement parting, and aloft, through the bright opening, the angel of liberty waves her banner and beckons the nation onward and higher, till the azure blue of God's sky, with all the stars shining in beauty, shall be over one people, united, happy and free![10]

Several preachers used their concluding words as one final opportunity to demand that stern justice be administered on the South. On April 16, Robert Lowry, an Episcopalian from New York City, concluded by declaring that no pardons must be issued for the "leaders of the rebellion."

This land is not large enough to hold the leaders of the rebellion. The flag they have sought to dishonor should not be allowed to cover them. They have forfeited, a thousand times over, the mercy of the government they assailed. And this last and vilest culmination of their crimes puts them beyond the possibility of pardon. Let us make this soil red-hot to the foot of every traitor. Let the warm breath of our holy indignation sweep from our cities every rebel sympathizer. Let us vow, in God's house to-day, that treason shall be destroyed, trunk and branch, root and rootlet, till not one hand be left to give the sword such a vintage of blood again. Then will our land be a land of peace and freedom. Then will our nation be the joy of the whole earth![11]

On the following Sunday, the Presbyterian Samuel T. Spear, also from New York City, echoed the words of Lowry in demanding justice.

We commend our suffering country to his care and keeping. We here pledge ourselves to each other, and call upon high heaven to witness the covenant, that to the cause for which Abraham Lincoln lived, and in which he died, we will be true to our last breath; we will never desert the Stars and the Stripes; we will never lay down the sword till the supremacy of this government is vindicated; we will never pause till the daring criminals who have brought this evil upon the land are themselves brought to merited justice. God helping us, we will crush treason and suitably punish traitors, cost what it may. Just now we are in no mood to be trifled with by that senseless philanthropism, that shallow and almost soulless sentimentality, that has no foundation in the moral nature of man, and none in the moral government of God. We are not dealing with wasps—perfectly harmless if we let them alone—but with traitors, with the enemies of public order, with men who have virtually raised the black flag over our defenceless and helpless soldiers captured in war, a fit representative of whom has just murdered our President. Such are the men who are at the head of this rebellion and with whom we have to do, and our duty in the premises is as clear as light. May the God of heaven prepare us for the work and crown it with his blessing.[12]

A few preachers, however, ended their sermons with pleas for reconciliation, mercy, and forgiveness. On April 16, Amory D. Mayo,
in the Church of the Redeemer of Cincinnati, made such a plea.

We are that American People, God's chosen people of these modern days
to lead the world to the freedom of all mankind. Every one of us must
be somewhat nobler now that our great leader is gone. Let no breath now
be wasted in barbaric curses; no power lost in indiscriminate vengeance.
It would be childish in us to go off into a frenzy, or drift into disorder,
or try to wash out his precious blood by spurning the corpse of the slave
aristocracy! No! Let that abomination alone! Begin, to-morrow morning, to build up the American home, American industry, American religion, American society, the American Republic, in all its vast extent,
with that decayed aristocracy left out and let alone. "Let alone" every
man and woman that ties to that dead body. The new age is here. Have
your doings, and sayings, and associations with living men and living
things. Everywhere do better than you have yet done. Stop not to weep;
but work and pray; and as you toil towards the new day the kindly face
of our dear, dear father shall smile upon us with the same love that used
to gleam out of those eyes, which assured us that when he did put off
that great earthy body he would put on the spiritual body of a saint
in heaven.[13]

Episcopal rector Stephen H. Tyng similarly urged his Northern
listeners to "open the arms of fraternal concord."

But in reality there has never been a time when this whole Northern
people have not been ready to meet the first offer of conciliation with the
most cordial response of kindness. Let that spirit now prevail. Open the
arms of fraternal concord. Spread through all the land the priceless bless-
ings of liberty and education to all the people. Give the full rights of
respected and acknowledged citizenship to all. Blot out, cover up the
last remnant of that slavery which has been the parent and the child of
every species of oppression—the one line of division between a free
North and a beggared South—and plant around the grave that holds the
monument and the memory of our beloved President a mingled grove of
the pine-tree and the palm, the orange and the apple, to flourish in immortal union, and to rival each other only in the beauty of their growth,

the abundance of their fruit, and the perennial verdure of their living foliage, that God may be glorified in all and by all for ever.[14]

Several preachers used their concluding words to turn their listeners' attention to the needs, fate, and future of the nation. George H. Hepworth likened the country's latest misfortune to a wrecked ship.

In my mind's eye, I see a stout and well-built ship, lying a wreck upon hidden rocks. Bravely she has breasted the storms of a score of winters. She has battled with the tornadoes of Indian seas, bending her proud masts until the frenzied wave threw its furious spray upon the highest sail; she has confronted Atlantic tempests; and, when she came into port at last, was just enough defaced to prove the terrible character of the struggles from which she had come in triumph. She has brought her rich cargo of hope and faith, of good laws and liberty; and, but yesterday, her cargo safely landed upon the wharf, she slipped her moorings and play-fully unbent her sails for an hour's enjoyment. But, alas! there were rocks, hidden rocks, in the way,—rocks not laid down upon any chart except the chart of Satan. She struck; and tears filled our eyes as we saw the noble vessel that had done her duty so well, lying there, the vic-tim of a mischief that could not have been foreseen. So is it with our country to-day.[15]

Most preachers had great hopes for the future of the nation in spite of, and partly because of, the recent tragedy. George Putnam looked forward to a renewed patriotism and national loyalty.

Perhaps at this moment, while we speak, they are lifting up the remains of our noble patriot, deliverer, martyr, to bear them from his palace-home to the dark and narrow house. In such a moment, of so great so-lemnity and tenderness, let the sacred fires of patriotism blaze up bright and aloft in millions of hearts; let hand clasp with hand in a solemn league and covenant of loyalty, and all true souls renew their vows of devotion to the country which he loved, and lived for and died for; and make that country, in its unity, its grandeur, and its peace, a fitting monument to his memory, worthy to record his earthly fame, and ac-ceptable to the contemplation of his glorified spirit.[16]

E. S. Atwood, on April 16 at the South Church in Salem, Massachusetts, used the Easter theme of resurrection—national resurrection—when delivering his concluding thoughts.

Above all, let us rise up with quickened faith in God, and the country's cause. He has rolled away the clouds before now—he will do it again. We are cast down but not destroyed—perplexed but not in despair. God lives, and while he lives we may hope and be strong. The nation stoops to day to drink of the stream of Marah, and cries out at the bitter draught, but to-morrow the waters will be sweet and clear. Our Flag is not all shrouded in mourning, we but border its edges with sable—and out of its funereal fringes, its radiant stripes still gleam with their symbolism of promise, its stars still shine from their field of azure. Our sorrow is not our history, only the dark hem that shades for a little its brightness. Over the sad pall that covers our buried hopes bloom the bright flowers of resurrection. [17]

Several preachers concluded their sermons with a millennial view of the nation's future. Such was the case with Leonard Swain.

If we learn the lesson well, and ponder it deeply and wisely, our sorrow shall yet be our redemption. We shall see that one man has died for the people, in order that the whole nation might not perish. We shall confess the hand of God. We shall turn to Him who has smitten us. We shall repent of our sins against Him, and make a new and everlasting covenant with Him. Then shall He return unto us and bless us. He shall heal all our woes, and bring upon us the good which, through all these years, He has been secretly preparing for us. He will make us His people, and He Himself will be our God. The nations that hated us shall come bending to us for His sake, and all the ends of the earth shall say, when they behold us, "Happy is the people that is in such a case; yea, happy is that people whose God is the Lord."

Similarly, A. P. Rogers concluded with a millennial vision.

Let the nation bow itself before God, who hath smitten, and he will raise us up. Through the darkness of the present I see the brightness of the future as the sun in heaven. I see the picture of a glorious land, her sins purged away, every blot removed from her stainless escutcheon—the home of civilization, liberty, and Christianity—a beacon light among the nations of the earth, the friend of the oppressed, the sun of the benighted, the messenger of a resurrection to all the slumbering hopes of humanity, the great benediction of God to the world. Oh! if this picture may be a reality, and if this awful catastrophe which has clothed us in mourning shall but help on the grand consummation, then, indeed, our lamented President will have blessed his country and the world far more in death than in his life, and this last climax of agony and blood will not have been reached in vain.[18]

On Easter morning April 16, Alonzo H. Quint brought his sermon to an end by tying together a millennial vision of the nation's future with the theme of resurrection. It was hopeful, optimistic, due to the "faithfulness" of Abraham Lincoln.

But the vision is yet to be realized. The promised land is to be enjoyed. God lives. I see before us, the country united; not with the sufferance of traitors,—for they, the Canaanites are to be driven with fire and sword. I see the millions of freedmen becoming American citizens, happy and loyal. I see a land of growing wealth, in towns and cities and harvest lands. I see the ocean whitened with sails, and the harbors forests of masts. I see a flag beloved at home, and honored abroad. I see this country the asylum of the oppressed from every land. I see the name of the great republic feared by despots as no name has been since Oliver Cromwell threatened they should hear the thunder of his cannon at the gates of Rome. I see religion flourish; churches multiplied; the tread of him who preacheth glad tidings; God's Spirit descending; and the nation, tried and purified by suffering, the people of God. This day, which many Christians hail as the day when Christ arose, is the auspicious omen of this country's resurrection.

We would he could have seen it. It seems due to his faithfulness. But God's will be done. A nation's tears fall to the memory of a beloved ruler. A nation's heart throbs painfully at his grave. A nation's gratitude cherishes the widow and the fatherless. And in that history which will do him justice, he will be inscribed, not only as an honest, a wise, a devout ruler; but, in the story of the hard trial out of which America emerged a great and just nation, his name will be linked with its record as its martyred leader in its sufferings and its glory.[19]

◆ ◆ ◆

Conclusion

THAT THE POST-ASSASSINATION sermons of the Northern clergy
were so political in nature should come as no surprise. The preachers, through their pulpits, as well as other means, had been heavily
involved in the public affairs of their time since the mid-1830s. They
had been instrumental in turning sectional differences into moral issues during antebellum days. The Northern preachers, as well as
their Southern counterparts, played significant roles in exciting the
sectional passions and debates that culminated in the Civil War. In
1857 historian Albert Barnes wrote of the influence of the clergy at
that time.

> In a country so extensively under the influence of religion as ours; where
> religion undeniably so much controls public sentiment; where so large a
> portion of the community is connected with the church; and where the
> Christian Ministry exerts so wide an influence on the public mind, it
> cannot be an unimportant question what the church is doing, and what
> it ought to do, in reference to an evil [slavery] so vast, and so perilous
> to all our institutions. . . . In our country there is no class of men who
> exert more influence than the ministers of the gospel.[1]

Religion was a dominant influence in mid-nineteenth-century
America and as such played a significant role in private and public
life. In the 1830s, the perceptive French visitor to America, Alexis
de Tocqueville, observed that there was "no country in the world
where the Christian religion retains a greater influence over the souls
of men than in America." Irving H. Bartlett, in his brief but in-
sightful study *The American Mind in the Mid–Nineteenth Century*, has

written that "theology was a primary concern of the American mind at least through the middle of the nineteenth century."[2]

The era was an especially invigorating time for those concerned with religious questions and answers. It was a time of marked theological change as ministers and theologians attempted to mold religion to a more liberal and democratic American mind without destroying some fundamental foundations. American Christianity was breaking away from the inflexible determinism of Calvinism to an increasing emphasis on free will, which meant personal and national responsibility. Yet, for those Americans whose thoughts were always buttressed by theology, there was a great desire to believe in a Providence who was still in control. The preachers quoted in Chapter 5 are examples of a deeply held faith in and conviction about Providence. Even such an evil deed as the assassination of the beloved Lincoln was within the parameters of the will of God. Though free will and Providence seemed to be such a contradiction, most mid-nineteenth-century Northern preachers were able to cherish and hold both ideas in tandem. Bartlett has noted the paradox: "The celebration of human will is hardly consistent with a belief in Providence, yet both ideas were of central importance to Americans in the pre–Civil War period, a time when men could place unbounded confidence in their own efforts to improve a world controlled by God."[3]

This belief in Providence is found in the thought patterns of Lincoln himself. Pounded out upon the anvil of suffering—the loss of his son Willie in 1862 and the suffering of the nation throughout the war—Lincoln's concept of Providence was powerfully and beautifully expressed in his Second Inaugural Address, delivered a month and a half before his death. After declaring that "the Almighty has His own purposes," Lincoln continued:

> If we should suppose that American slavery is one of those offenses which, in the providence of God, must needs come, but which, having continued through His appointed time, He now wills to remove, and that He gives to both North and South, this terrible war, as the woe due to those by whom the offense came, shall we discern therein any departure from those divine attributes which the believers in a Living God always ascribe to Him? Fondly do we hope—fervently do we pray—that this mighty scourge of war may speedily pass away. Yet if God wills that

it continue . . . as was said three thousand years ago, so still it must be said the judgments of the Lord are true and righteous altogether.

A series of events in the ten years prior to the war moved many Northern preachers from non-involvement to high moral indignation and action, so that when Fort Sumter was fired upon in April of 1861, the great majority of the clergy was adamant in its denunciations of slavery, secession, and the South and was a strong supporter of the war. The Fugitive Slave Law (1850), the Kansas-Nebraska Act (1854), the caning of Charles Sumner on the floor of the United States Senate by Preston Brooks of South Carolina (1856), the Dred Scott decision by the Supreme Court (1857), the move toward secession (1860–61), and the firing on Fort Sumter (1861)—all and each brought forth an increasing involvement of the Northern pulpits into the public arena of their times. Illinois senator Stephen A. Douglas, who co-authored the Kansas-Nebraska Act, was stung by the clerical opposition to the bill. Calling the clergy ignorant men and liars and declaring that they were disgracing themselves and their profession by such political intrusions, Douglas intoned:

> It is presented by a denomination of men calling themselves preachers of the Gospel, who have come forward with an atrocious falsehood and an atrocious calumny against the Senate, desecrated the pulpit, and prostituted the sacred desk to the miserable and corrupting influence of party politics. I doubt whether there is a body of men in America who combine so much profound ignorance on the question upon which they attempt to enlighten the Senate as this same body of preachers.[4]

Not all Northern clergymen, however, were politically involved. Whether from cowardice, conviction, or the desire to maintain denominational unity, there were several who declared that the pulpit was not the place to discuss public matters. Nearly all representatives of the Roman Catholic Church strongly supported the non-involvement position. In 1852, Archbishop John Hughes admonished his clergy "to abstain from all interferences in politics." A "Pastoral Letter" of May 1858, signed by Archbishop Kenrick, Bishop Neumann, and Bishop McGill, warned not only against political involvement but in taking a position on a controversial public issue such as slavery.

In the great political struggles that have agitated the country on the subject of domestic slavery. . . . among us there has been no agitation on the subject. Our clergy have wisely abstained from all interference with the judgment of the faithful, which should be free on all questions of polity and social order, within the limits of the doctrine and Law of Christ. . . . venerable brethren . . . Do not in any way, identify the interest of our holy faith with the fortunes of any party.[5]

Joining the Catholic Church in advocating silence on political issues were the Protestant Episcopal Church and the Lutheran Church. The Catholics and Episcopalians, for the most part, maintained their silence throughout the war, while the Lutherans changed their position and began to speak out. However, there were individual Episcopalian and Lutheran ministers who defied their denominations' official stances and spoke directly to and about public issues. It is interesting to note the readiness of several Episcopalian rectors to address political issues in the post-assassination sermons referred to in this volume. Were emotions and convictions, long restrained by denominational policies, finally unleashed and expressed because of the traumatic experience of Lincoln's brutal murder?

One of those Episcopalian clergymen who maintained a virtual pulpit silence on public issues in the years before and during the Civil War, yet upon the death of Lincoln delivered a powerful political sermon, was the renowned Phillips Brooks. In a sermon delivered on April 23, while the body of Lincoln was lying in state in Philadelphia, Brooks preached what was for him an atypical sermon, which was to become his most-remembered sermon. In it he delivers an eloquent eulogy of Lincoln, castigates the South, and blames the institution of slavery for the assassination.[6] It should be noted that in future years Brooks continued to express strong reservations about the progress of Reconstruction, especially as it pertained to black suffrage, long after most Northern ministers had lost interest and were occupied with other matters.

Though Brooks had proceeded cautiously on social issues, he was far in front of the stance taken by the Episcopal Church. Brooks was impatient with his denomination. In the fall of 1862, after the meeting of the General Convention of the Episcopal Church in New York City, Brooks, in a letter to George A. Strong, wrote that he was disappointed "to see those old gentlemen putting their heads together to make some resolutions that would please the Union people and not hurt the feelings of the dear rebels. . . . It's a miserable business and they won't satisfy either side." In the May 1864 meeting of the Pennsylvania diocesan convention in Pittsburgh, Brooks was among those who asked for a resolution stating that treason was wicked and slavery a sin. Later, writing to his brother, Brooks complained that he was ashamed when the convention

> substituted some feeble platitudes done up in rhetoric which meant nothing and said it. I was ashamed of my church. Never mind; the salvation of the country does not depend on the Episcopal Church, and glad as I should have been to see her boldly on the right side now, she will have to come there by and by when it will be no honor to herself. Oh, how I hate this miserable conservatism. I almost cried for the church at Pittsburgh.[7]

It is known that though Brooks was hesitant to use sermons as a means of addressing social issues he did feel strongly about the pressing matters of his time. He hated slavery and was a strong supporter of Abraham Lincoln and the Union. The evidence for this comes from letters he wrote, actions he took, and the few sermons that did speak out. It would seem, after observing the post-assassination sermons, that there were other Episcopalian rectors whose sentiments and experiences were similar to Brooks's.

Most Protestant ministers, several of them very slowly, but ever so certainly, became more and more involved in the issues of the times. In 1854, the Reverend Eden B. Foster of Lowell, Massachusetts, proclaimed that the Christian minister had not only the right but the duty to speak out on public matters: "how could you forgive the minister, who is the watchman of the Lord, who is the expounder of the Bible. . . . who does not enforce these lessons. . . . who does not lift up the warning cry if he sees the laws of justice prostrated?" And with the coming of the war in the spring of 1861, most Northern Protestant preachers dropped their last reservations about speaking on secular topics. In September of that year, Henry Ward Beecher thought that he detected a change in the reluctance of Northern preachers to speak on public and political issues. "The sublimest history of the Church of Christ, I think, within the last twenty-five years, has taken place during the last three or four months, when the ministers of churches have with one accord so far broken away from the shackles that have bound them as to discuss secular topics in the light of the Gospel."[8]

Historians agree with Beecher's assessment. Dunham writes that various events in addition to the secession crisis that began in December of 1860 conspired to bring about the change.

> The effects of the Compromise of 1850 and the Fugitive Slave Law, of the Kansas-Nebraska Act of 1854, and the Dred Scott decision of 1856, were transforming the Northern movement for the overthrow of slavery, from the secular, almost infidelic, radical idea of abolition, into a civic and sacred ideal, supported by an increasing number of leading clergymen and government officials.

A concurring note comes from John R. McKivigan, who writes that "in the decade and a half before the beginning of the Civil War . . . there was a significant growth of antislavery sentiment in many northern denominations. . . . By the war's end . . . only Catholics and Episcopalians had failed to condemn slavery and to demand its speedy destruction."[9]

An indication of political involvement was the Northern clergy's influence in the 1860 election of Abraham Lincoln to the presidency. Beecher openly and vigorously campaigned for Lincoln. William G. McLoughlin has stated that the Finney revivals were "significant and important in the election of Lincoln," and Beecher and Charles G. Finney were typical of many other Northern churchmen. "The growing willingness of northern churchmen to act against slavery contributed significantly to Lincoln's election." Once Lincoln was elected, both Beecher and Finney, along with several other Northern clergy, attempted to exert pressure on the President to act more quickly and boldly on emancipation. McKivigan has acknowledged that the Northern clergy played an important role in persuading Lincoln to draw up a statement of emancipation.[10]

Stuart W. Chapman has summarized the political involvement of the Northern Protestant clergy in the years preceding and during the Civil War.

> In spite of the fact that there was no unanimity among the clergy and people regarding the duty of ministers in relation to politics, the vast

majority of the preachers of the large evangelical Protestant sects seemed to have accepted that field as a legitimate one for their operations. Those who occupied the field and defended their right to do so were much more numerous than those who did not. A wealth of sermons and articles in religious journals, even conservative ones, serve to show that the clergy were interested in political issues, followed them, and frequently expressed decided opinions regarding them.[11]

The post-assassination sermons of the Northern clergy demonstrated a high degree of hostility toward the South. Though the demand for harsh punishment upon the South was greatly intensified because of the assassination, the Northern ministers had, for some time, looked upon Southerners as inferior in morals, religion, education, and culture. In an 1851 sermon, Theodore Parker, the eloquent Unitarian from Boston, mocked Southern culture. "Ask the Southern States of America," he intoned, "to show us their rapid increase in riches, in civilization; to show us their schools and their scholars, their literature, their science, and their art." In an 1854 sermon, Horace Bushnell depicted the North as being far superior in learning, culture, art, and letters: "The scholarship, the philosophic and esthetic culture, the originative art . . . are barbarized of necessity by the element of slavery and make a very sorry figure in the world of letters. . . . some honorable exceptions are dinners, horses, hounds and pistols. . . . a certain power of harangue which is not oratory, and as much political skill as does not amount to statesmanship."[12]

For Henry Ward Beecher there was a fundamental difference between Northern and Southern character. In his novel, *Norwood,* he had two leading characters: Heywood, prototype of the South, and Cathcart, prototype of the North. As Beecher compared the two men, the advantage was always given to Cathcart. The Northerner was deep natured and persevering, whereas the Southerner appeared superficial, flashy, and short winded. In an 1865 sermon, Beecher came close to declaring that the reason for these differences was some vague kind of social or environmental determinism. "Why was the North valid, healthful? . . . It was not because we were by nature more virtuous than the people of the South; but we were under the influence of great organic laws that were inciting us to conduct which was wiser and better than we individually knew or purposed."[13]

Chester Dunham has summarized the attitude of the Northern clergy toward the South in the years preceding and during the Civil War.

> In general the Northern Clergy who treated the theme of Southern Philosophy or the Southern Way of Life, believed it was based upon a civilization of despotism, a social order of caste, a barbarous slavocracy, widespread immorality, and a static religion. Southern philosophy was believed to be a menace because it endangered both the North and the South. In the North, it tended to undermine the ideals of democracy and equality expressed through free speech, free thought, free pulpit, free press, free schools, and free labor. In the South, it tended to disintegrate the personality, the character, and the morals of all classes of whites and blacks. [14]

Because this kind of disposition toward the South was an attitude of long standing, having roots that extended back several years before the Civil War, it is no wonder that the post-assassination sermons of the Northern preachers were so acrimonious and so harsh in their demands for swift, certain, and unmerciful justice.

Most post-assassination sermons were so vindictive, harsh, and judgmental toward the South that the Northern clergy represented the most punitive and radical views of any group in the North. Charles J. Stewart, in his study of post-assassination sermons, has noted that "the proposals made by these clergymen were of a much severer nature than those made by the so-called 'Radicals' in Congress. Charles Sumner, Thaddeus Stevens, and Benjamin Wade desired stern measures, but they did not go to the extent of wholesale executions as did a great many preachers." Stewart wrote that over 61 percent of the sermons he studied "demonstrated harsher actions against the South than did the 'Radicals.' " Stewart continued: "A majority of these ministers then proposed methods of Reconstruction far more severe than the so-called Radicals of Congress dared to set before the public. Many of these plans were unbelievably vengeance-minded." A similar evaluation comes from Thomas Reed Turner: "If the Radicals [in Congress] have been criticized for vindictiveness, the clergy in sheer weight of numbers, influence, and level of harshness, 'out-radicaled' the Radicals."[15]

Contemporaries also noted the excessively harsh judgments of the post-assassination sermons. George Templeton Strong wrote in his diary about attending church services at Trinity (Episcopal) Church in New York City on April 16. "Trinity was never so full. . . . The crowd packed the aisles and even occupied the choir steps and the choir itself nearly to the chancel rails." What captured Strong's attention even more than the crowd was the severe tones of Dr. Francis Vinton's sermon. "What should we have said four years ago," Strong asked, "of Vinton earnestly enforcing on us the duty of hewing the [Southern] Agag in pieces before the Lord, not from personal animosity, but as a sacred obligation, to be neglected only at peril of divine punishment, public and private?" Similarly, Orville Hickman Browning, Whig politician from Illinois and friend of Lincoln, recorded in his diary his April 16 experience of attending the Capitol Hill Presbyterian Church in Washington, D.C., and listening to the sermon of John Chester. "At church," he wrote, "the Rev. Mr. Chester delivered an inflammatory stump speech—the first one I ever heard in an old school Presbyterian Church. He thought the President might have been removed because he was too lenient, and trusted that we now had an avenger who would execute wrath." [16] Both Strong and Browning thought the sermons they heard on April 16 to be out of character to the kind and tenor of sermons they were accustomed to hearing.

Lloyd Lewis wrote that throngs of people crowded the churches that dark Easter morning seeking and expecting to hear words of consolation and hope from the pulpits.

> Instead, there came down from the pulpit a clarion call for "vengeance," the old battle-call of the Covenanters to be up and at the sinful aristocrats. It was not of Jesus and the resurrection of love that the dominies talked most this Easter Sunday; it was of the stern and bitter Jehovah who stood in the great gloom waiting for more and ever more "rebel" atonement.
>
> Lincoln, the man, was never so dead as on "Black Easter," his policies drowned in his own blood. Here were the preachers, those vicars of Christ's mercy, as they claimed, calling more loudly than the Radicals of Congress for the doom of the slaveholding South. With almost unanimous accord they held up Lincoln's murder as the one final proof that the Confederacy was not yet dead and that villainous sedition was still afoot—still thriving as unchastened as before the war. [17]

Most congregations, however, not only accepted their preachers' inflammatory accusations, but enthusiastically approved them. On the evening of April 16, speaking to a crowd of over four thousand listeners at Pike's Opera House in Cincinnati, the Reverend Maxwell P. Gaddis exclaimed that "For every drop of blood that flowed from the veins of this great and good man, at least one leading Rebel must die, or be banished from this country forever." Someone who was at the opera house described the audience's reaction to these particular words: "The scene that followed this cannot be described. Hundreds rose to their feet; thousands of handkerchiefs waved all over the hall, and it was many seconds ere the eloquent preacher could proceed." "Continued cheering" followed these words from Gaddis: "I demand that this climax of their terrible iniquity be wiped out at the hands of the sternest justice that this nation is capable of administering." When Gaddis thundered, "Now, the adder must die!" the listeners responded with "immense applause."[18]

Several newspapers throughout the North became involved in the charges and severe remedies suggested by the preachers, an indication of the attention these sermons were receiving.

Normally, journals that were progovernment tended to agree with the sermons that expressed vindictive sentiments. . . . The Easton (Pa.) *Free Press* chided the Democratic Easton (Pa.) *Argus* for its criticism of overzealous ministers and went on to say that "the preacher or the editor that counsels leniency towards such infamous assassins as Booth and all his accomplices, is secretly rejoicing at the death of Mr. Lincoln, and that such a man is no better than Booth himself." The opposition press, like the Easton (Pa.) *Argus* and Columbus (Ohio) *Crisis,* generally supported a more moderate view. The Easton (Pa.) *Sentinel* remarked editorially, "We have a class of preachers in this country who have been not inappropriately termed 'Bloodhounds of Zion,' in consequence of their persistent cry for blood."[19]

Yet in their cries for vengeance, several of the sermons are marked by a flagrant inconsistency. In one breath the preachers call out for revenge in highly emotive words, but in the next breath they deny that they are doing so. In the words of Wayland Hoyt, "Brand treason, own child of slavery, as the last and unpardonable crime. Burn the gallows marks deep into it forever. With calm judicial voice, let the arch traitor and his colleagues answer for their crimes by the felon's death—yet still remembering always those great closing words— 'With malice towards none; with charity for all.' " John E. Todd declared that Confederate leaders "are men to be hunted down like wild beasts, and sent to prison and the gallows; that secession is not to be vanquished by leniency and kindness, but is to be stamped out with the iron heel." In the very next sentence, though, he offered a disclaimer: "This is said, not in any spirit of vengeance and wrath, but from a solid conviction that the true interests of the country, and true humanity and religion, require the prosecution of a vigorous policy of extermination and utter subjugation." Robert H. Williams asked: "Can we look upon the corse, the mangled corse of our honored chief, and not cry for vengeance upon the perpetrators of the bloody deed?" Yet later in the sermon he admonished his listeners that they should harbor no feelings of vengeance. On the same date, O. H. Dutton, after vividly describing the alleged atrocities and barbarities of the Confederacy, then exclaimed: "God forbid that we should say any thing to inflame the passions of men, or excite desires for carnal vengeance."[20] It seems inconceivable that Hoyt, Todd, Williams, Dutton, and so many other Northern preachers—well-educated men who well knew the rules and power of rhetoric—did not understand that their emotive words would arouse their listeners to intense and justifiable feelings of revenge.

There is no way of truly measuring the effect of these harsh and vindictive sermons upon public opinion. But recalling the authority of the pulpits in the mid–nineteenth century, the fact that a vast majority of these pulpits were demanding harsh penalties against the South, and considering the highly emotional manner and volatile words of the preachers and the vulnerability of their congregations, one can only surmise that the weight these discourses carried was considerable. The radicals in Congress needed public support for their programs, and the preachers more than did their part in providing that support. In the congressional elections of 1866, Republicans, most of them favoring radical reconstruction, took such a control of Congress that they were able to push through any program they desired and easily override any presidential veto by Andrew Johnson. The preachers, most of whom did not hesitate to become involved in politics, certainly helped to create the kind of climate that achieved such election results as those of 1866. Victor B.

Howard has written that "The Republicans won in part because of the mobilization of the church going people. They believed that the country faced a crisis as great as that of the war." It can only be a matter of speculation as to how different Reconstruction and other postwar policies might have been if a majority of preachers had called for forgiveness and leniency with the same fervor that they cried out for harsh justice. With great insight, Turner has written: "If one grants to ministers the influence that some feel they had in the nineteenth century, it is again logical to maintain that sermons recounting southern atrocities and involvement in the assassination had a much more important influence in arousing people than Stanton ever thought of having. However, Stanton is heaped with blame, and most historians ignore sermons almost completely."[21]

The harsh measures advocated by the Northern preachers suggest that the Civil War had caused a reentrenchment in America of a conservative concept of society and government. In place of prewar individualism was a renewed emphasis on institutionalism. Maintenance of law and order was substituted for humanitarian reform. The imperatives of nationalism had replaced the dictates of personal conscience. Civil obedience was deemed a higher virtue than Thoreau's civil disobedience. Conformity was valued over Emersonian nonconformity. George M. Frederickson, who has written in detail of this transformation, has commented that "Americans, in the course of putting down a popular uprising in their own country, had perhaps learned by painful experience that sovereignty must be defined and acknowledged, so that governments can govern and citizens obey."[22] The preachers were reflecting an American spirit that had grown weary and even suspicious of experimentation, of revolution, of rapid change, of risk taking, of each person answering to his and her own inner light; they longed for a return to authority and a renewal of a faith in the formal institutions of churches, laws, and government.

The assassination provided many preachers with the opportunity to stress and re-preach some of their favorite themes. Castigating and chastising the South was only one of them. Many ministers had been concerned for some time about what they perceived as a growing permissiveness in American society, an often-repeated pulpit theme in every generation, it would seem. The assassination, for several preachers, was strong evidence that permissiveness had been carried too far in the nation. William Adams, a Presbyterian minister in New York City, declared on April 16 that "there is too much . . . mawkish sentimentalism abroad." He assailed "rose-water religion" that denied future punishment and argued for "universal salvation." Adams deplored government that would "dispense with all the severities of justice." Fellow Presbyterian Samuel Spear, in the same city on the same day, asserted, "away with mawkish sympathy that ignores justice, and ruins government. It is alike stupid and cruel." That day in Boston, Congregationalist Edwin B. Webb complained of "a miserable, morbid, bastard philanthropy" and blamed many of the nation's problems and troubles on "mawkish leniency."[23] "Mawkish" was a popular adjective in the vocabulary of post-assassination sermons.

George Duffield declared that "As a people, we have, of late years, lost sight of the great end and obligation of civil government, designed of God, as His ordinance, for the punishment of crime and the promotion of the general good. Law has lost its sacredness." Several of the preachers emphasized that much of this unwarranted permissiveness, with all its dire consequences, had its roots in a mistaken and perverted theology. Thus, Rufus S. Cushman declared that "mistaken views of Christian mercy has poisoned and demoralized so many minds and hearts among us," and David Murdock warned against a false theology that would ignore "justice" and speak "only of mercy."[24]

The assassination also provided a number of Northern ministers with the opportunity to stress the need for and importance of capital punishment and to verbally attack those who opposed it. At this point in the nation's history, some states had abolished capital punishment and others were considering doing so. George Duffield addressed the issue at some length. "In the North a spurious self-righteous humanitarianism, claiming to be wiser and more benevolent than the God of the Bible, has sympathized with the perpetrators of evil, in the indulgence of a mawkish and murderous charity, so-called, denouncing capital punishment, destroying the sanctions of law, and underminding the authority of government." He continued by accusing "pseudo-philanthropists" in the North of "insulting the God of the Bible" by attempting to "disannul the death penalty." The assassination was needed, claimed Duffield, "to bring the public mind to a just and proper estimate of human life, and demand the restoration of the death penalty to the place a God of justice and mercy has assigned it in the administration of the government."[25]

Other preachers echoed similar sentiments in favor of the death penalty. John Dudley argued hard on behalf of capital punishment, declaring that if the people had not been timid about the death penalty there would have been fewer violent deaths and quite possibly Lincoln himself would not have been killed. Andrew Beveridge referred to sentiments that would do away with capital punishment as "sickly humanitarianism," and Warren Randolph said that those who opposed capital punishment were guilty of "sickly sentimentalism." On June 1 at the German Reformed Church of Clearspring, Maryland, Henry Harbaugh vigorously defended capital punishment. "This is the supreme law of the land," he said. "It rests on divine authority (Romans 13:1–4). This is an infinitely better law, than that mawkish, frothering and vaporing of washy and watery sentimentalism, which has its foundation in the shallow pools of Gotham."[26]

The assassination also provided the preachers with an opportunity to expound on the various sins, both private and public, that they perceived as endangering individuals and society. In Chapter 2 it was noted that the fact that Lincoln was killed in a theater, opened the doors for many clergymen to vent their strong opposition to the theater, theater attendance, and actors. George Junkin summed up the feelings of many clergymen when he declared: "Our theatrical exhibitions are a stench in the nostrils of high Heaven. These dens of pollution, these synagogues of Satan, collect in and around them, the concentrated abomination of all immorality and crime." Thomas Laurie spent four pages of his sermon on his concern over Lincoln attending a theater and why he perceived the theater as such an evil institution. Laurie was hopeful that because Lincoln had been murdered in a theater, and by an actor, that others would be deterred from attending such a place.[27]

Several preachers assumed that the assassination was a judgment from God upon a people that was guilty of a great host of sins. In addition to permissiveness, a failure to support capital punishment, and theater going, those sins included drunkenness (alcohol was an instigator in Booth's crime), idolatry (the people had turned to Lincoln more than they had turned to God), lack of humility (especially for Northern military victories), dishonoring the Sabbath (some battles in the war had actually taken place on Sunday), dishonesty and greed (there were those who had reaped great profits from the war), gambling, profanity, licentious literature, and infidelity. All of these were themes that the ministers had preached on many times in the past, and the assassination provided the opportunity to preach on them again with a greater verve, immediacy, and authenticity than ever before.

There was another theme that had been of vital importance to the clergy in the North for many years, and Lincoln's death only confirmed that theme. Most of the preachers were ardent patriots who believed strongly in the Union and the republican form of government for which it stood. The very worst had happened—civil war and the assassination of a much-loved and trusted chief executive— yet the Republic still remained, strong and unmoved. B. Hawley noted that though God had removed Lincoln he did not destroy the government. And Henry Ward Beecher declared that "Republican institutions have been vindicated in this experience as they never were before. . . . God, I think, has said, by the voice of this event, to all the nations of the earth, 'Republican liberty, based upon true Christianity, is firm as the foundation of the globe.' " Edwin B. Webb also exuded hope when he noted that "such is the happy structure of our government that no assassination can arrest its wheels." Similarly, Benjamin Watson affirmed that the assassination had demonstrated the superiority of republican government to "decadent European governments."[28]

This writer located only two sermons that thought the assassination had, in some way, harmed the American form of government. J. Hazard Hartzell, at the Universalist Church of Buffalo on April 16, complained that "This assassination of the President discloses a recklessness and a depravity, that must be humiliating to every American. It is the revealment of that contempt for law and order, which must lower the Government in the minds of Europeans." Another preacher who feared that Lincoln's murder brought great disgrace to the nation, from which it would take generations to recover, was Joseph D. Strong, who asserted: "Our enemies will point to [the assassination] as the culmination of democratic weakness and folly. It will take generations of good order and wise behavior on our part, to wipe out this reproach in the estimation of mankind. . . . Even our own faith in our institutions is jostled, if not shaken."[29] But Hartzell and Strong, in their display of pessimism for the reputation of America's form of government, represented only a tiny minority of the American preachers.

Closely allied to the preachers' pride in the nation's republican form of government was the cherished faith in America's role in issuing in the Kingdom of God on earth, the millennium. Such a faith had been a vital part of American theology since the Puritan vision of "the city upon a hill." America was the New Israel, chosen by the Eternal God to set before the world an example and to lead all humankind to some future glory. The Civil War had been a part of that vision, for the Kingdom, the preachers announced, could come only through suffering and a titanic struggle between good and evil, the new and the old. "God was violently overturning the old, corrupt order and was bringing the disparate forces of history to a climatic resolution in one place and time. It had been granted to Americans to fight the definitive battle that would ensure the future happiness of the nation and the world."[30]

In the latter years of the war, as a Union victory seemed more and more assured, the millennial vision of the Northern preachers was heightened. On Thanksgiving Day 1863, Henry Clay Fish predicted a Union victory and described his vision of the new America:

I see it. I see it. The war successfully ended; the bondman everywhere a freeman; the degraded white man everywhere educated and ennobled; the diverse elements in the national composition fused and welded inseparably together; local jealousies and animosities at an end; treason and traitors expelled from the country; the heresy of state sovereignty and secession killed; . . . a school house and church in every district; the people talking the highest type of civilization—intelligent, God-fearing, liberty-loving, self-governed, and bound together in one tender and beautiful brotherhood.[31]

The following year at Thanksgiving time, Sherman Canfield spoke of the importance of going through the fire on the way to the millennium. "On its way towards the millennium," Canfield exclaimed, "the Kingdom of Christ occasions strifes and conflicts by causing a portion of a world laying in wickedness to differ from the rest. The very goodness, frankness, and courage which it produces in its subjects, renders them odious to evil doers." And when the war was over, James T. Robinson, pastor of the First Baptist Church in North Adams, Massachusetts, announced that "The great Republic, tried by fire . . . but terrible and glorious, ascends through smoke and flame to unending sway and splendor."[32]

For most of the preachers, the assassination of Lincoln enhanced, not darkened, the millennial vision. "The death of President Lincoln by an assassin's bullet on Good Friday, 14 April 1865, was widely interpreted as the final blood sacrifice by which the nation was purified and reborn to its high mission." Joel Bingham declared on the evening of May 7 that "The life of the just departed Lincoln, after having wrought out the painful salvation of the Republic, has been offered a bloody sacrifice, upon the altar of human freedom and the happiness of his fellow countrymen."[33]

Gilbert Haven drew descriptive parallels between Holy Week, the Passion of Jesus, and Lincoln's final days. Lincoln's humble but triumphal entry into Richmond was analogous to Jesus' humble but triumphal entry into Jerusalem, and the enemies of Lincoln were compared to those of Jesus. "As Christ entered into Jerusalem, the city that above all others hated, rejected, and would soon slay Him . . . so did this, His servant [Lincoln], enter the city that above all others hated and rejected him, and would soon be the real if not intentional cause of his death." Good Friday, challenged Haven, had become a sacred day, not just for the Church, but for the nation.

> The great day of the Church has become yet more solemn in the annals of America. Let not the 15th of April be considered the day of his death, but let Good Friday be its anniversary. For then the fatal blow was struck. . . . We should make it a moveable fast, and ever keep it beside the cross and the grave of our blessed Lord, in whose service and for whose gospel he became a victim and a martyr.[34]

Haven, along with so many other preachers in the North, also used the assassination to once again raise the millennial vision that had been an integral part of American theology since the early seventeenth century. The assassination, as well as the Civil War, was a part of the Almighty's plan to bring in the Kingdom of God using the United States of America as the primary component of that future glory.

Phineas Densmore Gurley, pastor of the New York Avenue Presbyterian Church in Washington, D.C., delivered the sermon at Lincoln's funeral service in the White House on April 19. Gurley stayed with Mrs. Lincoln on the night of the assassination and tried to console her. (Courtesy of the Presbyterian Historical Society, Philadelphia)

The New York Avenue Presbyterian Church in Washington, D.C., as it looked in Lincoln's time. Pastored by Phineas D. Gurley, it was the church most often attended by Lincoln during his presidency. (Courtesy of the Illinois State Historical Library)

Andrew Johnson, Lincoln's successor. The Northern preachers praised him in their post-assassination sermons but turned on him with a vengeance a year later when they perceived Johnson as being far too lenient in his policies toward the South. (Courtesy of the Illinois State Historical Library)

George Washington and Abraham Lincoln were linked together by many Northern preachers as the two greatest Americans. This sketch, perhaps inspired by one of the post-assassination sermons, depicts Washington welcoming Lincoln to his eternal home. (Courtesy of the Illinois State Historical Library)

Left document (cover)

THE LESSON OF THE HOUR.

JUSTICE AS WELL AS MERCY.

A DISCOURSE

PREACHED ON THE SABBATH FOLLOWING THE

Assassination of the President,

IN THE

CAPITOL HILL PRESBYTERIAN CHURCH,

WASHINGTON, D. C.,

BY THE PASTOR,

REV. JOHN CHESTER.

WASHINGTON CHRONICLE PRINT.
1865.

Right document (inside leaf)

WASHINGTON, *April 17, 1865.*

REV. JOHN CHESTER.

Reverend and Dear Sir :

The undersigned, of the Congregation and Members of the Capitol Hill Presbyterian Church, being impressed with the importance of the truths conveyed in your eloquent and appropriate discourse of last Sabbath, on the assassination of the honored and beloved President of the Republic, Abraham Lincoln, and believing that the thoughts therein conveyed are worthy of perusal and careful consideration by a more extended circle, respectfully request a copy of it for publication.

WALTER L. NICHOLSON,
C. H. PARSONS,
ROBERT LEITCH,
CHAS. E. LATHROP,
J. S. KELLOGG,
JAS. M. GORDON,
JOHN R. ARRISON
JOHN TAYLOR.

To Messrs. Walter L. Nicholson, C. H. Parsons, Robert Leitch, Charles E. Lathrop, and others.

GENTLEMEN :

I cheerfully yield to your kind request, if you deem this humble offering of affection, laid on the altar of our beloved President's memory, capable of benefiting a wider circle. It was intended as a calm appeal, not to the passions, but to the consciences of all who desire the integrity of the Union, maintained on the principles of Justice.

Very truly yours,

JOHN CHESTER.

The cover and inside leaf of John Chester's April 16 sermon. Note the black border on the cover; though some post-assassination sermons carried a similar black border, most did not. The inside leaf depicts the request from leaders of the congregation to have the ser- mon printed and Chester's response to that request. This printing of request and response was typical of most post-assassination sermons. (Courtesy of Special Collections, Milner Library, Illinois State University)

Henry Ward Beecher was the best-known and most popular preacher in America during the mid–nineteenth century. He openly campaigned for Lincoln in the 1860 and 1864 elections, and during Lincoln's presidency he put pressure on the chief executive to take a firmer stand on emancipation. (Courtesy of the Indiana Historical Library)

Phillips Brooks, the eloquent Episcopalian rector of Holy Trinity Church in Philadelphia and author of "O Little Town of Bethlehem," delivered his most memorable sermon, simply titled "Abraham Lincoln," on April 23 when the body of Lincoln lay in state in Philadelphia. (Courtesy of the Archives of the Episcopal Church, Austin, Texas)

A drawing of the Methodist bishop Matthew Simpson, Lincoln's close friend who delivered the funeral oration at the tomb in Springfield on May 4. (Courtesy of the Illinois State Historical Library)

The post-assassination sermons covered in this volume span a short period of time, the seven weeks immediately following Lincoln's death. It was a time of pervasive grief, bitter anger, and wrenching frustration; a time when passions overruled the rational, inspired both noble and caustic words, and dictated radical actions. Such emotionalism could not long be sustained, and it was not.

In the months that followed, the attitudes of the Northern clergy began to change. One of those changes was in their perspective of Andrew Johnson. In the post-assassination sermons, the preachers were nearly unanimous in their praise and support of the new president. Within a year's time, the same preachers who had praised Johnson began to condemn him; voices that had supported the chief executive turned to undermining him. The preachers, along with Congress and much of the public, perceived Johnson as inconsistent, ineffective, and, most damaging of all, far too lenient in his policies toward the South—the same complaint many preachers had of Lincoln.

Paul C. Brownlow has written of three basic tactics used by the Northern clergy in the years 1866 to 1868 to discredit President Johnson. The most frequently used tactic was to accuse the "acting President" of being "morally unfit and a national disgrace." Whereas, in 1865, the preachers had made light of and excuses for Johnson's "drunkenness" on inauguration day, in 1866 and 1867 they pointed to the incident as being truly indicative of Johnson's character. On Thanksgiving Day 1867, O. A. Burgess, of the Indianapolis Christian Church, declared: "We must bow our heads in sackcloth and ashes that the wicked still rule, and that the highest office in our land is a foul and bespotted blotch upon the morale of our nation, rather than an example of official dignity, personal integrity, and moral purity." In a second tactic, the preachers asserted that Johnson had "betrayed the North and the Union." James Cruickshanks, on Thanksgiving Day 1866, asserted that "The President's affiliations southward reveal a dark page in the history of the present administration. He has catered to the lowest passions of rebel leaders. He has received, at the Executive Mansion, on the most friendly terms, delegations from the very heart of secession, and dismissed them pouring oil into their wounds, and giving them hope even of a better time coming." On that same day W. S. Studley, who earlier in this volume spoke so highly of Johnson, now accused Johnson of betraying "the high and honorable course of his illustrious and immortal predecessor." A third tactic used by Northern pulpits was to label Johnson as an "unprincipled dictator and ambitious tyrant." In 1868, Alexander Clark, at the First Methodist Church of Pittsburgh, described Johnson as "a king," "a proclaimer of vetoes," and a "presumptious pronoun." According to Brownlow, "In mid-nineteenth century America, the Northern Protestant pulpit spoke with authority to an attentive public. . . . The pulpit, along with the press, excited the people and aroused their passions. Had Johnson been able to win sufficient support from either group of opinion leaders, his fate might have been far different."[35]

Of even greater importance and significance was the change in the Northern preachers' outlook on Reconstruction. In the post-assassination sermons, most preachers were demanding harsh judgments upon the South, in many cases even asking for the death penalty upon Confederate leaders such as Jefferson Davis and Robert E. Lee. Over time, however, those demands began to decrease and eventually, for the most part, ceased altogether. As the passions aroused by Lincoln's assassination began to subside, the Northern preachers began to lose interest in the whole process of Reconstruction, in their desire to promote the welfare of the freedmen, and in their concern to inflict harsh penalties on the South. It is difficult to point to a specific time when this transition took place for the Northern preachers; there seemed to be no single event that triggered the conversion. By the time of Andrew Johnson's impeachment in the spring of 1868, many preachers and much of the Northern populace had begun to wonder if radicalism had not been carried too far. From that point onward, other matters increasingly diverted attention away from the South and Reconstruction.

Henry Ward Beecher, who in the post-assassination days was in the minority in recommending leniency toward the South, within a short period of time found himself in his accustomed place among the majority. Beecher had not changed his position; others had come to share his views on Reconstruction. Speaking of relationships between the North and South after the war, Beecher asserted that "The only cause of antagonism was slavery; and now that slavery is destroyed there is no ground for conflict."[36] For Beecher the fight was over. The slaves had been emancipated. But it would take time for the freedmen to become the social equals of whites.

In a letter addressed to three army officers, Beecher advised:

Civilization is a growth. None can escape that forty years in the wilderness who travel from the Egypt of ignorance to the promised land of civilization. The freedmen must take their march. I have full faith in the results. If they have the stamina to undergo hardships which every uncivilized people has undergone in its upward progress they will, in due time, take their place among us.

But he failed to say what their "place" was, or how long "in due time" was supposed to be. Beecher did not believe that citizenship made the freed slave the social equal of whites, and such racial views help explain why he could support President Johnson's veto of the Freedman's Bureau and why he did not press for full black suffrage without restrictions. The black man was on his own and he must prove himself. In taking such a position, Beecher stood with many of the Northern clergy. The primary motive for most Northern clergy in taking a stand against slavery was expediency rather than true antislavery commitment, and "Because of these fragile origins, the churches' commitment to the welfare of blacks proved no better than that of other northern institutions to weather the storms of Reconstruction."[37]

Beecher and many other Northern clergy were beginning to reflect a social philosophy that would come to have great importance in postwar America—social Darwinism. Society, as in nature, was determined by evolutionary forces: the fit survive, progress, and grow stronger; the weak fall by the way. Society was governed by this deterministic force over which man had no long-lasting control, and one could only bend to the immutable laws of nature and society. Frederickson has written, "The new Darwinist view of social processes warned against a paternalistic approach to the Negro problem."[38] The voices of reform, so dominant in the prewar era and even for a short time after the war, though not mute, were barely heard in the land.

An example of a clergyman who was once an ardent antislavery proponent, but who after the war lost interest in the black cause, was the Unitarian Thomas Wentworth Higginson. Greatly influenced by Theodore Parker, Higginson led an assault on the Boston courthouse to free a fugitive slave in 1854. In 1856 he went to Kansas, took up arms, and fought for the free-state forces. He helped to subsidize John Brown and became an officer in the Union army after the war

began. Yet soon after the war, Frederickson asserts, Higginson became disinterested in the freedmen's cause and showed "surprizingly
little interest in the problems of Reconstruction after 1868."

> . . . he made no significant contribution to the discussion of events in
> the South until 1878, when he made a tour of South Carolina to inquire
> into the condition of the freedmen under "conservative" rule. Higginson
> found all going well enough for the Negro, despite the fact that he was
> now at the mercy of the Southern whites. His final answer to the great
> problems to which he had devoted many years as an abolitionist and
> commander of Negro troops was "local self-government" for the South-
> ern states, trusting to the benevolence of Southern gentlemen . . . or, in
> the event that matters got out of hand, to the ability of the Negro to
> emigrate from areas where his life was intolerable.

Frederickson wrote that Higginson was typical of many Northern intellectuals who "ignored the whole problem and turned to other
things." Eventually, Howard has written, "white people become
largely indifferent to the fate of black Americans until interest in human rights revived after World War II."[39]

Perhaps the greatest consequence of the post-assassination sermons from the Northern Protestant pulpits was the contribution
they made to the immortalization of Abraham Lincoln. "Undoubtedly, the numerous post-assassination discourses played a considerable part in the future fame of 'the martyr president.' " Sermons
that gave to Lincoln a status at least equal to that of George
Washington, the only authentic universal American idol up to that
time in national history; that spoke of the slain executive as "one of
the most faultless examples of true manhood every prominently exhibited to the world. . . . while he possessed all virtues he was free
from all vices," "absolutely incorruptible," "something greater than
greatness itself," and one of "inflexible integrity"—all these pronouncements and evaluations aided in making Lincoln something
bigger than life itself, someone who had achieved a superhuman
quality.[40] The preachers played a prominent role in the transformation of Lincoln from man to myth.

Well over half of the preachers emphasized that Lincoln's death—
or, more precisely, the manner of his death—had insured for him a
prominent place in America's Hall of Fame. Richard Edwards, a

Unitarian minister and president of Normal University on the prairies of Illinois, spoke eloquently of the assassination's role in the remembrance of Abraham Lincoln: "And how sublimely great was he in his glorious death! Dying as he did, in so noble a cause, his immortality, the sweet memory of him in the hearts of his countrymen, in the literature of his country and of the world, wherever the names of the good and great are treasured as rich gifts from the past, is secured beyond doubt or peradventure." Several preachers were of the opinion that the assassination had not only immortalized Lincoln but had preserved him from future actions, decisions, or policies that might have tarnished his unblemished fame and reputation. Edward P. Powell rendered a typical expression of this conviction.

> There is a time in every earnest noble life, when its work is just complete. Happy the man who dies then. Lincoln died without having unravelled a single thread of the good he accomplished. Had he lived a few weeks more, he might, in the kindliness of his disposition, have misjudged the needs of the time, and ruined much, that a firmer hand would have compacted and strengthened.[41]

The preachers accurately predicted the future fame of Lincoln. In many ways their predictions were self-fulfilling prophecies, for the preachers in no small way helped to bring about and perpetuate the very thing they had predicted and proclaimed.

❖ ❖ ❖

Appendix

"SOUTHERN CHIVALRY, *and What the Nation Ought To Do With It," was delivered by Alonzo Hall Quint on Sunday afternoon, April 16, at the North Congregational Church of New Bedford, Massachusetts, where Quint served as pastor. Quint preached a morning sermon that was basically a eulogy of Lincoln, which meant that he prepared two discourses on very short notice. The reason for choosing the sermon on "Southern Chivalry" is that it may well be the most vitriolic post-assassination sermon from a Northern pulpit in its attitude toward and prescriptions for the South.*

Quint was a pastor who was actively involved in the public affairs of his day. At the same time he held a pastorate during the Civil War, he also served as chaplain of the 2d Massachusetts infantry from 1861 to 1864. He served on the Massachusetts Board of Education from 1855 until 1861 and was a member of the state legislature from 1881 to 1883. Quint had an avid interest in history and was a member of several historical and genealogical societies. He was the author of several publications, including The Potomac and the Rapidan, or Army Notes From the Failure at Winchester to the Re-enforcement of Rosecrans (1864), The Records of the Second Massachusetts Infantry, *1861–1865* (1867), *and* First Parish in Dover, New Hampshire (1883).

Quint's sermon in this appendix is an attack upon Southern character, which he calls "Southern Chivalry." The "Southern Gentleman," Quint asserted, had long been regarded as "the perfection of humanity." It took a long time to discover that such a perception was a "delusion." Southern chivalry, in fact, was characterized by "slavery," "barbarism," "robbing," "stealing," "perjury," "murder," "rebellion," and "treason." Quint summarized Southern chivalry by saying that "Their customs, their laws, their practices, were all of hell. Over that Southern land the genius of hell has long brooded."

As the war drew to a close, Quint proclaimed, the North stood ready to be magnanimous toward the South. The assassination, however, had brought charity and lenity to an end. *"We would,"* he said, *"foolishly, have spared them, but they would not. It took this last blow to show the tiger, and arouse the overflowing scourge."* The sermon demanded harsh penalties upon the South: unconditional surrender, the exile and death of certain Rebel leaders, confiscation of property, and the sending of missionaries into the South to correct *"a corrupted gospel."*

This sermon demonstrates the extreme to which vindictiveness could be carried in the North. Few, if any, of the other Northern sermons could surpass Quint in bitterness, anger, hyperbole, vengefulness, and provincialism. This sermon is included in this volume so that the reader might understand some of the most radical feelings in the North following Lincoln's assassination.

Southern Chivalry, and What the Nation Ought to do With It
ALONZO H. QUINT
Sunday Afternoon, April 16, 1865

Because ye have said,—
We have made a covenant with death,
And with hell are we at agreement; . . . .
When the overflowing scourge shall pass through,
Then shall be ye trodden down by it.
From the time that it goeth forth, it shall take you;
For morning by morning shall it pass over,
By day and by night.
—Isaiah 28:15, 18,19.

You have seen men who have trained tigers. They reclaim, they discipline, they conquer their appetite. But, by and by, the tiger gets a taste of human blood. From that moment, the master is powerless. The eyes are the eyes of a tiger. The teeth are the teeth of a tiger. The thirst is the thirst of a tiger. Beware! Trust him not! He is a tiger! He was a tiger all the time, a quiet tiger; now he has had a taste of blood.

I told you, last Thursday, of the sin of our country. I thought it well nigh expiated. I said, "happy is the nation whose chief is imbued with such a principle," as to desire to be on the Lord's side. But little did we think that the next day's night should witness a scene which should shock the world. The expiation was not complete. I had to take the nation's chosen, beloved need.

I told you that unless the nation should do justice, there would be trouble; but not this trouble,—we did not dream of it; but either future war, or the return of rebels to power in Southern states. I think that God felt this. I think that His providence saw that the people were forgetting justice,—both to the traitor, in the way of penalty, and to the oppressed, both black and white. I feared it; and I tried to interpret to you what I knew you must feel, that the nation was in great danger of forgetting to secure what it had bought by the blood of its martyrs; and, in the tide of a too lavish generosity, omitting to exterpate the sin.

Is not God talking to us to-day? Has He not let this strange event come to startle the nation out of its weakness? Does He not say there can be no parleying with sin, no hesitation to do justice? Does He not appeal to us, not to cherish cruel revenge, but to feel that it was a tiger with whom we thought to live in peace, a tiger fired with blood? Do you want its teeth again at your throat?

This I take to be the providential lesson of the day. And believing it to be such, as a christian minister, and as one, too, who has seen treason in the time of battle, in the throngs of wounded, and in the burial of the dead, as such do I treat it. And what I wish to show you, is What Southern chivalry is, and what the Nation ought to do with it.

It was long the feeling that a Southern gentleman was the perfection of humanity. He was a noble, generous man, above mean and petty acts. He was no Yankee, to love a dollar. A kind of patriarchal protector, in his lordly mansion, to the attached and happy servants who could not take care of themselves. Rather passionate, but that was the natural fault of high toned feeling. His honor was proverbial. His hospitality was boundless. In government, he took the offices,—not for money, but because he was educated to statesmanship. At northern watering places, of a summer, he was feted and petted,—the generous, chivalric, Southerner. He had a right to look down on "northern mudsills" and "greasy mechanics."

It took time to find out that this was a delusion. That he was, with exceptions of course, revengeful, treacherous, murderous. That he was a liar and a cheat. That he loved money dearly, and wrung it out of the tears of his bondmen. That his lordly mansion was, nine times in ten, unfit for a sty of northern pigs. That his slaves were chained, and whipped, and branded. That his statesmanship was mere craft, to get salaries on the one hand, and, on the other to enable him to get and keep more negroes. That he was lazy, and selfish, and often stupidly ignorant. That his hospitality always wanted pay for the wayfarer's dinner, except when his ruling principle, vanity, prevented.

It took time to learn this. It did, me. I had known some honorable Southerners, so far as a slave holder can be honorable; and I thought they were samples. But I saw the reality, in Southern lands.

But we had not really felt all this, even after this war, plotted by perjurers and felons, and carried on by barbarians. And so, to impress it upon our minds, we have had this last, this crowning evidence, of what Southern Chivalry is. It is to assassinate an unarmed man. It is to enter the room of a sick man on lying pretences, and while he lies helpless in his bed, plunge a dagger into his throat.

It was not warfare. Allowing that these people had the right to make war,—this was not war. To kill in fight is lawful; to assassinate is murder. An enemy, unresisting, is sacred. War, hard as it is, does not justify every means of injury. A soldier is an honorable man.

Nor does war justify mere revenge. When defeat comes, it cannot be repaid by useless vengeance; it is to be accepted. A deed which would not add a single arm to the rebel force, nor weaken the hand of a single loyal soldier, which was only the work of hate and spite after remediless defeat, is not war. It is barbarism.

Nor, if revenge was ever to be palliated, could it be in this case. It was wreaked on a good, true, man; his only fault that he was observing the oath he had taken. He had never been harsh or vindictive. That very evening he had "spoken kindly of Lee and his army." He had just decided to forgive Virginia. He was planning a wide amnesty. He would not inflict lawful punishment. Then he was murdered.

But it matters not what manner of man he was. The act was the crime, on whomsoever perpetrated. That act shows us Southern Chivalry.

I. Southern Chivalry contains the elements which ensure just such deeds as this. I say "Chivalry" and not "slavery," because "Chivalry" is the sentiment back of slavery. The Slavery is an incident; the Chivalry is the principle. The Slavery does not create, it fosters only, the spirit of Chivalry. The Chivalry merely finds Slavery one method of showing itself. Slavery is only the evidence of the rottenness of the Southern spirit.

To rob is the first characteristic of the Chivalry. The Southern Gentleman lives by robbing. His property, when he is a slave-master, is a robbery in itself. He makes men work without adequate wages. He accumulates out of toil he has stolen.

To rule without law is another characteristic. His own passions are, virtually, his only control. Law themselves vicious, seldom enforced when good in any feature, are no restraint. He grows up a tyrant. "Every master of slaves," said George Mason of Virginia, "is born a petty tyrant." He does not, as years go on, belie the old truth that "the child is father to the man." Hence, with unrestrained passions, licentiousness is inevitable. One has only to glance at the color of the depressed race, to see the evidence. Oppression is inevitable, too. Blows and cruel punishments are at his option. He is answerable to nobody.

To kill without law, is another prerogative; or rather, it is according to law, to kill lawlessly. With "moderate chastisement" he could ensure death, and he himself harmless.

With such rights and such elements of character, it is no wonder that the slave-master should carry the disposition he has shown into general life. Moral principle was eaten out. Slavery, when made legal, poisoned truth.

When men were taught that it was right to rob blacks, it was no great stretch of principle, to rob whites. Nor to violate treaty obligations, by seizing Cuba; nor to send pirates and robbers mildly called "fillibusters," to Central America. Without law, it was not a strange thing to carry pistols and bowie-knives; assassinate in houses and streets; lynch men who happened to think differently from the Chivalry; raise mobs to violate obligations of the Constitution in Charleston; inflict barbarous penalties; kidnap and sell free persons.

I have seen the gashes in the flesh of a slave-girl. Her father and her mother were both children of her master. I have seen seven hundred fugitives, in one regiment; whose scars and injuries, their surgeon told me, and he showed me specimens, were beyond description. You have heard of the spots where they burned people at the stake. It was all too true. You have seen the spot where sat a Senator, at his desk in the Senate House; where there came up behind him, a Representative of chivalric South Carolina, and beat the defenceless Senator on the head, until the brain was feared for. All this was Southern Chivalry. It was only carrying into general life, the barbarities, the cruelty, the lawlessness of education.

II. Southern Chivalry has been doing such things all through this war.

It began with perjury. Nothing more totally destitute of every sentiment of honor, than the conduct of these men while plotting treason, can be found in history. Oaths of office were nothing. They who had sworn to defend the Constitution continued to hold office to the last moment, so as to use the advantages of their official position to pull down the government. Senators, Representatives, Cabinet Officers, and small officials, with oaths fresh upon their lying tongues, were conspirators. Soldiers, educated at the expense of the nation, sworn to support the government, wearing its uniform, supported by its money, violated every oath and obligation of honor. The Lees, and Magruders, the old Twiggs, and the Beauregards, were all traitors together. It began with stealing. Stealing moneys at Washington, at New Orleans, at Savannah; it was only the question which could steal fastest and most. Stealing vessels, where they could find the remnant. Stealing arms, handily planned by a Virginia perjurer, who showed his Chivalry by afterwards boasting of it. Stealing forts built and armed by the nation. Stealing, even, in their condescention of littleness, mail-bags and pouches. Anything that was "portable property" was acceptable. Stealing money honestly due to northern creditors for goods furnished. Stealing all they could steal.

That was how they began; Southern Chivalry.

But they were allowed belligerent rights. How have they acted in war? For war has its rules; and no decent soldier ever violates them.

In Eastern Tennessee there were multitudes of loyal people. They must be put down. So they shot and hung offending citizens. They led round gray haired men 'till they died of exposure. They seized their property and reduced them to starvation. When they could not find the men, they hung the women in front of their homes. That was Southern Chivalry.

In Northern cities are great hotels. Full of women and children. Southern leaders plot at home, and Southern emisaries come to the cities. Here is congenial employment. It is natural to the men that have raised babies for the market; and whipped and violated women; and imprisoned women for teaching children to read. Set fire to their hotels! Do it in the night! Half a dozen at once, to make the murders surer in the confusion! Hundreds will perish in the flames! That is Southern Chivalry.

In ambulances are wounded men. The battle is over. The wounded are quietly moving on the road. Southern riders come along, open the ambulances, and shoot the helpless, unresisting captives. That was done at Fort Royal. It was done in the West. I don't know how many times.

Near Tallahassee, rails are pulled up. It will destroy a train. The cars are seized and burnt. I saw the smoke. There are blacks employed on the road. They are taken out one side, and shot in cold blood. This is Southern Chivalry.

There is a fort. After heroic bravery, the garrison yields to overwhelming force. Then begins the slaughter. Surrendered men are butchered. Wounded men are made to stand up, to be shot. One is fastened to a floor by nails through his clothes; another to the side of a building; and burnt to death. The wounded are in tents and huts; and the tents and huts are set on fire. Some are burned alive, and some of them escaped to tell the tale. The murder of more than three hundred unresisting men, is the count of the good day's work. That is Southern Chivalry.

Down South there are prisoners. The captured are sent there. First, they are robbed. Then, deliberately the rebel power sets itself to destroy them by degrees. They are left shelterless, or, if sheltered, in places where they can hardly breathe; and if they go to a hole called a window to get air they are shot. They are starved. What live, are skeletons; and the dead, thus cruelly and purposely murdered are counted at more than fifty thousand. That is Southern Chivalry.

Do you wonder at these things? The wonder would be if these things did not happen. For these men were trained to this kind of work, by seven generations of oppressing,—just as they trained their blood hounds to chase men.

III. Southern Chivalry killed the President.

Possibly there are some few who yet cannot believe that this murder was anything more than the frantic idea of a single man, or a few men. The Southern leaders would not do such a thing! My friends, the Southern leaders have been doing such things for years. It is their nature and their practice. The vile rebel at the head,—is he not a traitor, and is not that enough to tell his corruption?

But look you at the drift.

Examine the circumstances, the letters, the remarks, attending the crime. Do they not all point to a plot which had its centre in Richmond?

All along the current for four years, you have seen this thing cropping out. When the President went to Washington four years ago, who does not now know that the plot to assassinate him, then laughed at, was a reality, eluded only by skill? In Alabama, they openly said that if he reached Washington, his life was not worth a week's purchase. In Georgia, a reward was offered for his death. In repeated instances, a Brutus has been demanded to rid them of this tyrant. But a few weeks since, a Richmond paper said an event would soon happen which would "startle the world." In northern states, even among certain classes, it has been said that he would never be inaugurated. And even a northern newspaper, in 1864, distinctly uttered the hope that the knife of the assassin might take his life.

If this particular plot was, ingeniously, ignored by Southern leaders, they cannot ignore the drift and demand of Southern feeling. Nor can the South now disclaim an act to which, at the least, their constant appeals excited the assassins. They are responsible, even if, which nobody can seriously believe, the murder was not planned in Richmond, for a mixture of English blood and Southern Chivalry to execute.

Would that this spirit was all at the South! But it is not so. In northern towns, in the old Bay State, citizens are found, so mean, so traitorous, so murderous, as to cheer when they heard that the President was assassinated! Where was the spirit of the outraged patriots of such a town, when they did not say that upon our soil such miscreants shall not live?

I have not spoken, now, of the fact that these men had no right to make war; but only of their violation of all the laws of war. Allow them belligerent rights, and their conduct is still infamous and barbarous. But I beg you to remember that they had no right to make war at all. Every act of the war was a crime.

The rebellion was wholly wrong. It had not an atom of apology. The Constitution was the Supreme law of the land. It was binding, and has been all these years, upon the whole country, and upon every man in it. If there had been any infraction of justice on the part of administration, there was a peaceable way of deciding it, by a court itself in the interest of the South; and there was a Senate in which the Southern interest was still dominant. But there was no infraction. It was under Buchanan's administration, and the only infraction was in the scoundrelly tyranny which found that illustrious tool a ready instrument. A constitutional election of a man pledged by himself and his party to noninterference with the legal claims of slaveholding wickedness, was no injustice. Only Southern pride was offended because it could no longer make free men beasts of burden. The war was unprovoked, and simply a crime.

The setting up of a pretended government was a crime. It had not a shadow of right. It gave to its projectors no more legal authority than they had as individuals. It could authorize them to do no act which its movers had not a lawful right to do without it; that is, its authority was wholly imaginary. It justified none of them in anything done against the constitutional authority.

Hence, every act done under this treason against the government, or against citizens, was a crime. There was no law to authorize any such act. Every man, doing such an act, was a criminal. For instance, government has the right to take property, under certain restrictions. But citizens have not. A citizen who takes it, is a robber, and his act is robbery. Hence, when the rebels confiscated property, they were merely robbers.

Government has a right to destroy, in case of disturbance. But citizens have not. Hence, when the rebels burned Chambersburg, they were guilty of arson.

Government has a right to take life, for crime or in war. But citizens have not. Hence, when the rebels have killed one of our soldiers, they were murderers, and their act was murder. Every battle has been on their part, wholesale murder; nothing else, because they had no authority to take life.

All this depends on the simple principle that their pretended government was illegal, wrong, and without the shadow of authority. The fact that their act was under the color of a pretended law, does not help the matter; their pretended law was a crime.

Now add to this, that their crime was embodied in treason, was made possible by perjury, and was begun in stealing,—all to establish the infamous sin of human slavery,—and you have the Southern Gentleman. The four years of war are four years of robbery and murder by the Southern Gentleman. All to establish the rights of the Southern Gentleman, which were to breed babies for market, trade in helpless victims of lust, whip and maim human bodies, and starve human souls.

It was, therefore, only the trained spirit of Southern Chivalry to add brutalities forbidden by the laws of war. When they sent their paroled men from Vicksburg directly into other armies, what should they care for the honor of their word, if they could defeat us at Chicamauga? A few lies more or less were of no consequence. When they shot Union soldiers after a surrender, what did they care, if it might wreck vengeance? A few murders more or less were of no consequence. What were rules of honorable warfare to men who plotted treason in the Senate chamber?

Truly the text which I have chosen is appropriate. They have made a covenant with death, and with hell are they at agreement. Their customs, their laws, their practices, were all of hell. Over that Southern land the genius of hell has long brooded. It was written in two hundred years of wronged men ground down by the slave master. It was in the cries of the scarred and crippled. It was in the gory backs of men and women. It was in the blinded souls of their victims. It was in the ashes of the funeral stake.

Then it passed into treason, and murder.

Then it added to the crimes of their treason engendered, butchered prisoners; slain women; fires at night.

Now it has shown itself in a cold-blooded, deliberate assassination of the President.

In all their course, it has, most of all, exhibited itself in its blasphemous appeals to Almighty God to defend and bless their cause!

But equally applicable is the second part of this text "When the overflowing scourge shall pass through, then shall ye be trodden down by it. From the time that it goeth forth, it shall take you. For, morning by morning shall it pass over; By day and by night."

That is God's vengeance. Faithful and true is He that promised. The cries and tears of the millions have been heard by God. They waited. They cried "is there a God?" Generations passed on; but vengeance came at last. The oppressors were crazy. In their pride they rebelled. They were their own executioners. Their stupendous crime could be reached only by their stupendous folly. "If the North fights," said Davis in 1861, "they shall smell Southern powder and feel Southern steel." Ah, they made good the boast. The wrath of God let them pile up their guilt. All the blood shed in this war lies at their door. Fearfully has it been repaid. The Southern woman dresses in black. The sons of the South lie on every battlefield. Its pride—though not its venom—is quenched in blood. Their wealth is destroyed. Their towns are garrisoned by the once despised African, and negro sentinels halt the haughty Southron in Charleston and Savannah.

But it is not enough. We would, foolishly, have spared them, but they would not. It took this last blow to show the tiger, and arouse the overflowing scourge.

This blow has said to the nation,—Have you forgotten the old crimes? Have you forgotten the Senate chamber? Have you forgotten then the graves of your slaughtered sons? Have you forgotten Tennessee, and Pillow, and Andersonville? Have you forgotten Justice? Did you think kindness would tame them? Have you wanted no security?

Come, then. Stand by this bedside. Here is a sick man. He has done his country faithful service. This is his house. Hark! there is one at the door. He will come in. There is a lie in his mouth. He comes to the bedside. He stabs the sick man, in the neck.

Come, again. Here is your President. His wife is with him. He has just let a rebel army go home, whose leaders ought to have been hung. He is going to pardon. See; there steals in an assassin. He shoots. The ball enters the head. The noble, faithful man is dead.

Southern Chivalry did it. Did you want this last lesson to tell you what Southern Chivalry is?

What else does it tell you?

It tells you, you have always been too lenient. You were too kind. You have played at war. Barbarians respect only force. You have not treated them rightly. In the very beginning, when Baltimore fired on our troops, you should have made a street a mile wide through Baltimore. When they hung men in Tennessee, you should have hung men in Louisiana. When they shot McCook, you should have shot Buckner. When they burnt Chambersburg, you should have burned Huntsville. When they shot black prisoners at Pillow, you should have shot white prisoners in South Carolina. That is hard? It is war. War is not play; it is not for women; it is not a lullaby for your children.

It tells you to be the instrument in God's hand of cleansing the land of its pollution. You were willing to leave the freedman without a voice, to the cruelty of the old rebels, were you? You were going to leave the property and life of loyal white men to the disposal of the arch traitors, were you? You were going to let those men come back to Congress, and you would take, in yours, the hand red with your brother's blood, would you? The voice of Providence says, you must have no fellowship with iniquity.

It tells you, you must secure the country. There is but one way,— let the boys and the ignorantly deluded go; they will learn better by and by; but for the leaders, Justice!

There are practical things to do.

1. When armies fall into our hands, it should be by unconditional surrender. There should be no terms given which give to the leaders the rights of prisoners. It is a false sentiment which thinks these generals are not criminals. They are traitors, every one of them. They are murderers all. The prison should be their temporary home. The court should sit, and the judge preside; the witnesses should appear, and tell the tale; and the halter should say that treason is a crime. Rebel judges should be judged, too. Rebel statesmen should reap the reward of their plots. Without this, you are parleying with treason. You are conniving at crime.

They threaten guerrilla war. Their disbanded soldiers will rob and murder. Then let a short shrift and a sure cord be their instant fate.

2. Let the land be cleansed of persistent, sullen, rebels and households. Say to Southern Chivalry, Go; for this, our lines are open. Carry your perjuries to other shores; England is a good place for you. This land is sick of your presence. Your a stench in the nostrils of

honest men. Go, Virginian descendants of transported convicts. Go, you who have lived by oppression and robbery. Never return. Your heritage is gone. Return, and the rope awaits your first step upon our shores.

3. The lands of convicted rebels should be taken. Their strength was in their possessions. Break up their estates. There are Union men by scores of thousands, who have been robbed of their all. Repay them from Southern property. There are millions of unpaid laborers at the South. Give them their arrears of wages. Place them in the lands of their birth, as owners. There are soldiers who deserve well of their country. Give them, each, a tract of land. Endow each with the musket he has faithfully borne, and tell the colonies to hold their possessions as they have held their honor and their loyalty. The men that have caused this war,—leave them landless and penniless, to do what they have despised us for doing,—earn an honest living by the sweat of the face.

4. Let the bondmen have their rights. I told you of this last Thursday. I tell you again. It has been weighing on my mind these many days. Make these loyal men voters. It is indispensable to our security. If there are any loyal whites in the Gulf states, they ought to be glad of such reinforcements of votes as will forever secure their own safety. If there are no loyal whites there, then the blacks are all you can re-organize States with. Justice demands it, also. These men are our friends. They have been true to the government, and they ought to be trusted. They are men, and they are entitled to the rights of citizens. Put the power in their hands. Make them governors, judges, generals. Have you any doubt whether, with arms and ballots in their hands, they could hold the land? The blood which held Hayti against the power of the first Napoleon can now hold the Carolinas against whipped Southerners. The men of Wagner and Olustee are the ones to place in charge of Sumpter, and Mobile, and St. Philip.

5. Christianize that land. They need missionaries. The masses have been deceived by a corrupted Gospel. New churches are wanted there, which will acknowledge God. They need teachers, too, and schools, and civilizing processes. There is no reason to doubt the capacity of the poor whites to be elevated to the scale of humanity. They have good elements; they are brave, true to their convictions, and patient. They are not the Chivalry. You can make something of them, if you begin right and persevere.

Such things should we look to. Government will answer the wish of the people. God's providences are strange. They killed the President; but they failed to kill the one who succeeds; a man trained in Tennessee, and in all the horrors of its warfare; a man from the people, not of the Chivalry; a man who believes in reimbursing the losses of loyal men out of the property of the disloyal; a man who advocates Justice; a man who said to his black fellow citizens, when they demanded it, that he would be their Moses.

We will rally around this man. He, when generals said Nashville could not be held, sent the citizens into the trenches, and held it, and kept the flag flying. He will defend the flag as well now, and will man the ramparts with faithful men. The kindly heart is gone; the avenger has come.

By the graves of our dead comrades, by the scarred battleflags, by the sturdy muskets, by the ashes of dwellings, let us swear eternal hatred to Southern Chivalry. In the fear of God Almighty, let us never pander to treason. Let no rebel generals be feted on our soil. Let the land be cleansed. Let the sword and the scaffold do their righteous work. Let treason die, that the country may live. By prayer, and vote, and our right arm, let us say, treason must perish. And, that treason may never have a resurrection, let Southern Chivalry be destroyed, root and branch, twig and leaf.

In the memories of this day, and because men who have violated every law, human and divine, are the enemies of God, I dare, as a Christian minister, to quote the words of the Almighty:

Arise, O God; let Thine enemies be scattered.
Pour out their blood by the force of sword.
Let their children be scattered;
Let their wives be widows;
Let their men be put to death;
Let their young men be put to the sword.
Deal with them, in the time of Thine anger.
Wickedness is in their dwelling;
Give them according to the wickedness of their endeavors.
Give them according to the work of their hands.
Let them be as chaff before the wind.
Let their way be dark and slippery.
Let death seize upon them.

The second sermon in the Appendix was prepared by Matthew Simpson, bishop of the Methodist Episcopal Church, for Lincoln's burial service at Springfield, Illinois, on May 4, 1865. Though harsh in its attitude toward the South, the sermon is of a different spirit than Quint's sermon.

Simpson, in his varied career, had practiced medicine, been a college president and professor, edited a religious journal, served as a local pastor and bishop. Prior to the Civil War, he was the best-known and most influential Methodist minister in the United States. Few public speakers of his day were Simpson's equal. Such was his power over his audience that during his sermons people would often leap to their feet, applaud, laugh, or weep. He spoke frankly and forcefully on public matters, especially those relating to slavery. During the war he was a powerful and unrelenting advocate for the Union cause. He was consulted by Secretary of War Edwin Stanton and President Lincoln. Simpson and Lincoln formed a strong bond of friendship, and for this reason Simpson was asked to deliver the eulogy at the President's burial.

His eulogy spent much time on Lincoln's character, drawing attention to his mental abilities, moral powers, administrative skills, and religious qualities. Lincoln's greatest heritage, according to Simpson, was the issuing of the Emancipation Proclamation. The sermon demonstrates a strong belief in the Providence of God and the assassination as a part of the providential plan. Simpson urged that harsh measures be administered upon the Southern leaders, but "to the deluded masses we will extend the arms of forgiveness." The sermon, personal in nature, is an example of high prose. Its tone and demeanor is much more typical of the majority of post-assassination sermons than is the sermon by Quint.

Oration
at Lincoln's Burial at Springfield, Illinois
BISHOP MATTHEW SIMPSON
May 4, 1865

NEAR THE CAPITAL of this large and growing State of Illinois, in the midst of this beautiful grove, and at the open mouth of the vault which has just received the remains of our fallen chieftain, we gather to pay a tribute of respect and to drop the tears of sorrow around the ashes of the mighty dead. A little more than four years ago he left his plain and quiet home in yonder city, receiving the departing words of the concourse of friends who, in the midst of the dropping of the gentle shower, gathered around him. He spoke of the pain of parting from the place where he had lived for a quarter of a century, where his children had been born, and his home had been rendered pleasant by friendly associations, and, as he left, he made an earnest request, in the hearing of some who are present at this hour, that, as he was about to enter upon responsibilities which he believed to be greater than any which had fallen upon any man since the days of Washington, the people would offer up prayers that God would aid and sustain him in the work which they had given him to do. His company left your quiet city, but, as it went, snares were in waiting for the Chief Magistrate. Scarcely did he escape the dangers of the way or the hands of the assassin, as he neared Washington; and I believe he escaped only through the vigilance of officers and the prayers of his people, so that the blow was suspended for more than four years, which was at last permitted, through the providence of God, to fall.

How different the occasion which witnessed his departure from that which witnessed his return. Doubtless you expected to take him by the hand, and to feel the warm grasp which you had felt in other days, and to see the tall form walking among you which you had delighted to honor in years past. But he was never permitted to come until he came with lips mute and silent, the frame encoffined, and a weeping nation following as his mourners. Among the events of history there have been great processions of mourners. There was one for the patriarch Jacob, which went up from Egypt, and the Egyptians wondered at the evidences of reverence and filial affection which came from the hearts of the Israelites. There was mourning when Moses fell upon the heights of Pisgah and was hid from human view. There have been mournings in the kingdoms of the earth when kings and princes have fallen, but never was there, in the history of man, such mourning as that which has accompanied this funeral procession, and has gathered around the mortal remains of him who was our loved one, and who now sleeps among us. If we glance at the procession which followed him, we see how the nation stood aghast. Tears filled the eyes of manly, sunburnt faces. Strong men, as they clasped the hands of their friends, were unable to find vent for their grief in words. Women and little children caught up the tidings as they ran through the land, and were melted into tears. The nation stood still. Men left their plows in the fields and asked what the end should be. The hum of manufactories ceased, and the sound of the hammer was not heard. Busy merchants closed their doors, and in the exchange gold passed no more from hand to hand. Though three weeks have elapsed, the nation has scarcely breathed easily yet. A mournful silence is abroad upon the land; nor is this mourning confined to any class or to any district of country. Men of all political parties, and of all religious creeds, have united in paying this mournful tribute. The archbishop of the Roman Catholic Church in New York and a Protestant minister walked side by side in the sad procession, and a Jewish rabbi performed a part of the solemn services.

Here are gathered around his tomb the representatives of the army and navy, senators, judges, governors, and officers of all the branches of the Government. Here, too, are members of civic processions, with men and women from the humblest as well as the highest occupations. Here and there, too, are tears, as sincere and warm as any that drop, which come from the eyes of those whose kindred and whose race have been freed from their chains by him whom they mourn as their deliverer. More persons have gazed on the face of the departed than ever looked upon the face of any other departed man. More races have looked on the procession for 1,600 miles or more—by night and by day—by sunlight, dawn, twilight, and by torchlight, that ever before watched the progress of a procession.

We ask why this wonderful mourning—this great procession? I answer, first, a part of the interest has arisen from the times in which we live, and in which he that had fallen was a principal actor. It is a principle of our nature that feelings, once excited, turn readily from the object by which they are excited, to some other object which may for the time being take possession of the mind. Another principle is, the deepest affections of our hearts gather around some human form in which are incarnated the living thoughts and ideas of the passing age. If we look then at the times, we see an age of excitement. For four years the popular heart has been stirred to its inmost depth. War had come upon us, dividing families, separating nearest and dearest friends—a war, the extent and magnitude of which no one could estimate—a war in which the blood of brethren was shed by a brother's hand. A call for soldiers was made by this voice now hushed, and all over the land, from hill and mountain, from plain and valley, there sprang up thousands of bold hearts, ready to go forth and save our national Union. This feeling of excitement was transferred next into a feeling of deep grief because of the dangers in which our country was placed. Many said, "Is it possible to save our nation?" Some in our country, and nearly all the leading men in other countries, declared it to be impossible to maintain the Union; and many an honest and patriotic heart was deeply pained with apprehensions of common ruin; and many, in grief and almost in despair, anxiously inquired, What shall the end of these things be? In addition to this wives had given their husbands, mothers their sons, the pride and joy of their hearts. They saw them put on the uniform, they saw them take the martial step, and they tried to hide their deep feeling of sadness. Many dear ones slept upon the battle-field never to return again, and there was mourning in every mansion and in every cabin in our broad land. Then came a feeling of deeper sadness as the story came of prisoners tortured to death or starved through the mandates of those who are called the representatives of the chivalry, and who claimed to be the honorable ones of the earth; and as we read the stories of frames attenuated and reduced to mere skeletons, our grief turned partly into horror and partly into a cry for vengeance.

Then this feeling was changed to one of joy. There came signs of the end of this rebellion. We followed the career of our glorious generals. We saw our army, under the command of the brave officer who is guiding this procession, climb up the heights of Lookout Mountain and drive the rebels from their strongholds. Another brave general swept through Georgia, South and North Carolina, and drove the combined armies of the rebels before him, while the honored Lieutenant-General held Lee and his hosts in a death-grasp.

Then the tidings came that Richmond was evacuated, and that Lee had surrendered. The bells rang merrily all over the land. The booming of cannon was heard; illuminations and torch-light processions manifested the general joy, and families were looking for the speedy return of their loved ones from the field of battle. Just in the midst of this wildest joy, in one hour—nay, in one moment—the tidings thrilled throughout the land that Abraham Lincoln, the best of Presidents, had perished by the hands of an assassin; and then all the feelings which had been gathering for four years, in forms of excitement, grief, horror, and joy, turned into one wail of woe—a sadness inexpressible—an anguish unutterable. But it is not the times merely which caused this mourning. The mode of his death must be taken into the account. Had he died on a bed of illness, with kind friends around him; had the sweat of death been wiped from his brow by gentle hands, while he was yet conscious; could he have had power to speak words of affection to his stricken widow, or words of counsel to us like those which we heard in his parting inaugural at Washington, which shall now be immortal—how it would have softened or assuaged something of the grief. There might, at least, have been preparation for the event. But no moment of warning was given to him or to us. He was stricken down, too, when his hopes for the end of the rebellion were bright, and prospects of a joyous life were before him. There was a cabinet meeting that day, said to have been the most cheerful and happy of any held since the beginning of the rebellion. After this meeting he talked with his friends, and spoke of the four years of tempest, of the storm being over, and of the four years of pleasure and joy awaiting him, as the weight of care and anxiety would be taken from his mind, and he could have happy days with his family again. In the midst of these anticipations he left his house never to return alive. The evening was Good Friday, the saddest day in the whole calendar for the Christian Church—henceforth in this country to be made sadder, if possible, by the memory of our nation's loss; and so filled with grief was every Christian heart that even all the joyous thought of Easter Sunday failed to remove the crushing sorrow under which the true worshiper bowed in the house of God.

But the great cause of this mourning is to be found in the man himself. Mr. Lincoln was no ordinary man. I believe the conviction has been growing on the nation's mind, as it certainly has been on my own, especially in the last years of his administration, that, by the hand of God, he was especially singled out to guide our Government in these troublesome times, and it seems to me that the hand of God may be traced in many of the events connected with his history. First, then, I recognized this in the physical education which he received, and which prepared him for enduring herculean labors. In the toils of his boyhood and the labors of his manhood, God was giving him an iron frame. Next to this was his identification with the heart of the great people, understanding their feelings because he was one of them, and connected with them in their movements and life. His education was simple. A few months spent in the school-house gave him the elements of education. He read few books, but mastered all he read. Bunyan's Progress, Aesop's Fables, and the Life of Washington were his favorites. In these we recognize the works which gave bias to his character, and which partly molded his style. His early life, with its varied struggles, joined him indissolubly to the working masses, and no elevation in society diminished his respect for the sons of toil. He knew what it was to fell the tall trees of the forest and to stem the current of the broad Mississippi. His home was in the growing West, the heart of the Republic, and, invigorated by the wind which swept over its prairies, he learned lessons of self-reliance which sustained him in seasons of adversity.

His genius was soon recognized, as true genius always will be, and he was placed in the Legislature of his State. Already acquainted with the principles of law, he devoted his thoughts to matters of public interest, and began to be looked on as the coming statesman. As early as 1839 he presented resolutions in the Legislature, asking for emancipation in the District of Columbia, when, with but rare exceptions, the whole popular mind of his State was opposed to the measure. From that hour he was a steady and uniform friend of humanity, and was preparing for the conflict of latter years.

If you ask me on what mental characteristic his greatness rested, I answer, on a quick and ready perception of facts; on a memory unusually tenacious and retentive; and on a logical turn of mind, which followed sternly and unwaveringly every link in the chain of thought on every subject which he was called to investigate. I think there have been minds more broad in their character, more comprehensive in their scope, but I doubt if ever there has been a man who could follow step by step, with more logical power, the points which he desired to illustrate. He gained this power by the close study of geometry, and by a determination to perceive the truth in all its relations and simplicity, and, when found, to utter it.

It is said of him in childhood, when he had any difficulty in listening to a conversation to ascertain what people meant, if he retired to rest he could not sleep till he tried to understand the precise points intended, and when understood, to frame language to convey it in a clearer manner to others. Who then has read his messages fails to perceive the directness and the simplicity of his style? And this very trait, which was scoffed at and decried by opponents, is now recognized as one of the strong points of that mighty mind which has so powerfully influenced the destiny of this nation, and which shall, for ages to come, influence the destiny of humanity.

It was not, however, chiefly by his mental faculties that he gained such control over mankind. His moral power gave him pre-eminence. The convictions of men that Abraham Lincoln was an honest man led them to yield to his guidance. As has been said of Cobden, whom he greatly resembled, he made all men feel a sense of himself—a recognition of individuality—a self-relying power. They saw in him a man whom they believed would do what is right, regardless of all consequences. It was this moral feeling which gave him the greatest hold on the people, and made his utterances almost oracular. When the nation was angered by the perfidy of foreign nations in allowing privateers to be fitted out, he uttered the significant expression, "One war at a time," and it stilled the national heart. When his own friends were divided as to what steps should be taken as to slavery, that simple utterance, "I will save the Union, if I can, with slavery; if not, slavery must perish, for the Union must be preserved," became the rallying word. Men felt the struggle was for the Union, and all other questions must be subsidiary.

But, after all, by the acts of a man shall his fame be perpetuated. What are his acts? Much praise is due to the men who aided him. He called able counselors around him—some of whom have displayed the highest order of talent, united with the purest and most devoted patriotism. He summoned able generals into the field—men who have borne the sword as bravely as ever any human arm has borne it. He had the aid of prayerful and thoughtful men everywhere. But, under his own guiding hands, wise counsels were combined and great movements conducted.

Turn towards the different departments. We had an unorganized militia, a mere skeleton army, yet, under his care, that army has been enlarged into a force which, for skill, intelligence, efficiency, and bravery, surpass any which the world has ever seen. Before its veterans the fame of even the renowned veterans of Napoleon shall pale, (applause), and the mothers and sisters on these hill sides, and all over the land, shall take to their arms again braver sons and brothers than ever fought in European wars. The reason is obvious. Money, or a desire for fame, collected those armies, or they were rallied to sustain favorite thrones or dynasties; but the armies he called into being fought for liberty, for the Union, and for the right of self-government; and many of them felt that the battles they won were for humanity everywhere and for all time; for I believe that God has not suffered this terrible rebellion to come upon our land merely for a chastisement to us, or as a lesson to our age. There are moments which involve in themselves eternities. There are instants which seem to contain germs which shall develop and bloom forever. Such a moment came in the tide of time to our land, when a question must be settled which affected all the earth. The contest was for human freedom, not for this republic merely; not for the Union simply, but to decide whether the people, as a people, in their entire majesty, were destined to be the government, or whether they were to be subject to tyrants or aristocrats, or to class-rule of any kind. This is the great question for which we have been fighting, and its decision is at hand, and the result of the contest will affect the ages to come. If successful, republics will spread in spite of monarchs, all over this earth. (Exclamations of "Amen." "Thank God.")

I turn from the army to the navy. What was it when the war commenced? Now we have our ships-of-war at home and abroad, to guard privateers in foreign sympathizing ports, as well as to care for every part of our own coast. They have taken forts that military men said could not be taken, and a brave admiral, for the first time in the world's history, lashed himself to the mast, there to remain as long as he had a particle of skill or strength to watch over his ship, while it engaged in the perilous contest of taking the strong forts of the rebels.

Then, again, I turn to the treasury department. Where should the money come from? Wise men predicted ruin, but our national credit has been maintained, and our currency is safer to-day than it ever was before. Not only so, but through our national bonds, if properly used, we shall have a permanent basis for our currency, and an investment so desirable for capitalists of other nations that, under the laws of trade, I believe the center of exchange will speedily be transferred from England to the United States.

But the great act of the mighty chieftan, on which his fame shall rest long after his frame shall molder away, is that of giving freedom to a race. We have all been taught to revere sacred characters. Among them Moses stands pre-eminently high. He received the law from God, and his name is honored among the hosts of heaven. Was not his greatest act the delivering of three millions of his kindred out of bondage? Yet we may assert that Abraham Lincoln, by his proclamation, liberated more enslaved people than ever Moses set free, and those not of his kindred or his race. Such a power, or such an opportunity, God has seldom given to man. When other events shall have been forgotten; when this world shall have become a network of republics; when every throne shall be swept from the face of the earth; when literature shall enlighten all minds; when the claims of humanity shall be recognized everywhere, this act shall still be conspicuous on the pages of history. We are thankful that God gave to Abraham Lincoln the decision and wisdom and grace to issue that proclamation, which stands high above all other papers which have been penned by uninspired men. (Applause.)

Abraham Lincoln was a good man. He was known as an honest, temperate, forgiving man; a just man; a man of noble heart in every way. As to his religious experience, I cannot speak definitely, because I was not privileged to know much of his private sentiments. My acquaintance with him did not give me the opportunity to hear him speak on those topics. This I know, however, he read the Bible frequently; loved it for its great truths and its profound teachings; and he tried to be guided by its precepts. He believed in Christ the Saviour of sinners; and I think he was sincere in trying to bring his life into harmony with the principles of revealed religion. Certainly if there ever was a man who illustrated some of the principles of pure religion, that man was our departed President. Look over all his speeches, listen to his utterances. He never spoke unkindly of any man. Even the rebels received no word of anger from him, and his last day illustrated in a remarkable manner his forgiving disposition. A dispatch was received that afternoon that Thompson and Tucker were trying to make their escape through Maine, and it was proposed to arrest them. Mr. Lincoln, however, preferred rather to let them quietly escape. He was seeking to save the very men who had been plotting his destruction. This morning we read a proclamation offering $25,000 for the arrest of these men as aiders and abettors of his assassination; so that, in his expiring acts, he was saying, "Father, forgive them, they know not what they do." As a ruler, I doubt if any President has ever shown such trust in God, or in public documents so frequently referred to Divine aid. Often did he remark to friends and to delegations that his hope for our success rested in his conviction that God would bless our efforts, because we were trying to do right. To the address of a large religious body he replied, "Thanks be unto God, who, in our national trials, giveth us the churches." To a minister who said he hoped the Lord was on our side, he replied that it gave him no concern whether the Lord was on our side or not, for, he added, "I know the Lord is always on the side of right," and with deep feeling he added, "But God is my witness that it is my constant anxiety and prayer that both myself and this nation should be on the Lord's side."

In his domestic life he was exceedingly kind and affectionate. He was a devoted husband and father. During his presidential term, he lost his second son, Willie. To an officer of the army he said, not long since, "Do you ever find yourself talking with the dead?" and added, "Since Willie's death I catch myself every day involuntarily talking with him, as if he were with me." On his widow, who is unable to be here, I need only invoke the blessing of Almighty God that she may be comforted and sustained. For his son, who has witnessed the exercises of this hour, all that I can desire is that the mantle of his father may fall upon him. (Exclamations of "Amen.")

Let us pause a moment in the lesson of the hour before we part. This man, though he fell by an assassin, still fell under the permissive hand of God. He had some wise purpose in allowing him to fall. What more could he have desired of life for himself? Were not his honors full? There was no office to which he could aspire. The popular heart clung around him as around no other man. The nations of the world had learned to honor our chief magistrate. If rumors of a desired alliance with England be true, Napoleon trembled when he heard of the fall of Richmond, and asked what nation would join him to protect him against our Government under the guidance of such a man. His fame was full, his work was done, and he sealed his glory by becoming the nation's great martyr for liberty.

He appears to have had a strange presentiment, early in political life, that some day he would be President. You see it indicated in

1839. Of the slave power he said, "Broken by it I too may be; bow to it I never will. The probability that we may fail in the struggle ought not to deter us from the support of a cause which we deem to be just. It shall not deter me. If ever I feel the soul within me elevate and expand to those dimensions not wholly unworthy of its Almighty architect, it is when I contemplate the cause of my country, deserted by all the world besides, and I standing up boldly and alone and hurling defiance at her victorious oppressors. Here without contemplating consequences, before high Heaven and in the face of the world, I swear eternal fidelity to the just cause, as I deem it, of the land of my life, my liberty, and my love." And yet, secretly, he said to more than one, "I never shall live out the four years of my term. When the rebellion is crushed my work is done." So it was. He lived to see the last battle fought, and dictate a despatch from the home of Jefferson Davis; lived till the power of the rebellion was broken; and then, having done the work for which God had sent him, angels, I trust, were sent to shield him from one moment of pain or suffering, and to bear him from this world to the high and glorious realm where the patriot and the good shall live forever.

His career teaches young men that every position of eminence is open before the diligent and the worthy. To the active men of the country, his example is an incentive to trust in God and do right.

Standing, as we do to-day, by his coffin and his sepulchre, let us resolve to carry forward the policy which he so nobly began. Let us do right to all men. To the ambitious there is this fearful lesson: Of the four candidates for Presidential honors in 1860, two of them— Douglas and Lincoln—once competitors, but now sleeping patriots, rest from their labors; Bell perished in poverty and misery, as a traitor might perish; and Breckinridge is a frightened fugitive, with the brand of traitor on his brow. Let us vow, in the sight of Heaven, to eradicate every vestige of human slavery; to give every human being his true position before God and man; to crush every form of rebellion, and to stand by the flag which God has given us. How joyful that it floated over parts of every State before Mr. Lincoln's career was ended. How singular that, to the fact of the assassin's heels being caught in the folds of the flag, we are probably indebted for his capture. The flag and the traitor must ever be enemies.

Traitors will probably suffer by the change of rulers, for one of sterner mould, and who himself has deeply suffered from the rebellion, now wields the sword of justice. Our country, too, is stronger for the trial. A republic was declared by monarchists too weak to endure a civil war; yet we have crushed the most gigantic rebellion in history, and have grown in strength and population every year of the struggle. We have passed through the ordeal of a popular election while swords and bayonets were in the field, and have come out unharmed. And now, in an hour of excitement, with a large majority having preferred another man for President, when the bullet of the assassin had laid our President prostrate, has there been a mutiny? Has any rival proffered his claims? Out of an army of near a million, no officer or soldier uttered one note of dissent, and, in an hour or two after Mr. Lincoln's death, another leader under constitutional forms, occupied his chair, and the government moved forward without one single jar. The world will learn that republics are the strongest governments on earth.

And now, my friends, in the words of the departed, "with malice towards none," free from all feelings of personal vengeance, yet believing that the sword must not be borne in vain, let us go forward even in painful duty. Let every man who was a senator or representative in Congress, and who aided in beginning this rebellion, and thus led to the slaughter of our sons and daughters, be brought to speedy and to certain punishment. Let every officer educated at the public expense, and who, having been advanced to position, perjured himself and turned his sword against the vitals of the country, be doomed to a traitor's death. This, I believe, is the will of the American people. Men may attempt to compromise, and to restore these traitors and murderers to society again. Vainly may they talk of the fancied honor or chivalry of these murderers of our sons—these starvers of our prisoners—these officers who mined their prisons and placed kegs of powder to destroy our captive officers. But the American people will rise in their majesty and sweep all such compromises and compromisers away, and will declare that there shall be no safety for rebel leaders. But to the deluded masses we will extend the arms of forgiveness. We will take them to our hearts, and walk with them side by side, as we go forward to work out a glorious destiny.

The time will come when, in the beautiful words of him whose lips are now forever sealed, "the mystic chords of memory, which stretch from every battle-field, and from every patriot's grave, shall yield a sweeter music when touched by the angels of our better nature."

Chieftain! farewell! The nation mourns thee. Mothers shall teach thy name to their lisping children. The youth of our land shall emulate thy virtues. Statesmen shall study thy record and learn lessons of wisdom. Mute though thy lips be, yet still they speak. Hushed is thy voice, but its echoes of liberty are ringing through the world, and the sons of bondage listen with joy. Prisoned thou art in death, and yet thou art marching abroad, and chains and manacles are bursting at thy touch. Thou didst fall not for thyself. The assassin had no hate for thee. Our hearts were aimed at, our national life was sought. We crown thee as our martyr—and humanity enthrones thee as her triumphant son. Hero, Martyr, Friend, FAREWELL!

* * *

Notes

INTRODUCTION

[1]For further discussion on the use of sermons as historical documents, see David B. Chesebrough and Lawrence W. McBride, "Sermons as Historical Documents: Henry Ward Beecher and the Civil War," 275–91. Thomas Reed Turner has noted that "Sermons preached after the assassination are an excellent means of gauging public reactions, yet they have been virtually unexamined by historians." *Beware the People Weeping: Public Opinion and the Assassination of Abraham Lincoln,* 77.

[2]Paxton Hibben, *Henry Ward Beecher: An American Portrait,* xiii–xiv; Theodore Parker, "The Slave Power," *Centenary Edition of the Works of Theodore Parker* 11:279.

[3]For a brief but excellent account of the role of Southern preachers in the years before and during the Civil War, see James W. Silver, *Confederate Morale and Church Propaganda.* Richard E. Beringer, Herman Hattaway, Archer Jones, and William N. Still, Jr., *Why the South Lost the Civil War,* 97.

[4]John C. Thompson, *In Memoriam,* 19.

[5]Lloyd Lewis, *Myths After Lincoln,* 79.

[6]As recorded in Charles J. Stewart, "A Rhetorical Study of the Reaction of the Protestant Pulpit in the North to Lincoln's Assassination," 13.

[7]An especially fine Jewish sermon, one which differed markedly from most Protestant sermons, was delivered on April 19 by Rabbi Sobato Morais before the Congregation Mikve Israel in Philadelphia. Contrary to most of the Protestant preachers, Morais exclaimed: "We shared not the intemperate zeal of such who laid against our General-in-Chief the charge of excessive leniency." Again contrary to most Protestant preachers, he urged for moderation in response to the assassination. "Our great Abraham," he emphasized, "would . . . prefer magnanimity to severity, forgiveness to vengeance" (*An Address,* 3, 6).

[8]John C. Thompson, *In Memoriam,* 3.

[9]Daniel Rice, *The President's Death—Its Import,* 1. Rice used the following texts: 2 Sam. 3:33, 35, 38; Matt. 7:2; Judg. 1:7; 1 Sam. 15:33; Isa. 33:1; Job 5:12–13; Ps. 79:12; Isa. 65:6; and Deut. 32:43.

[10]Robert Russell Booth, *Personal Forgiveness and Public Justice,* 7.

[11]Turner, *Beware the People Weeping,* 51; Robert James Keeling, *The Death of Moses,* frontispiece; *The Terrible Tragedy at Washington: Assassination of President Lincoln,* 114.

[12]Charles J. Stewart, "A Rhetorical Study," 11.
[13]Thomas Swaim, "Discourse," 4, 5.
[14]Phillips Brooks, "Abraham Lincoln," *Addresses,* 158.
[15]Charles J. Stewart, "The Pulpit and the Assassination of Lincoln," 300.

CHAPTER 1

[1]Edwin B. Webb, "Sermon," *Sermons Preached in Boston on the Death of Abraham Lincoln,* 146.
[2]Henry H. Northrop, *A Sermon,* 3; Edward Everett Hale, "Sermon," 273.
[3]A. P. Rogers, "Sermon XIII," 242.
[4]George Dana Boardman, "An Address," 52; Theodore L. Cuyler, "Sermon IX," 159; Rufus S. Sanborn, *A Discourse,* 2.
[5]Henry Lyman Morehouse, *Evil Its Own Destroyer,* 6–7.
[6]Leonard Swain, *A Nation's Sorrow,* 4; Morgan Dix, *The Death of President Lincoln,* 6.
[7]Jacob Thomas, "Sermon," 44–45. Another sermon depicting black grief can be found in this same volume, Joseph A. Prime, "Sermon," 151–57. Wallace Shelton, *Discourse Upon the Death of Abraham Lincoln,* 4.
[8]E. S. Atwood, *The Nation's Loss,* 3.
[9]Northrop, *A Sermon,* 3; Elias Nason, *Eulogy,* 4.
[10]John C. Thompson, *In Memoriam,* 17. The reference to prisoners is to that day when Lincoln's funeral train passed Sing Sing Prison and the prisoners stood with their hats off in homage to the dead President.
[11]Nason, *Eulogy,* 5; J. B. Wentworth, *A Discourse on the Death of President Lincoln,* 11; James Reed, "Address," 302; Charles Carroll Everett, *A Sermon,* 5. Several preachers referred to the orphan theme. E. S. Atwood said that by the stroke of assassination "millions are orphaned." *The Nation's Loss,* 4, 21–22.
[12]Isaac E. Carey, *Discourse,* 5.
[13]John E. Todd, "President Lincoln," 79; Gilbert Haven, "The Uniter and Liberator of America," 561; J. B. Wentworth, *A Discourse,* 19.
[14]William H. Herndon, *Herndon's Lincoln: The True Story of a Great Life* 3:466–67. See also, Edgar DeWitt Jones, *Lincoln and the Preachers,* 180–81.
[15]Jones, *Lincoln and the Preachers,* 90.
[16]James D. Liggett, "Our National Reverses," 253, 255.
[17]Israel E. Dwinell, *Hope for Our Country;* Frederick G. Clark, *Gold in the Fire: Our National Position;* J. E. Rankin, *The Battle Not Man's, But God's.*
[18]Byron Sunderland, *The Crisis of Our Times.*
[19]Gilbert Haven, "Three Summers of War," 407–20.
[20]William D. Potts, *Freemen's Guide to the Polls and a Solemn Appeal to American Patriots,* 3, 13, 46–47, 100–101. Potts's passionate arguments often defy logic. A summary of his accusations went: "Lincoln & Co., have no special regard for the Flag, the Constitution, or the Union, only as they subserve their selfish ends. . . . are the most dangerous Abolitionists in our country; and are opposed to the Government of our forefathers. . . . are the Authors of Secession; and compelled the South to secede. . . . are the Authors of the War. . . . forced the South to 'fire the

first gun'. . . . could have prevented the War. . . . aspire to free the slaves,—to enfranchise them,—to overthrow Democracy, and to establish a Monarchial Government" (4). Following the assassination, Potts would not have dared to issue a publication expressing this kind of sentiment.
    [21] O. T. Lanphear, *Peace by Power;* Jones, *Lincoln and the Preachers,* 58–59.
    [22] George Dana Boardman, "An Address," 52; Sanborn, *A Discourse,* 2, 3.
    [23] Northrop, *A Sermon,* 6; Todd, "President Lincoln," 83.

CHAPTER 2

    [1] Edward Searing, *President Lincoln in History,* 16, 18; George Dana Boardman, "An Address," 60, 61; Charles Carroll Everett, *A Sermon,* 17–20; Seth Sweetser, *A Commemorative Discourse on the Death of Abraham Lincoln,* 13.
    [2] Abram N. Littlejohn, "Sermon VIII," 150, 153–56. Those tests were, according to Littlejohn, the ability

    [1] to discharge immense responsibilities in times of change and peril, and to hand over a trust of extraordinary powers without even the suspicion of failure or abuse. . . . [2] to lead and to fashion, amid all possible elements of hazard and convulsion, an era of transcendent success in the life of empires or republics. . . . [3] to mould and govern the opinions of a free people. . . . [4] to win and to hold in high station and amid days of change and peril the confidence of millions. . . . [5] to preserve an original, uncorrupted individuality amid the frictions and abrasions of a rulership which makes the incumbent the depository of all men's notions, the prey of flatterers, deceivers and parasites, the victim of the menace or the blandishments of a dominant party. . . . [6] to enrich by character, deeds, and sufferings, the annals of a people, and to multiply their traditions of endurance, heroism, and triumph. . . . [7] to complete service by sacrifice; to attest by death what was toiled and fought for in life; and to add the martyr's crown to the patriot's work.

    [3] Joseph P. Thompson, "Sermon X," 173, 174.
    [4] Phillips Brooks, "Abraham Lincoln," 141, 150, 158–59; Alonzo H. Quint, "What President Lincoln Did For His Country," *Three Sermons,* 20.
    [5] Some good and interesting biographies are found in the following sermons: George Dana Boardman, "An Address"; Richard Eddy, *Three Sermons,* 9ff; Amory D. Mayo, "Abraham Lincoln," *Two Discourses;* Searing, *President Lincoln in History;* and Hiram Sears, *The People's Keepsake.* One of the reasons, of course, that many of the events and stories in the preachers' "biographies" are not found in full-length biographies is because those contemporary accounts are found to be unreliable, too often based on popular rumors rather than substantiated facts. These rumored stories, however, are important, as they colored contemporary perceptions of Lincoln.
    [6] Thomas Mears Eddy, *A Memorial Discourse,* 8–17.
    [7] Haven, "The Uniter and Liberator," 570; Samuel C. Baldridge, *The Martyr Prince,* 10; Sidney Dean, *Eulogy,* 15; E. S. Atwood, *The President's Record,* 27; Thomas E. Bliss, *A Discourse,* 12. The Union Church was founded in 1863 when a

band of Federal soldiers decided to organize a Congregational church because there was no church of that denomination in Memphis. Bliss, an army chaplain, became the first pastor, serving from 1864 to 1870. The church did not have even one woman as a charter member.

[8]Quint, "What President Lincoln Did For His Country," 27.

[9]Mayo, "Abraham Lincoln," 25; George L. Chaney, "Sermon," 331–32; Elbert S. Porter, "Sermon XII," 237–38.

[10]Joshua T. Tucker, A Discourse, 5.

[11]Ibid., 12; Pliny H. White, A Sermon Occasioned by the Assassination of Abraham Lincoln, 7; J. B. Wentworth, A Discourse, 18; Charles Hammond, A Sermon on the Life and Character of Abraham Lincoln, 12, 13; Haven, "The Uniter and Liberator," 554, 555–56.

[12]Henry A. Nelson, "The Divinely Prepared Ruler," 18; Hammond, Life and Character, 13; Jeremiah E. Rankin, Moses and Joshua, 9.

[13]Baldridge, The Martyr Prince, 7, 8; Carey, Discourse, 2; Cuyler, "Sermon IX," 168.

[14]Brooks, "Abraham Lincoln," 144–45; Joseph P. Thompson, "Sermon X," 180; Matthew Simpson, "Oration," 400; George Dana Boardman, "An Address," 57, 58.

[15]L. M. Glover, The Character of Abraham Lincoln, 6; George Putnam, "Address," 314; Morris C. Sutphen, Discourse, 10.

[16]Cuyler, "Sermon IX," 167; Denis Wortman, A Discourse on the Death of Abraham Lincoln, 9–10.

[17]Tucker, A Discourse, 12; Andrew L. Stone, "A Sermon," 342.

[18]Joseph P. Thompson, "Sermon X," 188; Haven, "The Uniter and Liberator," 558.

[19]Simpson, "Oration," 399; George Hepworth, "Sermon," 114.

[20]Cuyler, "Sermon IX," 167–68; William Adams, "Sermon XIX," 331–32.

[21]Henry J. Fox, "Sermon XX," 347; Henry W. Foote, "Address," 185; Todd, "President Lincoln," 81; Atwood, The Nation's Loss, 5.

[22]Robert Lowry, "Sermon XVII," 312; Thomas Mears Eddy, A Memorial Discourse, 18; Cephas B. Crane, Sermon, 27.

[23]J. D. Fulton, "Sermon," 368; Foote, "Address," 189; Rufus Ellis, "Sermon," 242.

[24]Phineas Densmore Gurley, "Sermon," 24.

[25]Sears, The People's Keepsake, 13; Simpson, "Oration," 405; Gordan Hall, President Lincoln's Death: Its Voice to the People, 9–10.

[26]Baldridge, The Martyr Prince, 12; Cuyler, "Sermon IX," 169; Joseph P. Thompson, "Sermon X," 202; Nelson, "The Divinely Prepared Ruler," 21.

[27]Albert S. Hunt, "Sermon XVIII," 327; Northrop, A Sermon, 7.

[28]William J. Potter, The National Tragedy: Four Sermons, 37; Lowry, "Sermon XVII," 309, 310.

[29]Joseph A. Seiss, The Assassinated President, 20.

[30]Lowry, "Sermon XVII," 310; George Dana Boardman, "An Address," 61; Stone, "Sermon," 352–53; Fulton, "Sermon," 367; Sutphen, Discourse, 14; Glover, The Character of Abraham Lincoln, 19.

[31]Thomas Laurie, Three Discourses, 33; George Duffield, The Nation's Wail, 17; Lowry, "Sermon XVII," 310–11.

³²E. J. Goodspeed, *Funeral Discourse on the Death of Abraham Lincoln*, 11–12.

³³Laurie, *Three Discourses*, 33, 34–35.

³⁴Frederick Starr, Jr., *The Martyr President*, 13. Of all the sermons that addressed the subject of Lincoln's attendance at a theater, I have seen only one that sought to put the subject in any kind of positive reference. Edwin B. Webb noted: "Wearied with the duties of his high position, and the persistent annoyance of petty office-seekers, and unwilling to disappoint the people even in their unreasonable expectations, he sought an hour's recreation in the theater" ("Sermon," 147).

³⁵Charles Lowe, *Death of President Lincoln*, 18–19.

³⁶Henry Ward Beecher, "Abraham Lincoln," 702–3; Clement M. Butler, *Funeral Address*, 12; Samuel K. Lothrop, "Sermon," 252; Quint, "What President Lincoln Did For His Country," 18.

³⁷Beecher, "Abraham Lincoln," 712; Seiss, *The Assassinated President*, 42–43.

³⁸James M. Manning, "Sermon," 60–61; Cuyler, "Sermon IX," 160–61.

³⁹Goodspeed, *Funeral Discourse*, 5; Rogers, "Sermon XIII," 253.

⁴⁰This was done at some length by Bliss, *A Discourse*; Everett, *A Sermon*; and Nelson, "The Divinely Prepared Ruler."

⁴¹Tucker, *A Discourse*, 15; Sweetser, *A Commemorative Discourse*, 16; Sears, *The People's Keepsake*, 15; Wortman, *A Discourse*, 9.

⁴²Dean, *Eulogy*, 7; Joel F. Bingham, *National Disappointment*, 7; William R. Williams, "Sermon I," 18; John G. Butler, *Our Grief and Our Duty*, 9; Amory D. Mayo, "The Nation's Sacrifice," 10–11; Henry B. Smith, "Sermon XXI," 366.

⁴³Rollin H. Neale, "Sermon," 167; Searing, *President Lincoln in History*, 18–19. Another who proclaimed Lincoln a greater man than Washington was Richard Edwards, Unitarian minister and president of Normal University in Normal, Illinois. On April 19, Edwards, after speaking of Lincoln's role in the emancipation of the slaves, declared that "Lincoln the Liberator, contending for a grand unselfish and beneficent idea, is greater in his opportunities and his position, than Washington the Patriot, fighting for the freedom of his native land" (*The Life and Character of Abraham Lincoln*, 19).

CHAPTER 3

¹Samuel Thayer Spear, "Sermon XVI," 291; Dean, *Eulogy*, 5.

²Swain, *A Nation's Sorrow*, 5; Wilbur F. Paddock, *A Great Man Fallen*, 18; Goodspeed, *Funeral Discourse on the Death of Abraham Lincoln*, 10.

³Chester Forrester Dunham, *The Attitude of the Northern Clergy Toward the South 1860–1865*, 177; Albert G. Palmer, *A Sermon*, 2, 3.

⁴Morehouse, *Evil Its Own Destroyer*, 12; Alfred S. Patton, *The Nation's Loss and Its Lessons*, 10–11.

⁵Atwood, *The Nation's Loss*, 12–13; Quint, "What President Lincoln Did For His Country," 28.

⁶Tucker, *A Discourse*, 16; Dix, *The Death of President Lincoln*, 13–14.

⁷Stone, "Sermon," 344; Bingham, *National Disappointment*, 11–14.

⁸Duffield, *The Nation's Wail*, 11, 12.

⁹Alonzo H. Quint, "Southern Chivalry, and What the Nation Ought To Do With It," 32–33.

[10]Edward N. Kirk, "Be Still and Know That I Am God," 45; Marvin R. Vincent, *A Sermon on the Assassination of Abraham Lincoln*, 7–8; Fox, "Sermon XX," 346.

[11]Fox, "Sermon XX," 345; D. T. Carnahan, *Oration on the Death of Abraham Lincoln*, 17; Everett, *A Sermon*, 13–14; Baldridge, *The Martyr Prince*, 9; James Reed, "Address," 296.

[12]George M. Everhart, as quoted in Burke Davis, *The Long Surrender*, 87–88.

[13]J. Lansing Burrows, *Palliative and Prejudiced Judgments Condemned*, 3–8.

[14]Ibid.

[15]Vincent, *A Sermon on the Assassination of Abraham Lincoln*, 43; Patton, *The Nation's Loss and Its Lesson*, 11; Pliny B. Day, *Memorial Discourse*, 18; J. B. Wentworth, *A Discourse on the Death of President Lincoln*, 21; Vincent, *A Sermon on the Assassination of Abraham Lincoln*, 38; Augustine G. Hubbard, *In Memory of Abraham Lincoln*, 10.

[16]William R. Gordon, *The Sin of Reviling and Its Work*, 4, 6, 20, 21, 22.

[17]J. P. Daily, "Discourse," 8–9; George Mooar, *The Religion of Loyalty*, 13.

CHAPTER 4

[1]Lowry, "Sermon XVII," 314; Baldridge, *The Martyr Prince*, 10; Dix, *The Death of President Lincoln*, 11; Wortman, *A Discourse*, 20.

[2]Sweetser, *A Commemorative Discourse*, 27–28.

[3]Webb, "Sermon," 153–54; Adams, "Sermon XIX," 336.

[4]R. S. Cushman, *Discourse*, 12; William Ives Budington, "Sermon VI," 123; J. E. Rockwell, "Sermon XV," 281; Patton, *The Nation's Loss and Its Lessons*, 14.

[5]S. D. Burchard, "Sermon XIV," 269; Rankin, *Moses and Joshua*, 12.

[6]Warren Randolph, *The Fallen Prince*, 21; Vincent, *A Sermon on the Assassination of Abraham Lincoln*, 40; Rankin, *Moses and Joshua*, 12; Spear, "Sermon XVI," 298.

[7]Daniel C. Eddy, *The Martyr President*, 18; Quint, "Southern Chivalry," 43–45.

[8]Simpson, "Oration," 409; Swain, *A Nation's Sorrow*, 8.

[9]Swain, *A Nation's Sorrow*, 9.

[10]Tucker, *Discourse*, 17; Spear, "Sermon XVI," 292–93.

[11]Spear, "Sermon XVI," 293; Fulton, *Radicalism*, 39–40.

[12]Webb, "The Assassination of the President," 55; J. B. Wentworth, *A Discourse on the Death of President Lincoln*, 30.

[13]J. B. Wentworth, *A Discourse on the Death of President Lincoln*, 30–31; Richard Eddy, *Three Sermons*, 24.

[14]John Chester, *Justice As Well As Mercy*, 13; Henry B. Smith, "Sermon XXI," 378; J. B. Wentworth, *A Discourse on the Death of President Lincoln*, 29.

[15]Clement M. Butler, *Funeral Address*, 26; Henry E. Butler, *God's Way of Leading the Blind*, 21.

[16]Porter, "Sermon XII," 233; Fox, "Sermon XX," 352; E. S. Johnston, *Abraham Lincoln*, 11; Morehouse, *Evil Its Own Destroyer*, 9–10.

[17]Duffield, *The Nation's Wail*, 9; Booth, *Personal Forgiveness and Public Justice*, 11, 13, 17; Bingham, *National Disappointment*, 24, 27.

[18]Chester, *Justice As Well As Mercy*, 14; Charles S. Robinson, *The Martyred President*, 18–20.

[19]Quint, "Southern Chivalry," 32, 33, 42; Starr, *The Martyr President*, 17–18.

[20]Dunham, *The Attitude of the Northern Clergy*, 182–83; Goodspeed, *Funeral Discourse on the Death of Abraham Lincoln*, 20.

[21]Washington Gladden, *Recollections*, 152, 153.

[22]One of the best works on the role of Southern preachers in promoting sectional differences following the Civil War is Charles Reagan Wilson, *Baptized in Blood: The Religion of the Lost Cause, 1865–1920.*

CHAPTER 5

[1]Sweetser, *A Commemorative Discourse*, 25, 26; Spear, "Sermon XVI," 299–300.

[2]Laurie, *Three Discourses*, 20; Mooar, *The Religion of Loyalty*, 8; Duffield, *The Nation's Wail*, 4.

[3]Gurley, "Sermon," 18–19.

[4]James Reed, "Address," 299.

[5]Northrop, *A Sermon*, 6; Glover, *The Character of Abraham Lincoln*, 14; Hammond, *Life and Character*, 8.

[6]Pliny H. White, *A Sermon*, 12; Budington, "Sermon VI," 125; Sutphen, *Discourse*, 16–17; Morehouse, *Evil Its Own Destroyer*, 8.

[7]Laurie, *Three Discourses*, 21; Cyrus A. Bartol, "Address," 54–55; James Reed, "Address," 301; John C. Thompson, *In Memoriam*, 15; Fulton, "Sermon," 361; Chandler Robbins, "Sermon," 219.

[8]Lowry, "Sermon XVII," 312; Carey, *Discourse*, 7; Duffield, *The Nation's Wail*, 15.

[9]Warren H. Cudworth, "Sermon," 205; Thomas Mears Eddy, *A Memorial Discourse*, 20; Atwood, *The Nation's Loss*, 10; W. S. Studley, "Sermon," *Sermons Preached in Boston*, 230.

[10]W. S. Studley, "Sermon," 231; Booth, *Personal Forgiveness and Public Justice*, 16–17.

[11]Pliny H. White, *A Sermon*, 16; Wortman, *A Discourse*, 17–19. Wortman gave more space and time in his sermon to Johnson's inauguration-day drunkenness than any other sermon I have read; and before allowing the publication of this sermon, Wortman added a lengthy footnote about the incident. Budington, "Sermon VI," 126–27.

[12]John G. Butler, *Our Grief and Our Duty*, 12; Mayo, *The Nation's Sacrifice*, 13; Sweetser, *Commemorative Discourse*, 24; Rogers, "Sermon XIII," 253; Quint, "Southern Chivalry," 45; Webb, "Sermon," 159.

[13]Paul C. Brownlow, "The Northern Protestant Pulpit and Andrew Johnson," 248.

[14]Beecher, "Abraham Lincoln," 711; John McClintock, "Sermon VII," 140; James Eells, "Sermon XVI," 223; James Freeman Clarke, "Who Hath Abolished Death?" 102.

[15]William R. Williams, "Sermon I," 20, 26–27; Cudworth, "Sermon," 209.

[16]Thomas M. Hopkins, *A Discourse*, 5–6; George Dana Boardman, "Death, the Law of Life," *Addresses*, 39.

[17]Henry E. Niles, *Address*, 6; Richard Duane, *A Sermon*, 11; Henry W. Bellows, "Sermon III," 59; Booth, *Personal Forgiveness and Public Justice*, 7–8.

[18]Charles S. Robinson, *The Martyred President*, 25, 29; George Dana Boardman, "Death the Law of Life," 44–45.
[19]As recorded in Turner, *Behold the People Weeping*, 71.
[20]J. L. Janeway, "Discourse," 12.

CHAPTER 6

[1]Brooks, "Abraham Lincoln," 163.
[2]Beecher, "Abraham Lincoln," 712.
[3]Bingham, *National Disappointment*, 36.
[4]Todd, "President Lincoln," 87.
[5]John C. Thompson, *In Memoriam*, 19.
[6]Chester, *Justice As Well As Mercy*, 16.
[7]Simpson, "Oration," 410.
[8]Everett, *A Sermon*, 25.
[9]Seiss, *The Assassinated President*, 42–43.
[10]Sanborn, *A Discourse*, 6–7.
[11]Lowry, "Sermon XVII," 315.
[12]Spear, "Sermon XVI," 301.
[13]Mayo, "The Nation's Sacrifice," 13.
[14]Stephen H. Tyng, "Sermon IV," 84.
[15]Hepworth, "Sermon," 120–21.
[16]Putnam, "Address," 320–21.
[17]Atwood, *The Nation's Loss*, 15.
[18]Swain, *The Nation's Sorrow*, 11; Rogers, "Sermon XIII," 253–54.
[19]Quint, "What President Lincoln Did For His Country," 29–30.

CONCLUSION

[1]For information on and comments about the use of the pulpit, North and South, from 1830 to 1865, see David B. Chesebrough, *"God Ordained This War:" Sermons on the Sectional Crisis, 1830–1865.* Albert Barnes, *The Church and Slavery*, 10.
[2]Alexis de Tocqueville, *Democracy in America*, 303; Irving H. Bartlett, *The American Mind in the Mid–Nineteenth Century*, 8.
[3]Bartlett, *The American Mind*, 38.
[4]As quoted in Dunham, *The Attitude of the Northern Clergy*, 51.
[5]Rena Mazyck Andrews, "Archbishop Hughes and the Civil War," 40; "Pastoral Letter," *Records of the American Catholic Historical Society*, 1865, No. 4, pp. 283, 293, 339–44.
[6]Brooks, "Abraham Lincoln," 140–65.
[7]Raymond W. Albright, *Focus on Infinity*, 88, 103–4.
[8]Eden B. Foster, *Two Discourses*, 9–34; Henry Ward Beecher, *Sermons* 2:183–86.
[9]Dunham, *The Attitude of the Northern Clergy*, 67–68; John R. McKivigan, *The War Against Proslavery Religion: Abolitionism and the Northern Churches, 1830–1865*, 160.

[10]William G. McLoughlin, "Introduction," *The Antislavery Impulse, 1830–1844,* ed. Gilbert H. Barnes, viii; McKivigan, *The War Against Proslavery Religion,* 160, 191. The clergy was also heavily involved in the reelection of Lincoln in 1864. See Victor Howard, *Religion and the Radical Republican Movement, 1860–1870.* "The Republicans," wrote Howard, "carried almost all of the evangelical votes. The great majority of Baptist, Methodist, Congregational, Presbyterian, Quaker and pietist votes went for Lincoln, and there was a substantial increase in Unitarian and Universalist support for Lincoln in 1864" (89).

[11]Stuart W. Chapman, "The Protestant Campaign for the Union," 166.

[12]Theodore Parker, *Centenary Edition of the Works of Theodore Parker* 9:87; Horace Bushnell, *The Northern Iron,* 21.

[13]Henry Ward Beecher, *Norwood;* idem, *Patriotic Addresses,* 716.

[14]Dunham, *The Attitude of the Northern Clergy,* 108.

[15]Charles J. Stewart, "A Rhetorical Study," 137, 144; Turner, *Beware the People Weeping,* 78.

[16]George Templeton Strong, *The Diary of George Templeton Strong* 3:385, 386; Orville Hickman Browning, *The Diary of Orville Hickman Browning* 2:21. Chester's sermon was entitled, "Justice As Well As Mercy."

[17]Lewis, *Myths After Lincoln,* 79–80.

[18]Maxwell P. Gaddis, *Sermon,* 11.

[19]Turner, *Beware the People Weeping,* 87–88.

[20]Wayland Hoyt, "Sermon," 1; Todd, "President Lincoln," 84; Robert H. Williams, *A Time to Weep,* 4, 7–8; O. H. Dutton, "Sermon," 86.

[21]Howard, *Religion and the Radical Republican Movement,* 143–44. Howard describes in some detail the clergy's involvement in the election of 1866 (128–45).

[22]George M. Frederickson, *The Inner War: Northern Intellectuals and the Crisis of the Union,* 186–87.

[23]Adams, "Sermon XIX," 336; Spear, "Sermon XVI," 298; Webb, "Sermon," 154, 155.

[24]Duffield, *The Nation's Wail,* 9; Cushman, *Resolutions and Discourse,* 12; David Murdock, *Death of Abraham Lincoln,* 11.

[25]Duffield, *The Nation's Wail,* 41, 12, 39.

[26]John Dudley, *Discourse,* 19; Andrew Beveridge, *A Discourse,* 15; Randloph, *The Fallen Prince,* 19; Henry Harbaugh, *Treason and Law,* 21.

[27]George Junkin, "Sermon," 138; Laurie, *Three Discourses,* 33–35.

[28]B. Hawley, *Truth and Righteousness Triumphant,* 5; Beecher, "Abraham Lincoln," 711; Webb, "Sermon," 158; Benjamin Watson, "Sermon," 227–28.

[29]J. Hazard Hartzell, "The Nation's Bereavement," 92; Joseph D. Strong, *The Nation's Sorrow,* 9–10.

[30]James H. Moorhead, *American Apocalypse: Yankee Protestants and the Civil War, 1860–1869,* 43.

[31]Henry Clay Fish, *The Valley of Achor a Door of Hope, or, The Grand Issues of the War.*

[32]Sherman Canfield, *The American Crisis;* James T. Robinson, *National Anniversary Address.*

[33]Moorhead, *American Apocalypse,* 174–75; Bingham, *National Disappointment,* 36.

³⁴Haven, "The Uniter and Liberator," 578, 552.

³⁵Brownlow, "The Northern Protestant Pulpit," 255–59. For the ecclesiastical involvement in the impeachment of Johnson, see Howard, *Religion and the Radical Republican Movement*, 146–64.

³⁶Beecher, *Patriotic Addresses*, 718.

³⁷Ibid., 741; McKivigan, *The War Against Proslavery Religion*, 200. As to the churches and clergy involvement in the black suffrage movement and the passing of the Fifteenth Amendment, see Howard, *Religion and the Radical Republican Movement*, 165–214.

³⁸Frederickson, *The Inner Civil War*, 192.·

³⁹Ibid., 195; Howard, *Religion and the Radical Republican Movement*, 214.

⁴⁰Stewart, "A Rhetorical Study," 156; Searing, *President Lincoln in History*, 16, 18; George Dana Boardman, "An Address," 60; Joseph P. Thompson, "Sermon X," 173; Hammond, *A Sermon*, 12.

⁴¹Richard Edwards, *Life and Character of Abraham Lincoln*, 19; Edward P. Powell, "Sermon, Appropriate to the Obsequies of Abraham Lincoln," 10–11.

• • •
Bibliography

An Annotated List of Post-Assassination Sermons from Northern
Pulpits, April 16–June 1, 1865

Abbot, Francis E. "The Martyr of Liberty." *Lincolniana.* 1–7. On April 16,
at the Unitarian Church of Dover, New Hampshire, Abbot declared
that "To-day, the enemies of God and man rejoice: to-day, friends, there
is jubilee in hell." Abbot saw the assassination as a providential act.
Lincoln's death may have been the only means whereby his work could
be completed. His leniency could have sacrificed "the vital interests of
his country." There was stern work ahead. "Mild and forgiving to re-
pentent prodigals, we must be stern and uncompromising to conquered
rebels. Leniency to traitors means death to loyal men."
Adams, William. "Sermon XIX." *Our Martyr President, Abraham Lincoln:
Voices from the Pulpit of New York and Brooklyn.* 329–40. This sermon, by
a Presbyterian minister in New York City, was delivered on April 16.
Adams said, "There is too much of this mawkish sentimentalism abroad;
this milky, rose-water religion, which, beginning with a denial of future
punishment, and arguing for universal salvation against the explicit assertion of the Scriptures, which declare that God will turn the wicked
into hell, if they repent not, would dispense with all the severities of
justice, and resolve all government, human and Divine, into an aromatic
essence. One such act as that which now convulses the country was perhaps needful to correct all these meretricious notions."
Allen, Ethan. *A Discourse.* Baltimore: Wm. K. Boyle, 1865. Delivered at
the St. Thomas (Episcopal) Church, Homestead Baltimore Country,
Maryland, on June 1, the rector said that the assassination "was called
forth by our national sins." Allen drew an analogy between the murder
of Jesus and the murder of Lincoln.
Atwood, E. S. *The Nation's Loss.* Salem, Mass.: Salem Gazette, 1865. Allen
delivered this sermon on April 16 at South (Congregational) Church of

Salem. He claimed that the South would greet the news of the assassination with boundless glee.

————. *The President's Record.* Salem, Mass.: Salem Gazette, 1865. On June 1, Atwood declared: "Let Abraham Lincoln be known to posterity by no other name than that of the Great Emancipator, and his name is secure."

Babcock, Samuel B. *A Discourse.* Dedham, Mass.: John Cox, Jr., 1865. On April 19, in the Orthodox Congregational Church of Dedham, Babcock declared that the assassination was a judgment on a sinful nation.

Backman, Charles. *Abraham Lincoln, the World's Great Martyr.* Jamaica, N.Y.: Charles Welling, 1865. Delivered at the Methodist Episcopal Church of Jamaica on April 23, Backman concentrated on those qualities that made Lincoln great. He called upon the world to "look on and see whether we have borne this wonderful trial manfully or not. It has produced no revolution, only here and there have there been cases of personal violence and those seemed to be cases of righteous retribution."

Badger, Henry C. *The Humble Conqueror.* Boston, 1865. Preached to the Cambridge (Unitarian) Parish on April 23, Badger said: "To be just, but not vindictive; to punish, not for revenge, but for future security; to know when mercy is wisdom, and when it is criminal weakness,—was never so desirable or so difficult as now."

Bain, John W. *National Lessons from the Life and Death of President Lincoln.* Pittsburgh: W. S. Haven, 1865. On June 1, at the United Presbyterian Church in Canonsburg, Pennsylvania, the pastor asked for the deaths of Jefferson Davis and Robert E. Lee as just retribution against the South.

Baldridge, Samuel C. *The Martyr Prince.* Cincinnati: Jos. B. Boyd, 1865. At the Presbyterian Church of Friendsville, Illinois, on April 23, the pastor declared: "Mr. Lincoln, with the inborn goodness of his nature, was but poorly qualified to act as judge, and dispense the awful awards of justice and law upon the perjured and blood-stained leaders in treason. And from this he has been relieved, but in a manner that will ensure the ends of righteousness."

Barnes, Albert. *The State of the Country.* Philadelphia: Henry B. Ashmead, 1865. At the First Presbyterian Church of Philadelphia on June 1, Barnes declared that Lincoln's handling of the war proved that he would not be too lenient in dealing with Reconstruction matters.

Barnes, Samuel. *Discourse.* Baltimore: John D. Toy, 1865. This sermon eulogizing Lincoln was preached on April 19 at the Monument Street Methodist Episcopal Church in Baltimore.

Barr, T. H. *A Discourse*. Wooster, Ohio: Republican, 1865. This sermon, by a Presbyterian minister, was delivered at Canaan Center, Ohio, on April 19.

Bartol, Cyrus A. "Address." *Sermons Preached in Boston on the Death of Abraham Lincoln*. 51–56. On April 16, this Boston Unitarian minister could give thanks that the nation still lived, that slavery would die more swiftly and surely because of the assassination, and that Lincoln was allowed to finish his work.

Beecher, Henry Ward. "Abraham Lincoln." *Patriotic Addresses*. New York: Fords, Howard, and Hulbert, 1891. 701–10. Delivered on April 23 at the Plymouth Church in Brooklyn, Beecher's sermon addressed some positive implications arising out of the assassination. Men would hate slavery and love liberty more than ever. The government would be stronger. Lincoln would have a new and greater influence than ever before. There would be a new impulse of patriotism.

Bellows, Henry W. "Sermon III." *Our Martyr President*. 49–63. On April 16, at All Souls (Unitarian) Church in New York City, Bellows retained the Easter theme in his sermon with some references to the assassination. He asked: "May we not have needed this loss to sober our hearts in the midst of our National triumph, lest in the excess of our joy and pride we should overstep the bounds of that prudence and the limits of that earnest seriousness which our affairs demand?"

Benade, William H. *The Death of Abraham Lincoln; What It Represents*. Pittsburgh: W. G. Johnston and Co., 1865. Preaching before the First New Jerusalem Society (Swedenborgian) of Pittsburgh on June 1, Benade attempted to draw lessons from the great tragedy. The assassination proved that those who perpetuated the rebellion were "clothed in the dark and filthy rags of a lie."

Benedict, Andrew D. *Our Nation's Sorrow*. Racine, Wisc.: Journal Print, 1865. This eulogy was delivered on April 19 at the St. Luke's (Episcopal) Church in Racine.

Beveridge, Andrew M. *A Discourse*. Troy, N.Y.: A. W. Scribner, 1865. This sermon was delivered on the evening of April 16 at the First Presbyterian Church of Lansingburg, N.Y. Beveridge referred to sentiments and desires that would do away with capital punishment as "sickly humanitarianism."

Bingham, Joel F. *National Disappointment*. Buffalo: Breed, Butler and Company, 1865. Delivered on Sunday evening of May 7, at the Westminster (Presbyterian) Church of Buffalo, Bingham asserted that "April 14 was but striking a higher and more conspicuous note in the same dreadful harmony of hell, which has been playing half-muffled and in the distance, for the last four years, the name of which is 'Revenge and Ruin.' . . . The danger which chiefly threatens us lies not in the direction of severity, but in that of leniency."

Blackburn, William M. *The Crime Against the Presidency.* Trenton, N.J.: Murphy and Bechtel, 1865. On April 16 at the Fourth Presbyterian Church of Trenton, Blackburn blamed the assassination on the Copperheads. He blended the Old Testament and New Testament by uniting justice and mercy.

Blake, John Falkner. *A Sermon on the Services and Death of Abraham Lincoln.* New York: W. H. Kelley and Bro., 1865. This sermon was first delivered in Christ (Episcopal) Church in Bridgeport, Connecticut, on April 16 by the rector and then repeated in the North Congregational Church on April 19.

Bliss, Thomas E. *A Discourse.* Memphis: W. A. Whitmore, 1865. Bliss was a Union chaplain who began a Congregational church in Memphis. On April 23 he delivered a sermon eulogizing Lincoln and blaming slavery "as the real cause of rebellion." He claimed that the Emancipation Proclamation was that which brought God in on the side of the North. He called for justice and believed that Andrew Johnson would administer it.

Boardman, George Dana. "An Address" and "Death, the Law of Life." *Addresses.* Philadelphia: Sherman and Co., 1865. On April 16 at the First Baptist Church of Philadelphia, Boardman delivered "Death, the Law of Life," emphasizing the fruits and benefits stemming from the Civil War. On April 19, he delivered "An Address," which spoke of the qualities that made up the life and character of Lincoln: "rarely made mistakes," "infallible instincts," "absolutely incorruptible."

Boardman, George N. *The Death of President Lincoln.* Binghamton, N.Y.: F. N. Chase, 1865. This sermon was delivered at the Presbyterian Church of Binghamton on April 16.

Boardman, Henry Augustus. *The Peace We Need, and How to Secure It.* Philadelphia: James S. Claxton, 1865. This sermon was delivered on June 1 at the Tenth Presbyterian Church in Philadelphia.

Bogardus, W. E. *Sermon on the Death of Our Late President.* New York: Isaac J. Oliver, 1865. The sermon by this Reformed Dutch pastor was delivered on April 30 at Unionville, Westchester County, New York.

Booth, Robert Russell. *Personal Forgiveness and Public Justice.* New York: Anson D. F. Randolph, 1865. The theme of this sermon delivered on April 23 at the Mercer Street Presbyterian Church of New York City was that public justice must transcend private forgiveness.

Bradford, Benjamin F. *The Cause of the Rebellion: or, What Killed Mr. Lincoln.* Buffalo: A. M. Clapp and Co., 1865. In his sermon of April 20 at the First Congregational Church of Niagara City, Bradford said that God may have permitted the removal of the lenient Lincoln that a sterner Johnson might deal with the South.

Brakeman, Nelson L. *A Great Man Fallen.* New Orleans: New Orleans Times Book and Job Office, 1865. This sermon was delivered on April 23 by a Union chaplain at the First Methodist Church of Baton Rouge.

Brigham, Charles H. "The National Bereavement." *Lincolniana.* 8–20. On April 16, at the First Congregational (Unitarian) Church of Taunton, Massachusetts, Brigham noted that the assassination teaches the foolishness of conciliation with traitors by attempting to deal gently with them. The assassination did, however, unite the people of the North in their lamentation for the martyred president.

Brooks, Phillips. "Abraham Lincoln." *Addresses.* Henry Altemus, 1895. 140–65. This sermon, delivered at the Church of the Holy Trinity in Philadelphia on April 23, was Brooks's most noted sermon. The Episcopalian rector exclaimed that the character of Lincoln was in conflict with the character of slavery, and thus he was assassinated. The sermon, preached on the very day that Lincoln's body was lying in state in Philadelphia, closes with a moving and eloquent depiction of Lincoln as a shepherd who fed his flock.

Brown, S. D. "Sermon." *A Tribute of Respect by the Citizens of Troy.* 36–42. On April 16 at the State Street Methodist Episcopal Church in Troy, N.Y., Brown said: "God has a purpose in permitting this great evil. . . . may not another instrument, a man of different character be needed at the present moment? It is a singular fact, that the two most favorable to leniency to the rebels have been stricken. . . . We are prone to rely upon the human instrument. We relied on Lincoln and God took him."

Buckingham, Edgar. "Sermon[s]." *A Tribute of Respect by the Citizens of Troy.* 66–78, 229–37. On April 16 this Unitarian minister eulogized Lincoln and then reminded his audience that "the lives of great men work more after death than during life. . . . Mr. Lincoln's work on earth was done." On April 23, Buckingham emphasized in his sermon that "few men in public station have ever inspired so much confidence and secured so much attachment and love" as has Lincoln.

Buckley, Edwin A. *The Uncrowned Nation.* Plattsburgh, N.Y.: J. W. Tuttle, 1865. This sermon was preached on April 19 at the First Presbyterian Church of Plattsburgh.

Budington, William Ives. "Sermon VI." *Our Martyr President.* 111–27. This sermon, delivered at the Clinton Avenue Congregational Church in Brooklyn on April 16, is devoted to the theme that "the wrath of man shall praise God," by revealing the wickedness of rebellion, learning the wickedness of slavery and the folly and madness of sin, checking unchristian charity which denies the necessity of a penalty, and understanding that God has a right to the blood and life of his servants.

Burchard, S. D. "Sermon XIV." *Our Martyr President.* 255–72. On April 23, this Presbyterian cleric urged that there be no mercy to traitors or Rebels and demanded the complete eradication of slavery.

Burdick, C. F. *Slavery and Its Crimes.* Troy, N.Y.: A. W. Scribner, 1865. This sermon was delivered on June 1 at the Methodist Episcopal Church of Saratoga Springs, New York. Burdick made the point that slavery and rebellion culminated in the crime of assassination.

Burgess, Chalon. *The Life and Character of Abraham Lincoln, With Some Lessons From His Death.* Jamestown, N.Y.: Bishop Brothers, 1865. This sermon was delivered on April 30 at the Presbyterian Church of Panama, New York, by the pastor of the church. The sermon was a eulogy of Lincoln with comparisons to George Washington.

Burrows, J. Lansing. *Palliative and Prejudiced Judgments Condemned.* Richmond, Va.: Commercial Bulletin, 1865. Burrows, a leading Southern minister, delivered this sermon on April 23 at his church, the First Baptist Church of Richmond. He stated that Northern charges of Southern complicity in the assassination of Lincoln were ridiculous and un-Christian.

Bush, James S. *Death of President Lincoln.* Orange, N.J.: E. Gardner, 1865. This sermon was preached on April 16 at Grace (Episcopal) Church in Orange, New Jersey.

Butler, Clement M. *Funeral Address.* Philadelphia: Henry B. Ashmead, 1865. This sermon was preached at the Church of the Covenant (Episcopal) in Philadelphia on April 19. It is a eulogy of Lincoln that compares him to other greats in history. The preacher also charged that the Union dead at Bull Run had been buried "with the faces downward" and that their skulls had been converted into "drinking cups."

Butler, Henry E. *God's Way of Leading the Blind.* Burlington, N.Y.: Free Press, 1865. On April 23, at the Congregational Church of Keesville, New York, Butler made a plea for both justice and mercy.

Butler, John G. *Our Grief and Our Duty.* Washington, D.C.: McGill and Witherow, 1865. In this sermon at St. Paul's Lutheran Church in Washington, on April 16, Butler affirmed his own loyalty to the Union throughout the war in spite of pressure to do otherwise. He spoke of the responsibility of the Southern pulpit for the rebellion. He urged his listeners to support Johnson and asked for justice, but not revenge.

Carey, Isaac, E. *Abraham Lincoln: The Value to the Nation of His Exalted Character.* Freeport, Ill., 1865. This sermon was delivered at the First Presbyterian Church in Freeport on June 1.

————. *Discourse.* Freeport, Ill., 1865. On April 19, at the First Presbyterian Church, Carey said: "Our lamented President failed, I think, in one thing: He never seemed to comprehend fully the depravity and malice animating the rebellion and its leaders, and hence was perhaps inclined to extreme lenity. . . . Andrew Johnson comprehends it better. . . . [Lincoln] was himself incapable of depravity so devilish, and naturally found it hard to believe others capable of it."

Carhart, J. Wesley. "Sermon." *A Tribute of Respect by the Citizens of Troy.* 116–27. On Apr. 19 at the North Second Street Methodist Episcopal Church in Troy, Carhart noted that Lincoln's fame would continue to rise. "As the ages roll on, his fame will brighten."

Carnahan, David T. *Oration on the Death of Abraham Lincoln.* Gettysburg: Aughinbaugh and Wible, 1865. This sermon was delivered before the citizens of Gettysburg by the pastor of the Presbyterian church on June 1. The sermon does not mention the Gettysburg Address. It did say that emancipation "had not entered [Lincoln's] mind . . . when he assumed the reins of government; and was only adopted after Providence, by the irresistable logic of events, had educated both the people and himself up to its high necessity and righteousness." It is, however, this act that will cause Lincoln's name to "live through all coming time as the benefactor of his age, and a blessing to the human race."

Carrothers, J. J. "Funeral Oration on the Death of Abraham Lincoln." *Lincolniana.* 239–47. On April 19, before the mayor, city council, and citizens of Portland, Maine, this Congregational minister said that "Without impairing in the least the free agency of man, without mitigating in the least the guilt or just desert of human crime, the Sovereign Ruler of the universe is ever working out to their designed issues his purposes of judgment and mercy."

Chadwick, John W. "Abraham Lincoln." *Lincolniana.* 36–51. On April 23, this Unitarian clergyman delivered this sermon before his society in Brooklyn, New York. He asked: "Is it too much to say, that never in the annals of our modern life was there such deep and unaffected sorrow?" The sermon is very sensitive to the grief the slaves were experiencing. Chadwick rendered a touching eulogy of Lincoln and then concluded: "It was no single man that murdered him. . . . It was an institution. . . . the same that murdered Lovejoy and John Brown; the same that struck at Sumner from behind his back; and lit the fires of this rebellion, that it might burn up the hope of freedom and democracy."

Chaffin, William Ladd. *The President's Death and Its Lessons.* Philadelphia: King and Baird, 1865. This sermon was delivered before the Second Unitarian Society of Philadelphia by its pastor.

Chamberlain, Nathan H. *The Assassination of President Lincoln.* New York: G. W. Carleton, 1865. Preaching at St. James (Episcopal) Church of Birmingham, Connecticut, on April 19, Chamberlain declared: "The duty of the Church to the State is, first of all, obedience in things temporal. The correlated duty of the State is protection." Chamberlain further declared that "martyrdom for duty lifts a man out of days, to become a citizen of the ages." Lincoln's assassination "hath embalmed his fame and memory with his own blood."

Chaney, George L. "Sermon." *Sermons Preached in Boston.* 325–34. On April 16, this Unitarian clergyman declared that Lincoln never understood the hatred in the hearts of the Rebels. He bided his time on the Emancipation Proclamation because of his great respect for the Constitution.

Chester, John. *Justice As Well As Mercy.* Washington, D.C.: Washington Chronicle Print, 1865. In this sermon at the Capitol Hill Presbyterian Church on April 16, Chester sought to repudiate religious arguments for mercy and leniency toward the South. He made the point that the South needed to repent before it could receive mercy. He distinguished between the Confederate leaders and the "poor deluded followers."

Chubb, Rolla H. *A Discourse.* Mansfield, Ohio: Herald, 1865. This sermon was delivered on June 1 at the Greenwich Methodist Episcopal Church, Huron County, Ohio. Chubb declared that Lincoln "had finished his share of the programme—his work was done."

Clark, Alexander. *Memorial Sermon.* Cincinnati: Masonic Review Office, 1865. This sermon, by a Methodist minister, was delivered on April 19 at Union Chapel in Cincinnati. Clark declared that Booth represented a cause that must be completely conquered and subdued.

Clark, Daniel. *Eulogy on the Life and Character of Abraham Lincoln.* Manchester, N.H.: Mirror, 1865. In this sermon, Clark presented a detailed and vivid description of the assassination scene.

Clarke, James Freeman. "Who Hath Abolished Death?" *Sermons Preached in Boston.* 91–106. This sermon of April 16, by a Unitarian minister, delivered at the Indiana-Place Chapel in Boston, is an example of taking a prepared Easter sermon and adding the subject of assassination to it. The chief fault of Lincoln, Clarke claimed, was that he was "too forgiving." The assassination will unite the nation by convincing the public as to the real evil of slavery.

Claxton, Robert Bethell. *Sermons on the Death of President Lincoln.* Philadelphia: J. B. Lippincott and Co., 1865. These two sermons were preached on April 19 and 23 at the St. Luke's Episcopal Church in Rochester, New York. In the second sermon, Claxton offered a long list of sins for which the North was being punished: drunkenness, profanity, licentiousness, gambling, sabbath-breaking, dishonesty, avarice, greed, and idolatry.

Coit, Thomas W. "The Sword of the Lord." *A Tribute of Respect by the Citizens of Troy.* 268–79. On June 1, at St. Paul's Episcopal Church in Troy, Coit urged that Christianity take the lead in abolishing slavery.

Colman, George W. *Assassination of the President.* Boston: S. Chism, 1865. This sermon was delivered on April 16 at the Congregational Church in Acton, Massachusetts, and was repeated on June 1 in the Baptist Church of West Acton.

Cooke, Charles. *A Sermon.* Philadelphia: John Richards, 1865. This sermon was delivered on June 1 in Smyrna, Delaware.

Cooper, James. *The Death of President Lincoln.* Philadelphia: Jas. B. Rogers, 1865. This sermon was delivered on April 16 by the pastor of the Berean Baptist Church in West Philadelphia.

Corwin, Edward T. "Death of President Lincoln." *Lincolniana.* 52–62. At Millstone, New Jersey, on April 16, this Dutch Reformed minister proclaimed that the assassination was the work of a few individuals. Lincoln had fulfilled the work he was given to do. Corwin repeated the often-told story of Lincoln's conversion to Christianity after Gettysburg. "We mourn for the man. . . . But we will still rejoice, as we remember that the cause of God and of liberty can never die."

Craig, Wheelock. *A Sermon on the Fruits of Our Bereavement.* New Bedford, Mass.: E. Anthony and Sons, 1865. On April 16, this Congregational minister proclaimed that "The public heart is irritated. The land is vexed. A mighty nation is enraged, and each several community clamors for a victim; not merely the real culprit, for the whole world would rejoice to see him punished; but, in lieu of him, for any scapegoat on whom the stroke due to him may be inflicted."

Crane, Cephas B. *Sermon.* Hartford: Case, Lockwood and Co., 1865. This sermon, delivered at the South Baptist Church of Hartford on April 16, declared that from the day of the assassination on, every man or woman of the North who speaks against the government "deserves to be hanged ten thousand times higher than Hamon, and to sink ten thousand times deeper into the pit than he."

Crocker, Samuel L. *Eulogy Upon the Character and Services of Abraham Lincoln.* Boston: John Wilson and Son, 1865. Crocker urged moderation. "Let us not in our just indignation, read in it a lesson at variance alike with every principle of our religion, and with these qualities of his character which have especially endeared him to the memory of mankind."

Cudworth, Warren H. *Eulogy on the Life, Character and Public Services of the Late President Abraham Lincoln.* Boston: Wright and Potter, 1865. This Unitarian clergyman's review of Lincoln's life was delivered on May 8 before Council No. 33, Union League of America, at Sumner Hall in East Boston.

———. "Sermon." *Sermons Preached in Boston.* 199–212. This April 16 sermon is a powerful expression of personal and national grief. After eulogizing Lincoln, Cudworth said that God may have needed a sterner hand for the days ahead. Lincoln, in death, had more influence than in life. The assassination had revealed some of the hideous features of the slave society. The minister recounted some Southern atrocities.

Cushman, R. S. *Resolutions and Discourse.* Manchester, Vt., 1865. At the Congregational Church of Manchester on April 19, the pastor declared that the assassination was a part of "the permissive Providence of God." Cushman complained that "mistaken views of Christian mercy has poisoned and demoralized so many minds and hearts among us." It is important to remember that "God is just as well as merciful and He hath put the sword . . . into the hands of the legitimate rulers of the world."

Cutter, Edward F. *Eulogy on Abraham Lincoln.* Boston: D. C. Colesworthy, 1865. This sermon, delivered on April 19 in Rockland, Maine, by a Congregational minister, includes a detailed account of Lincoln's charity toward a young man from Vermont who was sleeping at his post. Cutter expressed a faith in Andrew Johnson if he "shall bring back every State to the Union and Freedom, crushing out treason and traitors with an iron hand."

Cuyler, Theodore L. "Sermon IX." *Our Martyr President.* 159–72. In this sermon delivered at the Lafayette Avenue Presbyterian Church in New York City, the pastor said that it was an extemporaneous discourse because his grief had been too great to write. After extolling the qualities of Lincoln's character, he compared Lincoln to William of Orange. He lamented, however, that Lincoln "never made any public confession of his faith in the Redeemer. This I regret from my inmost heart."

Daggett, Oliver Ellsworth. *A Sermon.* Canandaigua, N.Y.: N. J. Milliken, 1865. This sermon was first delivered on April 16, and then repeated the following Wednesday evening in response to a request, in the First Congregational Church of Canandaigua. The sermon says that God may have permitted the assassination to kindle sentiment against the "rose water philanthropy" growing in the land. Daggett also noted that "we first thought, this is the insanity of fanaticism; but since two murders were attempted at the same hour, we must reckon it the work of bribed conspirators."

Daily, J. P. "Discourse." *Discourses: Memorial of Abraham Lincoln.* 1–13. In a sermon on April 19, this Methodist minister of Flemington, New Jersey, referred to Booth as "one of the most miserable beings out of hell." The assassination had its roots in "speaking evil of political opponents, and especially of those in authority, though wide spread and of long standing, is the poison source of many of the bitter streams that reach all classes and all parties of our people, spreading blastine and mildew over all our social, political and moral interests."

Daily, William M. "Our Martyred Chieftan." *Discourses from the Pulpit.* Cincinnati: R. W. Carroll, 1865. On April 16, Daily, a Methodist army chaplain, delivered a sermon to Union soldiers at Benton Barricks in Missouri. It was an emotional appeal for severity in Reconstruction. "Sad day to patriots! But, sadder day to Rebels. In the death of Abraham Lincoln, they lost their best friend—and by their agency in his assassination, they cut themselves off from all pleas for leniency—and close the door to mercy! . . . if blood ran revulets, under Lincoln, if need be, it shall run rivers, under Andrew Johnson."

Darling, Henry. *Grief and Duty.* Albany: S. R. Gray, 1865. Delivered on April 19 in the Fourth Presbyterian Church of Albany, the sermon emphasized that such a depraved assassination could not have ripened in any but the congenial Southern soil.

Dascomb, Alfred Brooks. *A Discourse.* Montpelier, Vt.: Walton's, 1865. The eulogy delivered by this Congregational pastor on April 23 was a plea to young men to follow Lincoln's example and trust in God.

Davidson, Robert. *The Lessons of the Hour.* Huntington, N.Y.: Long-Islander Print, 1865. On April 19 at the First Presbyterian Church of Huntington, Davidson made a strong plea for sterner measures to be taken against the South.

Day, Pliny B. *Memorial Discourse.* Concord, Mass.: McFarland and Jenks, 1865. Delivered on June 1 at Hollis, New Hampshire, by the pastor of the Congregational church, this sermon declared that the assassination was necessary to arouse public sentiment in the North to bring justice to the leaders of the rebellion.

Dean, Sidney. *Eulogy.* Providence: H. H. Thomas and Co., 1865. The sermon was delivered by this Methodist minister on April 19 in the City Hall of Providence with the governor of Rhode Island and other dignitaries in attendance. Dean declared that Lincoln was George Washington's equal and a second Moses. He demanded justice upon the South, but not revenge; Confederate leaders such as Davis and Lee should be hanged, but the masses pardoned.

Demund, Isaac S. *Lamentation on the Death of Abraham Lincoln, President of the United States.* New York: John A. Gray and Green, 1865. This vivid description of the grief the nation was experiencing was delivered in May 1865 at the Reformed Dutch Church of Paramus, New Jersey.

Denormandie, James. *The Lord Reigneth.* Portsmouth, N.H., 1865. On April 16 the minister of the South Parish (Unitarian) Church in

Portsmouth insisted that Lincoln was murdered through calm delibera-
tion by the slave power and by every person who withheld his support
from repressing it.

Dexter, Henry Martyn. *What Ought to Be Done With the Freedmen and With
the Rebels?* Boston: Nichols and Noyes, 1865. Dexter, a Congregationalist who later became a noted church historian, delivered this sermon at
the Berkeley Street Church in Boston on April 23. He spoke of the necessity of dividing Rebel lands among the former slaves. Yet, the government must not interfere with questions of social equality: "If we can
trust the grass to grow . . . we can trust the great mass of emancipated
negroes to become thrifty farmers and mechanics, and valuable members
of the great industrial body, by natural promptings of opportunity and
self-interest, in the propitious air of freedom."

Dimmick, F. M. *Funeral Sermon.* Omaha, 1865. At the capitol building in
Omaha on April 19, this Presbyterian pastor spoke of an expressed fear
that there may have been a danger to the country in the clemency of
Lincoln's gentle and forgiving heart. Blaming the South for the assassination, Dimmick said: "O, how unwise! How inconsiderate, how impo-
lite! They have killed, they have assassinated, they have murdered their
best and truest friend."

Discourses: Memorial of Abraham Lincoln. Lambertville, N.J.: Beacon Office,
1865. A collection of sermons and other addresses delivered in response
to Lincoln's assassination.

Dix, Morgan. *The Death of President Lincoln.* Cambridge: Riverside Press,
1865. At St. Paul's (Episcopal) Chapel in New York City on April 19,
the rector declared that the assassination was a natural consequence of a
Southern slave society. Southerners needed to disclaim responsibility for
the assassination, but Dix feared they would not.

Douglas, James. *Funeral Discourse.* Pulaski, N.Y.: Democratic Job Press,
1865. The eulogy of Lincoln by this Methodist preacher was delivered on
April 19 at Pulaski, New York.

Drumm, John H. *Assassination of Abraham Lincoln, President of the United
States.* Bristol, Pa.: Wm. Bache, 1865. This sermon was delivered on
April 16 at the St. James (Episcopal) Church in Bristol by Drumm, the
rector of the parish.

Duane, Richard B. *A Sermon.* Providence: H. H. Thomas and Co., 1865.
On April 19, at St. John's (Episcopal) Church in Providence, the assis-
tant rector of the parish said that through the assassination, the Providence of God has saved us from "being exalted beyond measure by our
successes. . . . And there was another danger into which we were drift-
ing—into which some had already drifted, even our beloved President

himself. It was a mistaken leniency towards the leaders in the army or in the cabinet of the insurgents."

Dudley, John L. *Discourse*. Middletown, Conn.: D. Barnes, 1865. At the South Congregational Church of Middletown on April 16, the pastor spoke of the assassination as "slavery's last word." He argued hard for capital punishment: if people hadn't been timid about capital punishment, there would be fewer deaths by violence and Lincoln might not have been killed.

Duffield, George. *The Nation's Wail*. Detroit: Advertiser and Tribune Print, 1865. On April 16, the pastor of the First Presbyterian Church of Detroit accused the South of administering slow poison to Presidents Harrison and Taylor and attempting to do the same to Buchanan in order to keep the presidency out of Northern hands. He also accused the South of starving Northern prisoners and of importing yellow fever from the West Indies.

Dunning, Halsey. *Address*. Baltimore: John W. Woods, 1865. The sermon was delivered on April 19 at the First Constitutional Presbyterian Church in Baltimore.

———. *The Assassination: Its Lesson to Young Men*. Baltimore: John W. Woods, 1865. This sermon was delivered on May 7. In it, Dunning said that he believed God punished Booth by having him trip over the very flag he hoped to destroy, thus hampering his escape.

———. *The Nameless Crime*. Baltimore: John W. Woods, 1865. This sermon was delivered on April 23. Dunning said that he would have been more comfortable to think that the assassin was just mentally unbalanced, but that was not the case. Booth was motivated by his disloyalty to the government, by the bad company he kept, and by a desire for noteriety.

Dutton, O. H. "Sermon." *Lincolniana*. 76–88. At the Second Congregational Church of Holyoke, Mass., on April 19, Dutton engaged in an inconsistency demonstrated by many Northern preachers. After discussing and detailing the "barbarities" of the Confederacy, he continued: "God forbid that we should seem to say anything to inflame the passions of men, or to excite desires for a carnal vengeance."

Eddy, Daniel C. *The Martyr President*. Boston: Graves and Young, 1865. At the Baldwin Place Church of Boston, this Baptist preacher spoke to three issues: the North's need for God, the nature of the Southern people, and the need for additional guarantees to save the Republic.

Eddy, Richard. *Three Sermons*. Philadelphia: H. G. Leisenring, 1865. These three sermons were preached at the First Universalist Church of Philadelphia on April 16 and 19 and June 1. The three sermons speak of the national mourning over Lincoln's death, review the traits of Lincoln's character, and demand justice upon the leaders of the rebellion. The sermon on April 19 contains a moving review of Lincoln's life.

Eddy, Thomas Mears. *Abraham Lincoln: A Memorial Discourse.* Chicago: Charles Philbrick, 1865. This sermon, delivered at a Union meeting at the Presbyterian Church in Waukegan, Ill., on April 19, spoke of the four principles that governed Lincoln's policies: the union was incapable of division; government resides in the people; and all men have the right to freedom and a profound religious dependence.

Edgar, Cornelius Henry. *Josiah and Lincoln, the Great Reformers.* Easton, Pa.: Lewis Gordon, 1865. This sermon was delivered on June 1 in the Reformed Dutch Church of Easton.

Edwards, Henry L. *Discourse Commemorative of Our Late Illustrious Martyr.* Boston: Wright and Potter, 1865. This sermon attempts to unite the themes of love and punishment. It was delivered on June 1 before the Congregational Church of South Abington, Massachusetts. Edwards noted that had the people known that Lincoln would have to be replaced, Johnson probably would not have been their choice for vice-president.

Edwards, Richard. *The Life and Character of Abraham Lincoln.* Peoria: N. C. Nason, 1865. On April 19, Edwards, who was a Unitarian minister and president of Normal University in Normal, Illinois, declared at the university that such a calamity was needed in order to arouse the North from its complacency and reexamine its attitudes of leniency toward the South. "The distinction between treason and loyalty was to be obliterated in a glorious display of brotherhood and good feeling. From a dream so idle and mischievous, so foolish and criminal, God has aroused us by permitting this last crowning act of fiendish malignity."

Eells, James. "Sermon XI." *Our Martyr President.* 219–32. Delivered on April 16, this sermon by a Dutch Reformed minister stressed the providential aspect of the Civil War and Lincoln's assassination. Eells told a story that he said was evidence of Lincoln's conversion.

Egar, John H. *The Martyr President.* Leavenworth, Kans.: Bulletin, Job Printing, 1865. This sermon was first preached on April 23 at the Church of St. Paul (Episcopal) in Leavenworth; it was repeated, by request, on June 1. Egar seemed content to leave the future to God without expressing what that future policy should be.

Elliott, David T. "Discourse." *A Tribute of Respect by the Citizens of Troy.* 297–317. At the Third Street Methodist Episcopal Church on June 1, Elliott, after tracing the history of slavery, blamed the institution for the assassination. He then eulogized Lincoln and urged for justice, "pleading that nothing be done through revenge or in the spirit . . . of retaliation, but solely to promote the authority, stability and influence of law, and thus advance the best interests of all people. Treason is a crime and a sin against all people."

Ellis, Rufus. "Sermon." *Sermons Preached in Boston.* 235–42. This Unitarian minister, on April 16, tied together the Easter message with the assassination and urged the congregation to remember and practice Lincoln's spirit.

Everett, Charles Carroll. *Eulogy on Abraham Lincoln, Late President of the United States.* Bangor: Samuel S. Smith, 1865. On June 1, this Unitarian minister proclaimed that now that Lincoln was dead the true worth of his life could be measured.

————. *A Sermon.* Bangor: Benj. A. Burr, 1865. Delivered on April 16 at the Independent Congregational Church of Bangor, Everett advised: "In the fire of our patriotism, of our righteous indignation, of our stern justice, let us not forget the parting caution of our President. Let us be careful, that we do not crush a single germ, that may spring up into life, and into healthful, beautiful strength."

Farquhar, John. *The Claims of God to Recognition in the Assassination of President Lincoln.* Lancaster, Pa.: Pearsol and Geist, 1865. This sermon was delivered on June 1 at the Chanceford Presbyterian Church, Lower Chanceford, York County, Pennsylvania, by the pastor of the church. The preacher emphasized that the assassination was an act of God meant to rouse people to the danger of leniency to traitors.

Field, Thomas P. *Address.* New London, Conn.: C. Prince, 1865. On April 19, this Congregational minister, declared: "Not that I can think that the leaders in the rebellion would have counselled so dastardly a deed, but it was the slave spirit that awakened the hate and nerved the arm for the guilty work."

Foote, Henry W. "Address." *Sermons Preached in Boston.* 179–90. At King's Chapel in Boston on April 19, this Unitarian minister called George Washington the "Father of our Country" and Lincoln the "Saviour of our Country." The sermon is a mixture of eulogy for Lincoln and lessons to be learned from the assassination.

Fowler, Henry. *Character and Death of Abraham Lincoln.* Auburn, N.Y.: Wm. J. Moses, 1865. On April 23, the pastor of Central Presbyterian Church in Auburn declared that Lincoln was "slain by those for whom he was pleading."

Fox, Henry J. "Sermon XX." *Our Martyr President.* 341–57. A Methodist minister declared that the assassination had broken all possibilities of reconciliation with the South.

Freeman, George E. *God in Our National Affairs.* Boston: Alfred Mudge and Son, 1865. This sermon was delivered on April 16 at Trinity (Congregational) Chapel in Neponset, Massachusetts.

Fuller, Richard. *A City or House Divided Against Itself.* Baltimore, J. F. Weishampel, Jr., 1865. This sermon, delivered on June 1 at the Seventh Baptist Church in Baltimore, was a plea for reconciliation between the North and South. In antebellum days Fuller was an influential Baptist minister in South Carolina. Fuller argued that Lincoln was not removed by God because he was too lenient. "Impiously making God an accessory to their malignant passions, these ill omened harbingers proclaimed that he had removed an amiable man, because he had purposes of wrath, and needed an instrument more filled for the work of vengeance."

Fulton, J. D. "Sermon." *Sermons Preached in Boston.* 359–79. Delivered at the Tremont (Baptist) Temple in Boston on April 19, this sermon praises Lincoln but expresses sorrow that he was killed in a theater.

Gaddis, Maxwell P. *Sermon.* Cincinnati: Times, 1865. The pastor of the Sixth Street Methodist Church delivered this sermon in Pike's Opera House on April 16 because the church could not hold even a fourth of the people who wanted to attend.

Garrison, Joseph Fithian. *The Teachings of the Crisis.* Camden, N.J.: S. Chew, 1865. This sermon was delivered at St. Paul's (Episcopal) Church in Camden, N.J., on April 19.

Gear, D. L. *The Nation's Grief for Its Fallen Chief.* Philadelphia: Ringwalt and Brown, 1865. This sermon, a vivid description of the mourning of the nation, was delivered at the First Congregational Chapel of Philadelphia on the evening of April 23.

Gillette, Abram D. *God Seen Above All National Calamities.* Washington, D.C.: McGill and Witherow, 1865. On April 23, the pastor of the First Baptist Church of Washington blamed the assassination on the lack of Northern humility. He also singled out drinking as an important sin for which the nation was being punished.

Glover, L. M. *The Character of Abraham Lincoln.* Jacksonville, Ill.: Journal, 1865. This sermon was delivered at Strawn's Hall in Jacksonville on April 23 by the pastor of First Presbyterian Church, who declared that he was unable to discover lessons in the assassination. He wished that Lincoln had not been killed while attending a theater.

Goodspeed, E. J. *Funeral Discourse on the Death of Abraham Lincoln.* Chicago: Church, Goodman and Connelley, 1865. On April 23, the pastor of the Second Baptist Church in Chicago spoke of the evils of the theater and regretted that Lincoln was attending such a place. The lesson was: don't go to any place you would not wish to be found by death. He asked his listeners to remove all ideas of vengeance, to remember that we are all sinners and that we did not determine to be born in the North rather than the South.

Goodwin, H. M. "On the Assassination of President Lincoln." The Goodwin MSS Sermons, No. 393, Hammond Library, Chicago Theological Seminary, Chicago. At the Congregational Church in Rockford, Illinois, Goodwin said that the assassination was a "representative act" of slavery.

Goodwin, William. *Death of Abraham Lincoln*. Hartford, Conn.: David B. Mosely, 1865. On April 23, the pastor of the Baptist Church in North Colebrook, Connecticut, made a strong plea for more religion in politics. He claimed that two presidents, and possibly Stephen Douglas, were poisoned by the South and that the South boasts about it.

Gordon, William R. *The Sin of Reviling and Its Work*. New York: John A. Gray and Green, 1865. Gordon, who was the pastor of the Reformed Protestant Dutch Church of Schraalenberg, New Jersey, delivered this sermon on May 7. His theme was that "When any party succeeds in placing its men in power, it is the duty of all to cease opposition, and make the best of it. . . . It is the duty, inseparable for moral order, of every man to refrain from speaking evil of the Ruler of his people." Gordon also regretted that Lincoln was killed in the "devil's schoolhouse" and blamed the assassination on the Copperheads.

Gorman, Samuel. *Abraham Lincoln*. New York: C. A. Alvord, 1865. This sermon was delivered in the First Baptist Church of Canton, Ohio, on April 16. "While the blood of our beloved President, whom they have slain with wicked hands, is yet smoking upon the country's altar, is it not proper to denounce the hands that have so brutally shed it?"

Graeter, Abraham. *A Discourse*. Skippackville, Pa.: J. M. Schuenemann, 1865. This sermon, which was printed in both English and German, was delivered on April 21. The Lutheran pastor's theme was that like the Savior, Lincoln died to make men free.

Gray, George Zabriskie. *The Proper Use of the Memory of a Good Man's Life*. New York: Martin and Fulkerson, 1865. This sermon was delivered on June 1 at Trinity (Episcopal) Church in Bergen Point, New Jersey.

Gregory, Daniel S. "Sermon" and "Address." *A Tribute of Respect by the Citizens of Troy*. 47–66, 127–35. On April 16, Gregory assured his congregation that the omnipotent God still reigns. His truth shall endure and justice will prevail. At the Second Presbyterian Church of Troy on April 19, Gregory preached that man must die no matter how great or important he seems to be.

Gurley, Phineas Densmore. "Sermon." *Sermons Preached in Boston*. 16–28. Gurley, who was the pastor of New York Avenue Presbyterian Church in Washington, D.C., delivered this sermon on April 19 at Lincoln's funeral service in the Executive Mansion. Gurley noted, "we needed this stroke, this dealing, this discipline and, therefore, He has sent it."

————. *The Voice of the Rod.* Washington, D.C.: William Ballantyne, 1865. This sermon, delivered at the New York Avenue Presbyterian Church in Washington on June 1, was a summary of alleged Southern atrocities. Gurley spoke of "the diabolical capabilities and achievements of that combined spirit of treason and slavery." The assassination was also "a lesson touching the character and influence of the theater."

Hague, William. "Sermon." *Sermons Preached in Boston.* 129–42. The minister of the Shawmut Avenue Baptist Church in Boston, delivered an April 16 sermon that contained a poignant expression of the nation's grief and a belief in Providence. He claimed the South was rejoicing over the assassination. "True, indeed, our enemies still exult,—Gath and Askelon are yet merry; they rejoice in their secret cabals, in their hearts of insolence, in their guerilla dens, in their resorts of revelry and song."

Hale, Edward Everett. "Sermon." *Sermons Preached in Boston.* 267–75. This Unitarian minister delivered this sermon on April 16. It is mostly an Easter sermon with limited reference to the assassination. "To speak of [Lincoln]." said Hale, "I must seek some other hour." Hale emphasized that no matter what happened to presidents or what sorrow might come, belief in God would compensate for any reversals.

Hall, Charles H. *A Mournful Easter.* Washington, D.C.: Gideon and Pearson, 1865. In his sermon at the Church of the Epiphany (Episcopal) on April 16, Hall combined the joy of Easter and the tragedy of assassination.

Hall, Gordon. *President Lincoln's Death: Its Voice to the People.* Northampton, Mass.: Trumball and Gere, 1865. This sermon was delivered in the First Church of Northampton on April 19 by the pastor of Edwards (Congregational) Church, who said, "we know that Mr. Lincoln's continuance in office would not have been so favorable to God's plan as his removal. How do we know that? Because God removed him. This proves it. . . . [Lincoln was] too kind to deal with unscrupulous, truculent traitors— he has been taken to heaven, where there is a call only for gentle and loving ministries."

Hammond, Charles. *A Sermon on the Life and Character of Abraham Lincoln.* Springfield, Mass.: Samuel Bowles and Co., 1865. This sermon was delivered on June 1 at a united service of the Congregational and Methodist churches in Monson, Massachusetts, by the principal of Monson Academy. This Methodist clergyman rebuked those who claimed to know the divine purposes of the assassination. He also rebuked those who criticized Lincoln for being too lenient. He believed that Lincoln would have gained even greater fame if he had lived to carry out policies of Reconstruction.

Harbaugh, Henry. *Treason and Law*. Philadelphia: James B. Rogers, 1865. At the German Reformed Church of Clearspring, Maryland, on June 1, Harbaugh made an appeal for and a defense of capital punishment. "This is the supreme law of the land. It rests on divine authority (Ro. 13:1–4). This is an infinitely better law, than that mawkish, frothing and vaporing of washy and watery sentimentalism, which has its fountain in the shallow pools of Gotham."

Hart, Edwin J. *A Sermon*. Manchester, N.H.: Henry A. Gage, 1865. This sermon was delivered on April 16 at the First Congregational Church of Merrimack, New Hampshire.

Hartzell, J. Hazard. "The Nation's Bereavement." *Lincolniana*. 89–99. At the Universalist Church of Buffalo on April 16, Hartzell declared that "this assassination of the President discloses a recklessness and a depravity, that must be humiliating to every American. It is the revealment of that contempt for law and order, which must lower the Government in the minds of Europeans."

Haven, Gilbert. "The Uniter and Liberator of America." *National Sermons*. Boston: Lee and Shepard, 1869. 551–80. This is a sermon dealing with the character and accomplishments of Lincoln. It was delivered on April 23 at the North Russell Street Methodist Episcopal Church.

Hawley, B. *Truth and Righteousness Triumphant*. Albany, N.Y.: J. Munsell, 1865. This sermon, delivered on April 20 at the Washington Avenue Methodist Episcopal Church in Albany, declared that though God had removed Lincoln the government was intact; therefore, there was hope.

Hepworth, George H. "Sermon." *Sermons Preached in Boston*. 109–21. Delivered on April 16 by a Unitarian minister, this sermon contains a brief biography of Lincoln, one that emphasizes his simplicity, religious faith, and the fact that he was a representative man.

Hibbard, Augustine G. *In Memory of Abraham Lincoln*. Detroit: O. S. Gulley, 1865. This sermon was delivered on April 16 at the First Congregational Unitarian Church in Detroit by the pastor of the church. Hibbard suggested that Northern radicals and Copperheads helped to bring about Lincoln's death.

Hicks, William W. *An Address*. Frederick, Md.: Schley, Keefer and Co., 1865. This sermon was delivered on April 19 in the Methodist Church of Frederick City, Maryland, by the pastor.

Hillman, W. G. *National Calamities from God, and Thoughts on President Lincoln's Assassination*. Mansfield, Ohio: Herald, 1865. This sermon was delivered at the Presbyterian Church of Lexington, Ohio, on the evening of April 23. Hillman said, "Perhaps no man was ever so deeply and firmly embedded in the hearts of the people as Abraham Lincoln. . . . He merited it by his character and by his acts. His whole life was

simple, plain, honest, truthful and just, benevolent and kind." The
preacher went on to describe theaters as "cess-pools of all inquity."

Hitchcock, Henry Lawrence. *God Acknowledged in the Nation's Bereavement.*
Cleveland: Fairbanks, Benedict and Co., 1865. This sermon by a Presbyterian preacher, delivered in Hudson, Ohio, on April 19, acknowledged that God had permitted Lincoln's assassination to show the
barbarity of slavery and the need for punishing treason.

Hoffman, Eugene Augustus. *The Martyr President.* New York: C. A.
Alvord, 1865. This sermon was delivered on April 20 in the Grace
(Episcopal) Church of Brooklyn Heights. Hoffman said that God may
have taken Lincoln in order that "another may be entrusted the weighty
task of bringing order out of chaos which war has left in its track."

Homans, J. E. "Sermon." *Cincinnati Daily Commercial.* April 20, 1865. On
April 19, the rector of St. John's Episcopal Church in Cincinnati eulogized Lincoln by comparing him to Moses.

Hopkins, Thomas M. *A Discourse on the Death of Abraham Lincoln.* Bloomington, Ind., 1865. This sermon was delivered on April 19 at the
First Presbyterian Church in Bloomington. Hopkins called for a plan
of Reconstruction that would make full use of the death penalty. He
noted: "To such work our generous, forgiving President was greatly dis-
inclined. May it not, therefore, be well that the wise disposer of all
events should remove him and give the sword to others, that justice may
be done."

Hornblower, W. H. *Sermon.* Paterson, N.J.: Chiswell and Wurts, 1865.
This sermon was delivered on April 16 at the First Presbyterian Church
of Paterson.

Howlett, Thomas R. *The Dealings of God With Our Nation.* Washington,
D.C.: Gibson Bros., 1865. The theme of this sermon delivered on June
1 by the pastor of Calvary Baptist Church in Washington was that the
assassination was a new lesson in the diabolical nature of treason.

Hoyt, Wayland. "Sermon." *Cincinnati Daily Commercial.* June 2, 1865. At
the North Street Baptist Church of Cincinnati on June 1, Hoyt demonstrated an inconsistency of many Northern post-assassination sermons.
"Brand treason, own child of slavery, as the last and unpardonable
crime. Burn the gallows deep into it forever. With calm, judicial voice,
let the arch traitor and his colleagues answer for their crimes by the felon's death—yet still remembering always those great closing words—
'with malice toward none; with charity for all.' "

Hughes, D. L. "President Lincoln's Death." *Lincolniana.* 100–122. On
April 23 at the First Presbyterian Church of Des Moines, Hughes, calling attention to his text, "How are the mighty fallen" (2 Sam. 1:19),
reminded that even though Lincoln had fallen, even so was the rebellion,

slavery, and the aristocracy fallen. He lamented that Lincoln had fallen in a theater. "It is to me the only thing that tarnished his martyr-glory." Lincoln's work was done and Johnson was a fit man for the days ahead. We should all be prepared to someday meet God.

Hull, Moses. "Death of President Lincoln." *Lincolniana.* 123–33. Delivered before the Friends of Progress in Stuart's Hall in Battle Creek, Michigan, on April 19, Hull's sermon was basically a eulogy and history of Lincoln. He assured that Lincoln's "voice will ring more melodiously for freedom in the future than it ever has in the past." Hull, a Congregationalist-Presbyterian pastor, blamed the South for the assassination and called the Confederate government a "hell-born outbreak of slaveholding fiends."

Hunt, Albert S. "Sermon XVIII." *Our Martyr President.* 317–27. On April 16 this Methodist minister sought to point to a specific time of Lincoln's conversion to the Christian faith. He rejoiced that the nation lived on and urged support for the new president. He demanded justice, even death, upon the leaders of the rebellion.

Huntington, Frederick Dan. "Sermon." *Sermons Preached in Boston.* 193–96. On April 16, this Episcopalian rector declared that retribution must be left to God and the courts. He asked his listeners to heed the words of Jesus: "Father, forgive them."

Irvin, William. *A Sermon.* New York: John A. Gray and Green, 1865. This sermon was delivered on April 16 by the pastor of the Presbyterian Church in Rondout, New York.

Ives, Alfred Eaton. *Victory Turned Into Mourning.* Bangor: Wheeler and Lynde, 1865. In this sermon of April 16, delivered at Castine, Maine, Congregationalist Ives said that the assassination will mean that "more iron will enter into the nerve of every soldier, and new keenness into the edge of his sword." Ives also assured that "We had shown to the world, what had never before been known, the strength and capabilities of free government.

Jaggar, Thomas A. *A Sermon.* New York: R. C. Root, Anthony and Co., 1865. This sermon was delivered at the Anthon Memorial (Episcopal) Church of New York City on April 16.

Janeway, J. L. "Discourse." *Discourses: Memorial of Abraham Lincoln.* 1–22. On April 19, the pastor of the Presbyterian Church of Flemington, New Jersey, with words of high praise for Lincoln, commented that "above all, he was a Christian man." Janeway saw the assassination in a providential perspective but hesitated to proclaim what it meant. "I feel incompetent, brethren, to interpret God's providence. I prefer humbly to watch and wait the end, when God himself shall make plain what is now so dark and mysterious." He urged his congregation to "banish vengefull feelings," to "sustain the present magistrate," and to repress "party spirit."

Jeffery, Reuben. *The Mission of Abraham Lincoln.* Philadelphia: Bryson and Son, 1865. This sermon was delivered before the Fourth Baptist Church of Philadelphia on June 1.

Johnson, Herrick. *God's Ways Are Unsearchable.* Pittsburgh: W. G. Johnston and Co., 1865. This April 23 sermon was delivered before the congregation of the Third Presbyterian Church in Pittsburgh's Mozart Hall. Johnson noted that Lincoln's assassination "puts an eternal stigma" upon the South's cause and "sends it down to posterity loaded with infamy." He spoke of the danger of undue mercy toward Rebel leaders, but warned, "let it be justice, not vengeance."

Johnson, Samuel. *A Discourse.* Massachusetts: N.p., n.d. On April 19, Johnson, a Congregationalist from Massachusetts, stated: "He fails, the Nation's chief; but the Nation does not. It shows its mighty self-command. The wheels of State move on."

Johnson, William Melancthon. *Our Martyred President.* Troy, N.Y.: Daily and Weekly Times, 1865. This April 16 sermon by a Presbyterian minister was delivered in Stillwater, New York.

Johnston, Elias S. *Abraham Lincoln.* Harrisburg, Pa.: Theo. F. Scheffer, 1865. On June 1, this sermon was delivered at the Second English Evangelical Lutheran Church of Harrisburg. Johnston said, "It is neither wise nor safe for us to arrest the vengeance which does not belong to us, but to God."

Jordan, E. S. *Death of Abraham Lincoln.* Portland, Maine: David Tucker, 1865. On June 1, this sermon was delivered at the Congregational Church of Cumberland Centre, Maine.

Junkin, George. "Sermon." *Lincolniana.* 134–47. On June 1, Junkin, who had served as president of Washington College in Virginia, delivered this sermon in the Sixth Presbyterian Church of Philadelphia. He castigated the theater as a national sin. "Our theatrical exhibitions are a stench in the nostrils of high Heaven. These dens of pollution, these synagogues of Satan, collect in and around them the concentrated abomination of all immorality and crime." Other national sins for which the North was being punished were the failure to mention God in the Constitution; the appointment of a chaplain by Congress who denied "Christ as Mediator"; and profanity, drunkenness, gambling, sabbath-breaking, and debauchery.

Keeling, Robert James. *The Death of Moses.* Washington, D.C.: W. H. and O. H. Morrison, 1865. Keeling said of his April 23 sermon delivered at Trinity (Episcopal) Church in Washington, "It was delivered at night, to an intensely crowded audience tumultuous with excitement, and under circumstances connected with my parochial position and southern birth, that called for all the prudence and preparation possible."

Keith, Ormes B. *Address*. Philadelphia: King and Baird, 1865. This sermon was delivered on April 19 at the Church of Our Savior (Episcopal) in Jenkintown, Pa. Keith proposed that Confederate leaders should be hanged on Capitol Hill in the sight of Northern and Southern widows and orphans they had made and, once dead, "from the cannon's mouth they should be blown to the four winds of heaven."

Kennedy, Duncan. "Address." *A Tribute of Respect by the Citizens of Troy.* 136–51. On April 19, at the Second Presbyterian Church of Troy, Kennedy listed the characteristics of Lincoln as "a high measure of intellectual power" and "a well balanced character."

Kirk, Edward N. "Be Still and Know That I Am God." *Sermons Preached in Boston.* 33–47. Delivered on April 16, at the Mount Vernon Church of Boston, this Congregational minister asked that religious feeling might modify natural impulses of distress, murmurings, and vengeance. Near the end of the sermon, however, Kirk listed several debased Southern characteristics.

Krauth, Charles P. *The Two Pageants.* Pittsburgh: W. S. Haven, 1865. This sermon was delivered on June 1 at the First Evangelical Lutheran Church in Pittsburgh. Krauth emphasized that Lincoln had to die in order that people would understand that God was their only true leader.

Lamb, E. E. *Sermon on the Death of President Lincoln.* Rootstown, Ohio, 1865. In a sermon delivered on April 23 in the Congregational Church of Rootstown, Lamb said: "But yesterday the nation's heart was magnanimous—to-day vengeance has come down."

Laurie, Thomas. *Three Discourses.* Dedham, Mass.: John Cox, Jr., 1865. On April 16, 19, and 23 sermons were preached at the South Evangelical Church of West Roxbury, Massachusetts, by Laurie, who stressed the providential nature of the assassination. In the sermon on April 23, he spent about four pages with his concern about Lincoln attending a theater and why he perceived the theater to be such an evil place.

Leffingwell, C. S. *Strength in Sorrow.* Canandaigua, N.Y.: C. Jobson's Office, 1865. Delivered on June 1 at St. John's Episcopal Church in Canandaigua, the rector urged his listeners to allow the tragedy to toughen their lives.

Lincolniana. Boston: William V. Spencer, 1865. This is a collection of sermons, addresses, and essays that respond to Lincoln's assassination.

Littlejohn, Abram N. "Sermon VIII." *Our Martyr President.* 145–58. The basic theme of the sermon by this Episcopalian rector in New York City was how Lincoln met the standards of greatness.

Loring, George P. *The Present Crisis.* South Danvers, Mass.: Wizzard Office, 1865. "My friends, clemency was [Lincoln's] danger. And now that he has laid down his life, let us remember that danger and be warned by it." Great applause followed this statement.

Lothrop, Samuel K. "Sermon." *Sermons Preached in Boston.* 245–63. On April 16, this Unitarian minister from Boston urged that there be proof that Rebel leaders were behind the assassination before making accusations.

Love, William De Loss. *Smitten, But Not As Our Enemies.* Milwaukee: Daily Wisconsin, 1865. In this sermon delivered on June 1 at the Spring Congregational Church of Milwaukee, Love declared that the death of Lincoln did not compare to the losses that the South was experiencing.

Lowe, Charles. *Death of President Lincoln.* Boston: American Unitarian Association, 1865. Lowe, who was from Massachusetts, delivered this sermon on April 23 at the Unitarian Church on Archdale Street in Charleston, South Carolina. He declared that if there was to be true and lasting peace, the people of the South must give "unqualified submission and unreserved and unhesitating allegiance, with a determined purpose heartily to abide by it (for this mere sham of profession amounts to nothing), to the Constitution and Government of the United States."

Lowrie, John Marshall. *The Lessons of Our National Sorrow.* Fort Wayne, Ind.: Jenkinson and Hartman, 1865. Delivered on April 16 at the First Presbyterian Church in Fort Wayne, Lowrie declared that through the assassination, the Lord had exposed the true southern character. Emphasizing Providence, Lowrie proclaimed: "He who notices the falling sparrow has not allowed our Chief Magistrate to fall without a purpose."

Lowry, Robert. "Sermon XVII." *Our Martyr President.* 303–15. In this sermon delivered on April 16, this Episcopalian minister declared that the effect of the assassination upon the Northern populace was that "we have lost all sentiment of clemency." He demanded justice saying that there are those who are beyond the possibility of pardon.

Ludlow, James M. *Sermon Commemorative of National Events.* Albany: Weed, Parsons and Co., 1865. On April 23, at the First Presbyterian Church of Albany, the pastor declared: "That for which he labored in life, may be hastened to its accomplishment by the fact and circumstances of his death."

McAdam, Hugh P. "Discourse." *A Tribute of Respect by the Citizens of Troy.* 318–29. On June 1, at the United Presbyterian Church in Troy, McAdam drew some lessons from the assassination: by suffering, our hearts are turned to God; we are taught not to invade the sanctity of the Sabbath (some Civil War battles had been fought on the Sabbath); we have come to understand the enormity of the crime of slavery; we have learned that severe punishment needs to be dealt to traitors; "Men may pass away, but principle and truth will never decay."

McCabe, Francis S. *A Sermon.* Lafayette, Ind.: James P. Luse and Co., 1865. This sermon was delivered on April 19 at the First Presbyterian Church of Peru, Indiana.

McCarty, John W. *Lessons From the Life and Death of a Good Ruler.* Cincinnati: Jos. B. Boyd, 1865. On June 1, at Christ (Episcopal) Church in Cincinnati, McCarty declared that the assassination was the culmination of treason.

McCauley, James A. *Character and Services of Abraham Lincoln.* Baltimore: John D. Toy, 1865. On June 1 at the Eutaw, Maryland, Methodist Episcopal Church, McCauley stated: "Thenceforth two stars flamed in [Lincoln's] sky: Union—liberty conserved for those already free, and Emancipation—liberty decreed for the millions hitherto enslaved. . . . The fame of Mr. Lincoln will not be hurt—it will likely be helped—by the tragic close of his career."

McClintock, John. "Sermon VII." *Our Martyr President.* 129–44. In a sermon delivered at St. Paul's Methodist Episcopal Church in New York City on April 19, the preacher eulogized Lincoln's character and stated that there must be no place in Christian's hearts for revenge, vengeance, disorder, or mobs.

MacDonald, James M. *President Lincoln: His Figure in History.* New York: Charles Scribner and Co., 1865. This sermon was delivered on June 1 at the First Presbyterian Church of Princeton, New Jersey.

McGibbon, Andrew W. *Our Nation's Sorrow.* N.p., 1865. This sermon was delivered on April 19 before the Baptist, Methodist, Christian, and Presbyterian congregations in Berlin, Illinois, by the pastor of the Presbyterian church, who urged the congregation to pray for the inexperienced Johnson and affirmed that religion must guide the affairs of state.

Manning, James M. "Sermon." *Sermons Preached in Boston.* 59–72. At the Old South (Congregational) Church in Boston on April 16, Manning placed strong stress upon the assassination as a providential act. He paralleled Lincoln with the Dutch hero William of Orange. He suggested that Lincoln's heart may have been too tender for the stern work ahead.

Marshall, W. R. "Memorial Sermon." *Lincolniana.* 148–66. On June 1, at the First Presbyterian Church in Columbus, Ohio, Marshall emphasized three elements of Lincoln's character: his mental characteristics, his religious convictions, and his strong emotional nature.

Mather, D. D. *True Greatness.* Zanesville, Ohio: John T. Shryock, 1865. On April 19, this Methodist minister stated why and how Lincoln met the standards of greatness.

Mayo, Amory D. "Abraham Lincoln" and "The Nation's Sacrifice." *Two Discourses*. Cincinnati: Robert Clarke and Co., 1865. Both of these sermons were delivered in the Church of the Redeemer (Unitarian) in Cincinnati. "The Nation's Sacrifice" was preached on April 16, and in it the pastor declared that all shedding of blood is by God's permission. He urged his congregation not to waste time in cursing and passions for revenge. "Abraham Lincoln" was delivered on April 19, and in it Mayo stated that the reason Lincoln delayed in issuing the Emancipation Proclamation was for the education of the people.

Miner, Alonzo A. "Sermon." *Sermons Preached in Boston*. 279–91. On April 16 this Universalist minister from Boston and president of Tufts College emphasized that the assassination taught that we had trusted too much in men and have been too magnanimous toward the Rebels. He referred to the confederate government as "traitorous hordes" and "ambitious, crafty, and fiendish leaders."

Mitchell, Samuel S. *Address*. Harrisburg: Singerly and Myers, 1865. This sermon was delivered at the Presbyterian Church of Harrisburg on April 19. Mitchell stated that Lincoln was a sacrifice on the altar of liberty.

Mooar, George. *The Religion of Loyalty*. San Francisco: Towne and Bacon, 1865. In his sermon on April 23 at the First Congregational Church in Oakland, California, Mooar said that loyalty was a religious characteristic and that the war had taught Americans how important and virtuous that trait was.

Morehouse, Henry Lyman. *Evil Its Own Destroyer*. East Saginaw, Mich.: Enterprise Print, 1865. On April 19, the pastor of the First Baptist Church of East Saginaw, before a meeting of the Congregational and Baptist churches of the city, said: "We believe God has permitted [the assassination so] that the power of evil arrayed against us may be the more quickly and effectually crushed."

Morias, Sabato. *An Address*. Philadelphia: Collins, 1865. A Jewish sermon responding to the assassination of Lincoln.

Murdock, David. *Death of Abraham Lincoln*. Milford, Conn.: Northrop's Gallery of Art, 1865. This sermon was delivered on April 23 before the Congregational Church of New Milford, Connecticut. Murdock warned against a false theology that would ignore "justice" and speak "only of mercy." He speculated that leniency was Lincoln's "greatest defect" and perhaps the cause of his death.

Murray, William H. H. *Address*. New York: John F. Trow, 1865. This sermon was delivered on April 16 at the Second Congregational Church of Greenwich, Connecticut. Murray believed the plot to kill Lincoln had been hatched in the South as early as March 4, 1865.

Mussey, Charles F. *The Mighty Fallen.* Batavia, N.Y.: Daniel D. Waite, 1865. This sermon was delivered at the Presbyterian Church of Batavia on April 23.

Nadal, B. H. *National Reconstruction.* Washington, D.C.: Wm. H. Moore, 1865. This sermon was delivered at Wesley (Methodist) Chapel in Washington on June 1.

Nason, Elias. *Eulogy.* Boston: William V. Spencer, 1865. This sermon was delivered before the New England Historic-Genealogical Society on May 3. Nason, a Congregationalist, was a member of that society. He said, "let the martyr sleep. His mission is accomplished; and, because of his departure, there remains the more for us to do."

Naylor, H. R. *A Discourse.* Salem, Ind.: J. P. and T. H. Cozine, 1865. This sermon was delivered on April 19 at the Christian Church of Salem by the local Methodist minister.

Neale, Rollin H. "Sermon." *Sermons Preached in Boston.* 163–75. On April 16, this Baptist minister said that when Lincoln erred it was on the side of kindness. He suggested that Lincoln may surpass Washington in greatness and showed confidence in Andrew Johnson. He accused theatrical experience and liquor as the evils that drove Booth to his infamous deed.

Nelson, Henry A. "The Divinely Prepared Ruler" and "The Fit End of Treason." *Two Discourses.* Springfield, Ill.: Baker and Phillips, 1865. Both of these sermons were delivered on May 7, the Sunday following Lincoln's burial at Springfield, at the First Presbyterian Church by the pastor of the First Presbyterian Church in St. Louis. In the first sermon, Nelson compared Lincoln to King David and George Washington. He proclaimed that Lincoln was an honest believer even though he never joined a church. In the second sermon, Nelson spoke of the crimes and atrocities committed by the South and its leaders. He noted that there was a Christian obligation to impose justice.

Niccolls, Samuel J. *In Memoriam.* St. Louis: Sherman Spencer, 1865. This sermon was delivered on April 23 at the Second Presbyterian Church of St. Louis. Niccolls warned his listeners that they must not disconnect the assassination from its true source of slavery and rebellion. He described theaters as "schools of vice."

Nicholson, W. R. "Introduction." *Sermons Preached in Boston.* 125–26. In the introduction to the service of April 16, this rector of St. Paul's (Episcopal) Church announced that the church would go on with regular Easter worship in spite of the assassination. He did note that the assassination "is God's call to us for a yet deeper self-humilation."

Niles, Henry E. *Address.* York, Pa.: Hiram Young, 1865. This Presbyterian pastor delivered this sermon on April 19 in a community service in York.

Niles accused the South of having carved the "bones of fallen soldiers into trophies and charms." In regard to the assassination, he proclaimed: "O! what a wicked nation ours must be, when to the long catalogue of her martyred sons, must be added this illustrious name, fallen in sacrifice for popular sins. What occasion then for widespread resentence before God; and for united supplications for national forgiveness and purification."

Noble, Mason. *Sermon*. Newport: George T. Hammond, 1865. This sermon was delivered on April 19 by one of the chaplains at the United States Naval Academy.

Northrop, Henry H. *A Sermon*. Carthage, Ill.: Carthage Republican Print, 1865. This April 16 sermon by a Baptist preacher called the assassination one of the saddest moments in history. Realizing the anger in his congregation and in the nation, Northrop said: "Let us be Christians even in our wrath . . . be consistent with the religion of Jesus . . . forgive them." The sermon attempted to give evidence that Lincoln was truly a Christian.

Olssen, William W. *Sermon*. New York: C. S. Westcott and Co., 1865. In this sermon delivered on April 16 at the Church of St. James the Less (Episcopal) in Scarsdale, N.Y., Olssen declared that "Perhaps evil plottings have been now permitted to succeed because more is to be gained by the death than by the continued life of our President."

Our Martyr President, Abraham Lincoln: Voices from the Pulpit of New York and Brooklyn. New York: Tibbals and Whiting, 1865. This book contains twenty-one post-assassination sermons from New York City and Brooklyn. Most of the sermons were delivered on April 16, two days after the assassination.

Paddock, Wilbur F. *A Great Man Fallen*. Philadelphia: Sherman and Co., 1865. In this sermon delivered on April 23 at St. Andrew's Episcopal Church in Philadelphia, Paddock said that Booth was no more responsible than the pistol he held. "Let the law deal with the mere tools and agents of this awful crime according to the severity which justice demands." Lincoln's murder could only be avenged by destroying forever the spirit of slavery.

Palmer, Albert G. *A Sermon*. Wakefield, Mass.: D. Gillies, 1865. This sermon was delivered on April 16 at the Baptist Church of Stonington Borough, Connecticut. Treason and slavery were responsible for the assassination, which called for revenge—not on the people of the South, but on the slave power that is the "Antichrist." Palmer compared Israel's leniency and God's punishment of such action with the circumstances of Lincoln's assassination.

Parke, N. G. *The Assassination of the President of the United States Overruled for the Good of Our Country*. Pittston, Pa.: Gazette Office, 1865. This sermon was delivered on June 1 at the Methodist Episcopal Church of Pittston. Parke declared that God caused the assassination to show the South in its true light so that it might be properly punished.

Parker, Henry E. *Discourse.* Concord, N.H.: McFarland and Jenks, 1865. This sermon was delivered on April 16 at the South Congregational Church of Concord.

Patterson, Adoniram J. *Eulogy.* Portsmouth, N.H.: C. W. Brewster and Son, 1865. This sermon was delivered on April 19 at the Universalist Church of Portsmouth. Patterson said of Lincoln: "He was emphatically a Christian. The Christian spirit was the all-pervading spirit of his life."

Patterson, Robert M. *The Character of Abraham Lincoln.* Philadelphia: James S. Claxton, 1865. This sermon, which took the form of an obituary, was delivered on June 1 at the Great Valley Presbyterian Church of Philadelphia by the pastor.

Patton, Alfred S. *The Nation's Loss and Its Lesson.* Utica, N.Y.: Curtiss and White, 1865. In this sermon delivered on April 23 at the Tabernacle Baptist Church of Utica, Patton charged that the assassination was approved by the leading men of the South. He quoted from an advertisement from a Selma, Alabama, newspaper which offered to assassinate Lincoln, Andrew Johnson, and William Seward for fifty thousand dollars. Patton demanded "stern justice . . . hang them!" He could not understand the motives of Northern men who wanted mercy shown toward the South.

Peirce, Joseph D. *An Address.* Boston: Davis and Farmer, 1865. This sermon was delivered on April 19 at the Universalist Church of North Attleboro, Massachusetts, by the pastor.

Porter, Elbert S. "Sermon XII." *Our Martyr President.* 233–40. On April 16, this Dutch Reformed preacher maintained that high crimes awaken a corresponding indignation: this is the spirit of a just God; it is a virtue.

Potter, Henry C. "Sermon." *A Tribute of Respect by the Citizens of Troy.* 32–35. At St. John's Episcopal Church in Troy on April 16, Potter implored: "let not the notes of our mourning stifle those of gratitude and hope—gratitude and hope for him whom we have lost, and praise and thanksgiving to the Master, who, in this, as in all our sorrows, gives us, on this Easter morning, the clear and unclouded assurance of the life which is to come!"

Potter, William J. *The National Tragedy: Four Sermons.* New Bedford, Mass.: Abraham Taber and Brother, 1865. These four sermons delivered before the First Congregational society (Unitarian) of New Bedford, were titled: "The Assassination," "Discourse," "The Capacity and Historical Position of President Lincoln," and "The Dramatic Element in the Career of Abraham Lincoln." Potter asked of the assassination, "Is it possible, my friends, that we needed this awful calamity . . . to urge us to some duty that we are shrinking?" Potter called into question the stories of Lincoln claiming to become a Christian after Gettysburg. This may be the only recorded sermon that questions the veracity of those stories. Potter said: "I do not credit the account, recently published, of an interview with him by some Western clergyman, in which phrases are put into the President's mouth that sound very much like the exclamations heard in an excited meeting of revivalists."

Powell, Edward P. "Sermon, Appropriate to the Obsequies of Abraham Lincoln" and "Sermon, Appropriate to the Obsequies of Jefferson Davis, and the Southern Confederacy." *Sermons on Recent National Victories, and the National Sorrow.* Adrian, Mich.: Smith and Foster, 1865. On April 23, the pastor of the Plymouth (Congregational) Church in Adrian delivered two sermons pronouncing the demise of the confederacy: "in fact, the old giant, armless, headless, legless, a miserable truck of lies and sins and filth, only cumbers the ground till we can learn how best to bury it." Powell referred to Henry Foote as "that crafty old Mississippi rat."

Prime, George Wendell. *A Sermon.* Detroit: Advertiser and Tribune Print, 1865. In this sermon delivered in the Westminster (Presbyterian) Church of Detroit on April 16, Prime declared that Lincoln's assassination should "teach us all to know our end."

Prime, Joseph A. "Sermon." *A Tribute of Respect by the Citizens of Troy.* 151–57. On April 19 at the Liberty Street Presbyterian Church in Troy, Prime, a black preacher, preached to a black congregation, declaring, "But there is a class who feel this death more keenly than all the other classes combined. It is the colored people. None mourn or lament more sincerely than they. None feel that they have lost so true and tried a friend as the millions of bond and freedmen of the South. . . . It was slavery that killed our President, and the blood of the murdered President will cry out against slavery as long as there is a bondman to sigh for freedom."

Purinton, Jesse M. *A Discourse.* Philadelphia: J. A. Wagenseller, 1865. This sermon was delivered on June 1 at the Baptist Church of Smithfield, Pennsylvania. Purinton recalled the grief that was demonstrated upon hearing the news of the assassination. "The tidings of the President's martyrdom . . . fell like a shock upon the public ear. . . . With a partial recovery from the shock the nation awoke to mingled grief and indignation. The grief was general and heartfelt." The preacher called the Confederate government, whom he held responsible for the assassination, a "loathsome reptile."

Putnam, George. "Address." *Sermons Preached in Boston*. 309–21. Putnam declared that Lincoln was as tenderhearted as a woman, as gentle as a child. He would have forgiven his slayer. However, the assassin and the spirit which inspired him must be brought to justice. Putnam, a Unitarian, delivered this sermon before the citizens of Roxbury, Massachusetts, on April 19. He declared that what was needed was "not a better or greater man, but a sterner nature and a more iron hand than his, to do what yet remains to be done."

Quint, Alonzo H. *Three Sermons*. New Bedford, Mass.: Mercury Job Press, 1865. All three of these sermons were delivered before the North Congregational Church of New Bedford. The first sermon was preached prior to the assassination. The second sermon, "What President Lincoln Did For His Country." was delivered on the morning of April 16. Quint remarked that Lincoln took the reigns of a ruined country and made it strong. He found the country a slave state and made it free. The third sermon, "Southern Chivalry, and What the Nation Ought To Do With It," was delivered in the afternoon of the same day. It is one of the most vitriolic of all Northern sermons in its accusations toward and prescriptions for the South.

Randall, E. H. *An Address*. Montpelier, Vt.: Walton's, 1865. This Episcopalian rector's sermon was delivered before the citizens of Randolph, Vermont, on April 19. Randall declared that the assassination was the penalty for depending on armies instead of on God.

Randolph, Warren. *The Fallen Prince*. Boston: J. M. Hewes, 1865. This sermon was delivered on April 16 at the Harvard Street Baptist Church in Boston. Randolph said that those who were opposed to capital punishment were guilty of "sickly sentimentalism."

Rankin, Jeremiah E. *Moses and Joshua*. Boston: Dakin and Metcalf, 1865. In this April 19 sermon, at the Winthrop (Congregational) Church of Charlestown, Massachusetts, Rankin demanded stern justice upon Confederate leaders. He claimed that if Calhoun had been hung, the nation would have avoided many troubles. He was sure that Andrew Johnson would adequately punish the South.

Ray, Charles. *A Sermon*. Buffalo: A. M. Clapp and Co., 1865. This sermon was delivered before the United Congregations of Wyoming, New York, on April 19 by the pastor of the Presbyterian church. Ray emphasized that "God would make the wrath of men to praise Him" and that men should not put their trust in princes. He then went on to eulogize Lincoln.

Reed, James. "Address." *Sermons Preached in Boston*. 295–305. On April 19, this Swedenborgian cleric said that the Lord permitted the assassination though he did not cause it. It was permitted for the good of the country and the race. Perhaps Lincoln was not the best man to deal with the problems to come.

Reed, Seth. *A Discourse.* Boston: Geo. C. Rand and Avery, 1865. In this April 19 sermon preached in the Methodist Church of Edgartown, Massachusetts, Reed blamed the assassination on Rebel leaders. He assured his congregation by pointing to the words of the new president, who had promised, "upon the leaders [of the rebellion] . . . I would execute the penalty of the law."

Reed, Villeroy D. *The Conflict of Truth.* Camden, N.J.: S. Chew, 1865. On April 19, at the First Presbyterian Church of Camden, Reed said that slavery must be abolished and treason must be punished. He warned, however, against a vengeful spirit that "may gain mastery of our loyal hearts."

Reid, Adam. *A Discourse.* Hartford, Conn.: Case, Lockwood and Company, 1865. This sermon was delivered on June 1 at the Congregational Church of Salisbury, Connecticut. Reid emphasized the lessons to be learned from the assassination.

Relyea, Benjamin J. *The Nation's Mourning.* New York: Jno. P. Prall, 1865. This sermon was delivered on June 1 before the Congregational Church and Society of Green's Farm, Connecticut. Relyea drew a vivid picture of the nation's grief in reaction to the assassination.

Reynolds, John V. *Sermon in Commemoration of the Virtues of Abraham Lincoln.* Meadville, Pa.: R. Lyle White, 1865. This sermon was delivered on June 1 at the First Presbyterian Church of Meadville.

Rhodes, M. *A Sermon.* Sunbury, Pa.: H. B. Masser and E. Wilvert, 1865. This sermon was delivered at the Evangelical Lutheran Church of Sunbury on April 19.

Rice, Daniel. *The President's Death—Its Import.* Lafayette, Ind., 1865. In this April 19 sermon given at the Second Presbyterian Church in Lafayette, Rice affirmed that the assassination was God's way of goading the people to vengeance, and he fully expected that President Johnson would exact that vengeance. Rice foresaw some benefits stemming from the assassination. "The whole nation could have done nothing, with all her resources, that would so exalt him, or so much promote the loyalty, the unity, and so the success of the cause dearest to his heart."

Rice, Nathan L. *Sermon on the Death of Abraham Lincoln.* New York: Wm. C. Bryant and Co., 1865. This sermon was delivered on April 19 at the Fifth Avenue Presbyterian Church in New York City. Rice developed his sermon around the lessons to be learned from the assassination.

Robbins, Chandler. "Sermon." *Sermons Preached in Boston.* 215–23. On April 16, the pastor of Second (Unitarian) Church noted the mysterious ways of Providence. Lincoln died at a time good for himself—the war was over, and he was at the height of his popularity and unstained by the problems of restoring the nation after the war.

Robbins, Frank LeBaron. *A Discourse on the Death of Abraham Lincoln.* Philadelphia: Henry B. Ashmead, 1865. This sermon was delivered on April 23 at the Greenhill Presbyterian Church by the pastor, who believed that had Lincoln survived he might have been too lenient toward the leaders of the rebellion.

Robertson, J. L. *A Sermon.* Geneva, N.Y.: Wm. Johnson, 1865. The pastor of the Presbyterian Church of Geneva delivered this sermon on April 19.

Robinson, Charles. *The Martyred President.* New York: John F. Trow, 1865. At the First Presbyterian Church of Brooklyn on April 16, Robinson asked for invoking to the utmost of the law against treason. The crime of assassination was the culmination of American slavery. Southern women had become barbarians under slavery's influence. Martyrdom has great power to fix principles.

Robinson, Thomas Hastings. *The Unveiling of Divine Justice in the Great Rebellion.* Harrisburg, Pa.: Ambrose Taylor, 1865. On June 1, this Presbyterian declared that the assassination bullet was fired not at a man but at a government. "In one foul deed . . . [people] see the whole nature and disposition of slavery."

Rockwell, J. E. "Sermon XV." *Our Martyr President.* 273–87. This Lutheran minister from Brooklyn declared that the growing disposition toward leniency in the nation was a bad sign. Justice must prevail. God demands it. However, we must discriminate between the Confederate leaders and the misguided followers. Rockwell declared that the North was being punished for such sins as dishonoring the Sabbath, infidelity, profanity, licentious literature, and "disregard for sound and wholesome laws."

Rogers, A. P. "Sermon XIII." *Our Martyr President.* 241–54. This sermon, by a Dutch Reformed preacher in New York City on April 16, was on the Providence of God and the assassination as a part of that Providence. This was not to be a reason, however, for leniency toward the perpetrators of the crime. The sermon concluded with a millennial vision of the nation.

Rowland, L. S. "Death of President Lincoln." *Lincolniana.* 177–85. On April 16 at the First Parish (Congregational) Church of Bangor, Maine, Rowland drew lessons from the assassination: teach us greater dependency on God and less on man; greater awareness of the atrocious nature of the Rebel cause; the need for greater sternness in dealing with traitors. "Even if [Confederate leaders] were not cognizant of the plan of the assassination, they should be held accountable for the crime as the legitimate issue of the wicked cause for which they are contending."

Russell, Peter. *Our Great National Reproach* and *The Counsel of Ahithophel Turned Into Foolishness.* Philadelphia: King and Baird, 1865. These two sermons were delivered at the St. James (Episcopal) Church of Eckley, Pennsylvania, on April 19 and June 1. In the first sermon, Russell said that the whole world was waiting for the South's reply to the assassination. In the second sermon, he said that as yet he had heard no Christian minister in the South raise a voice against the assassination.

Sabine, William Tufnell. *The Land Mourneth.* Philadelphia: W. P. Atkinson, 1865. In this sermon of April 16, delivered at the Church of the Covenant (Episcopal), Sabine made a plea that there be no compromise with traitors and for the shackles to be smitten from every slave.

Salisbury, S. *Sermon.* Eaton, Ohio: Eaton Weekly Register, 1865. On April 19, in West Alexandria, Ohio, Salisbury, a Methodist preacher, claimed that Lincoln's blood had cemented the nation and would do much to bring just punishment upon treason.

Sample, Robert, F. *The Curtained Throne.* Philadelphia: James S. Claxton, 1865. This sermon was first delivered on April 23 in the First Presbyterian Church of Bedford, Pennsylvania, and repeated, by request on April 30.

Sanborn, Rufus S. *A Discourse.* Ripon, Wisc., 1865. At the Universalist Church of Ripon on April 23, Sanborn said: "I tell you the people and the nation are at a white heat of righteous indignation against this dastardly act which has lascerated millions of souls, as well as the national feelings, and now is the time for traitors to beware."

Searing, Edward. *President Lincoln in History.* Janesville, Wisc.: Veeder and Devereux, 1865. On June 1, at the Congregational Church of Milton, Wisconsin, Searing, who was professor of languages at Milton Academy, had high praise for Lincoln's character. "While he possessed all virtues, he was free from all vices." Searing judged that Lincoln was even greater than George Washington.

Sears, Hiram. *The People's Keepsake.* Cincinnati: Poe and Hitchcock, 1865. This Methodist minister delivered this sermon in Mount Carmel, Illinois, on April 23. The sermons, which depicted Lincoln's character, declared that the assassination would inaugurate a wiser and more stringent policy toward the Rebels.

Seiss, Joseph A. *The Assassinated President.* Philadelphia, 1865. This sermon, delivered at St. John's Lutheran Church of Philadelphia on June 1, compared Lincoln to Moses and declared that the most virtuous and useful men are the most hated and abused in their lifetimes. Seiss concluded with a challenge as to what people can make of and do with their lives.

Sermons Preached in Boston on the Death of Abraham Lincoln. Boston: J. E.
Tilton and Company, 1865. Published together with the funeral services
in the East Room of the Executive Mansion in Washington are twenty-
four post-assassination sermons from Boston pulpits, most of them delivered on April 16. Also included is a sermon by Phineas Densmore
Gurley delivered at Lincoln's funeral service on April 19.

Sheldon, C. P. "Discourse." *A Tribute of Respect by the Citizens of Troy.* 104–
16. On April 19, at the North Baptist Church of Troy, Sheldon emphasized that "The Work of Abraham Lincoln was done, and God permitted
him to be removed. But so far as human hands and passions had to do
with it . . . we can never forget nor forgive. . . . In the death of
Abraham Lincoln, the nation has lost one of the wisest, purest, best of
rulers, and even the rebellious South, one of its truest friends."

Shelton, Wallace. *Discourse upon the Death of Abraham Lincoln.* Newport,
Ky.: W. S. Bailey, 1865. Delivered on April 19 in the Zion Baptist
Church of Cincinnati by this black Baptist preacher, the sermon lamented the passing of Lincoln and held out the hope that Johnson would
be God's instrument of vengeance to deal with traitors.

Silver, Abiel. "Sermon." *Lincolniana.* 204–11. At Wilmington, Delaware,
on April 16, this Swedenborgian pastor, after emphasizing the sorrow
surrounding the assassination, dealt with the causes, lessons, and consequences of the dreaded act.

Simpson, Matthew. "Oration." *Our Martyr President.* 393–410. This
Methodist bishop and personal friend of Lincoln's delivered the sermon
at the burial service in Springfield, Illinois, on May 4. Simpson proclaimed that the suppression of rebellion without recourse to a king or
dictator was a victory for democracy. He demanded stern punishment
upon Confederate leaders but asked for mercy for the masses. The sermon concludes with a moving paragraph in which Simpson bids his president and friend farewell.

Smith, Henry. *The Religious Sentiments Proper for Our National Crisis.* Buffalo:
Matthews and Warren, 1865. This sermon was delivered at the North
Presbyterian Church of Buffalo on the evening of April 23.

Smith, Henry B. "Sermon XXI." *Our Martyr President.* 359–81. On April
23, Smith, a Presbyterian clergyman from New York City, said that
though he greatly admired Lincoln, he felt that Lincoln may have stood
between the Rebels and the justice they deserved. Throughout history
the higher must live and die for the sake of the lower. If Confederate
leaders are allowed to live, it must not be in this country.

Smith, Isaac. *An Address.* Foxborough, Mass.: W. H. Thomas, 1865. Congregationalist Smith delivered this sermon in the Town Hall of Foxborough on April 19. He eulogized Lincoln, comparing him to Moses.

Southgate, Horatio. *The Death of Lincoln.* New York: John W. Amerman, 1865. This sermon was delivered on April 23 at the Zion (Episcopal) Church of New York City. It dealt with the lessons to be learned from the assassination.

Spear, Samuel Thayer. "Sermon XVI." *Our Martyr President.* 289–301. In this sermon delivered on April 16 at the South Presbyterian Church in Brooklyn, Spear blamed the upper class of the South for the war. He singled out Davis and Lee as especially deserving of punishment. "Away with mawkish sympathy that ignores justice." Recognizing the role of Providence, Spear said, "under his providence, all men are immortal till their work is done." God had permitted the great calamity for some wise reason.

Sprague, Isaac Newton. *President Lincoln's Death.* Newark, N.J.: Daily Advertiser Office, 1865. In this sermon of June 1 at the Presbyterian Church of Caldwell, New Jersey, Sprague declared that the Negro vote might be necessary to counteract the Catholic vote in the North. He asked that "justice be done though the heavens fall."

Sprague, William B. *A Discourse.* Albany: Weed, Parsons and Co., 1865. At the Second Presbyterian Church of Albany on April 16, Sprague emphasized that the best tribute to the departed Lincoln would be an abatement of party spirit. He was concerned with the North's trust in human leadership alone. Perhaps that was one of the reasons Lincoln was taken.

Sprole, William Thomas. *Our Departed President.* Newburgh, N.Y.: Cyrus B. Martin, 1865. This nonpolitical sermon was delivered at the First Presbyterian Church of Newburgh on April 19. Sprole asked for more faith in God as the lesson to be learned from the assassination.

Starr, Frederick, Jr. *The Martyr President.* St. Louis: Sherman Spencer, 1865. This sermon was first delivered on April 16 at the First Presbyterian Church of Penn Yan, New York. It was repeated by request at the North Presbyterian Church of St. Louis, where Starr was pastor-elect, on May 14. Starr asked: "Why hath God taken away the head of the nation? a To punish us for our sins. . . . b To compel us to rely on God alone. . . . c We have not prayed enough for our President and officers and rulers. . . . d God had fulfilled the earthly service and mission of Abraham Lincoln."

Stebbins, Horatio. "Oration." *Lincolniana.* 268–73. On April 19 in San Francisco, this Unitarian minister offered a sermon of hope. "Men are mightier in death than in their life when they die exponents of principles that live forever."

Steele, Richard Holloway. *Victory and Mourning.* New Brunswick, N.J.: Terhune and Van Anglen's Press, 1865. Delivered on June 1 at the First

Reformed Dutch Church in New Brunswick, Steele asserted that God intended to show that He alone gives victory. He asked that there would be no vengeance or wrath, and urged his listeners to support Andrew Johnson. He did believe, however, that Southern chivalry was capable of such a deed.

Steiner, Lewis H. *Abraham Lincoln: The Lessons Taught by His Life and the Obligations Imposed by His Death.* Philadelphia: James P. Rogers, 1865. On April 23, at the Evangelical Reformed Church of Frederick City, Maryland, Steiner referred to the Confederate government as consisting of the "scum of cities and country towns" and added that they were "thoughtless penny-a-liners or briefless barristers."

Sterling, William. *The Martyr President.* Williamsport, Pa.: Bulletin Print, 1865. In his April 23 sermon, delivered before the Court house in Williamsport, this Presbyterian cleric spoke of the cruelties in Confederate prison camps. "Can you read the testimonies of these prisoners; can you look upon these shattered wrecks of men with their sunken eyes, and hard and shriveled and ashy skins, and wasted forms; can you behold these starved and fleshless, yet living skeletons; can you hear them tell the pitiful story of their fearful wrongs and suffering, and not feel your blood grow hot like fire in your veins? Can you read or hear their talk of woe, and not feel every nerve in your body quiver with agony and indignation?"

Stewart, Daniel. *Our National Sorrow.* Johnstown, N.Y.: J. D. Houghtaling, 1865. This printing is the substance of two sermons, delivered in the Presbyterian Church of Johnstown on April 16 and 19.

Stone, Andrew, L. "Sermon." *Sermons Preached in Boston.* 337–55. This sermon, delivered at the Park Street (Congregational) Church in Boston on April 16, declared that the spirit of slavery slew Lincoln. Stone made a listing of slavery's crimes and atrocities. Lincoln's future was safe, but the preacher wished that Lincoln had been stern enough for Reconstruction. He also wished that there had been a different setting for the assassination than the depraved theater.

Strong, Joseph D. *The Nation's Sorrow.* San Francisco: George L. Kenny and Co., 1865. In this sermon at the Larkin Street Presbyterian Church of San Francisco on April 16, Strong declared that the assassination was a punishment for the nation's sin and a way to show what needed to be stamped out. This was one of very few sermons that said that the assassination pointed to weakness in democratic government. "Our enemies will point to it as the culmination of democratic weakness and folly. It will take generations of good order and wise behavior on our part to wipe out this reproach in the estimation of mankind. . . . Even our own faith in our institutions is jostled, if not shaken."

Studley, W. S. "Sermon." *Sermons Preached in Boston.* 227–32. On April 16, at the Tremont Street Methodist Episcopal Church, Studley emphasized that Lincoln's heart was as tender as a woman's and that Johnson would be more stern than Lincoln in dealing with traitors, quoting from previous Johnson speeches to prove that point.

Sutphen, Morris C. *Discourse.* Philadelphia: Jas. B. Rodgers, 1865. In this April 16 sermon at the Spring Garden Presbyterian Church of Philadelphia, Sutphen asked, "is it not possible that the overflowing love of our late President would have made concessions to the rebels, calculated to imperil the peace and safety of the nation, and to tarnish the fair fame with which he will now descend to posterity."

Swaim, Thomas. "Discourse." *Discourses: Memorial of Abraham Lincoln.* 1–22. On April 19, the pastor of the Baptist Church of Flemington, New Jersey, quoted from the *New York Daily News* of April 17, which said, "it has rarely happened that a people have been visited with such a cause for lamentation." Swaim responded: "If this forcible expression from the leading journal of the most persistent opposition to the administration of our late president be a fair index of the feeling of the party represented, then we justly declare that a whole nation is mourning." Swaim went on to eulogize Lincoln with special praise for his part in the Emancipation Proclamation. He expressed great confidence that Andrew Johnson would administer stern justice on the South.

Swain, Leonard. *A Nation's Sorrow.* Providence, 1865. In this sermon on April 16 at the Central Congregational Church of Providence, Swain claimed that the assassination united the North in demanding harsh Reconstruction terms upon the South. "We had overpowered our enemy, and now we were to use magnanimity and mercy . . . waving all further retribution. . . . All this is brought to an end at once and forever by the dreadful event. . . . We shall hear no more talk of pardoning the leaders of the rebellion."

Sweetser, Seth. *A Commemorative Discourse on the Death of Abraham Lincoln.* Boston: John Watson and Son, 1865. On April 23 at the Central (Congregational) Church of Worcester, Mass., Sweetser said it would be presumptious to claim that Lincoln had no faults, but acknowledged that they were few. He asked for justice to be administered without hate or vindictive passion.

Swing, David. *The Death of the President.* Hamilton, Ohio: Hamilton Telegraph Print, 1865. This sermon was first delivered on April 16 at the Presbyterian Church of Hamilton, Ohio, and then repeated in Oxford, Ohio, on April 19.

Symmes, Joseph G. *To What Purpose Is This Waste?* New Brunswick, N.J.: Fredonia Book and Job Office, 1865. This sermon was delivered on June

1 before the Loyal Leagues of South Brunswick and Monroe, New Jersey, by the pastor of the First Presbyterian Church of Cranbury, New Jersey. Symmes stated that blacks may be too ignorant to vote but that opposition is unbecoming to those who have thrust the ballot into the hand of foreigners.

Talbott, J. J. "Easter Sunday." *Lincolniana*. 212–17. On April 16 at St. John's Episcopal Church in Louisville, Kentucky, Talbott made a plea for moderation in reaction to the assassination. "Never before in the history of the nation was there a time when, more than now, the spirit of moderation should rule in our hearts, dictate the words of our lips, and guide and conduct our actions. . . . no matter how our execrations may follow the assassin into the dens and caves of the earth, do not let them go beyond him. Let this be their limit. . . . Let the thoughts of your hearts be buried with the dead, and the spirit of calm moderation and kindness guide and control you in this trying hour."

Tansy, J. *From the Cabin to the White House*. Evansville, Ind.: Evansville Journal Co., 1865. This Methodist pastor delivered the sermon at New Harmony, Indiana, on April 19.

Taylor, Archibald Alexander Edward. *Our Fallen Leader*. Philadelphia: James S. Claxton, 1865. This sermon on June 1 at the Bridge Street Presbyterian Church in Georgetown, is non-vindictive and non-political in nature. The theme is that God wanted us to learn that no mere man who ever lived was essential to his purposes.

Thayer, Loren. *The Assassination*. Boston: T. R. Marvin and Son, 1865. In this June 1 sermon delivered at the Presbyterian Church of Windham, New Hampshire, Thayer declared that it was better to be Lincoln than Jefferson Davis, to be the murdered than the murderer.

Thomas, Arthur G. *Our National Unity Perfected in the Martyrdom of Our President*. Philadelphia: Smith, English and Co., 1865. This sermon was delivered by the army chaplain at the Filbert Street U.S. General Hospital in Philadelphia on April 19.

Thomas, Jacob. "Sermon." *A Tribute of Respect by the Citizens of Troy*. 43–47. On April 16, at the African Methodist Episcopal Zion Church in Troy, Thomas, a black pastor, spoke of the special bereavement felt by his people. "We, as a people, feel more than all others that we are bereaved. We had learned to love Mr. Lincoln as we have never loved man before. We idolized his very name. We looked up to him as our saviour, our deliverer. . . . The interest he manifested in behalf of the oppressed, the weak and those who had none to help them, had won for him a large place in our heart. It was something so new to us to see such sentiments manifested by the chief majestrate . . . that we could not help but love him."

Thomas, Jesse Burgess. *Light Out of Darkness.* New York: R. C. Root, Anthony and Co., 1865. This sermon was delivered at the Pierrepont Street Baptist Church in Brooklyn on April 16 and offered hope in times of despair, discouragement, and grief.

Thompson, Henry Post. *In Memoriam.* New York: John F. Trow, 1865. This sermon was delivered on April 16 at the Reformed Protestant Dutch Church of Peapack, New Jersey.

Thompson, J. Renwick. *The National Bereavement.* Newburgh, N.Y.: R. H. Bloomer and Son, 1865. This sermon was delivered on April 23 at the Second Reformed Presbyterian Church in Newburgh.

Thompson, John C. *In Memoriam.* Philadelphia: Stein and Jones, 1865. In this sermon delivered on June 1 in the Presbyterian Church of Pottstown, Pennsylvania, Thompson said: "No man in all the land so well personified the spirit of the nation, or could have furnished a more striking and perfect illustration of what man, with no antecedents but those of his inherent worth, may become under the benign influence of American Institutions than did Abraham Lincoln."

Thompson, Joseph P. "Sermon X." *Our Martyr President.* 173–217. On April 30, this Congregationalist minister from New York City said that it was not greatness but grandeur that characterized Lincoln. The sermon emphasized the mental and moral traits that dominated Lincoln's character. Thompson noted that a star of first magnitude had fallen but the pole remained unchanged.

Timlow, Heman R. *A Discourse.* Rhinebeck, N.Y., 1865. At a public gathering at Rhinebeck on April 19, this Dutch Reformed minister urged the people to curb their vengeful emotions.

Todd, John E. "President Lincoln." *Sermons Preached in Boston.* 75–87. This sermon by the pastor of the Central Congregational Church dealt with the emotions and passions of the hour—horror, grief, rage, and anxiety. Of Lincoln, he said, "He was, to all appearance, a Christian man, and in the sense in which we understand the term."

Tousey, Thomas. *Discourse.* Rochester, N.Y.: C. D. Tracy and Co., 1865. This sermon was delivered on April 19 at the Presbyterian Church of Palmyra, New York, by the Methodist pastor from the same city. Shall murderers and traitors be welcomed back to the privileges and immunities of citizenship?

Tribute of Respect by the Citizens of Troy, A. Troy: Young and Benson, 1865. This book contains many post-assassination sermons delivered by ministers from several denominations in Troy, N.Y.

Tucker, Joshua T. *A Discourse.* Holliston, Mass.: Plimpton and Clark, 1865. On June 1 at the First Parish (Congregational) Church of Holliston, Tucker said that though Lincoln prevented the assassination of the nation he could not prevent his own. Rebellion was a crime of high treason and the leaders of the Confederacy must die.

Tustin, Josiah P. *Fast Day Sermon.* Grand Rapids, Mich.: Daily Eagle Office, 1865. This sermon was delivered on June 1 at St. Mark's (Episcopal) Church in Grand Rapids. Tustin affirmed: "We must follow, and not anticipate, and not force the openings of God's will."

Twombly, A. S. *The Assassination of Abraham Lincoln.* Albany: J. Munsell, 1865. On April 16, at the State Street Presbyterian Church of Albany, Twombly declared that God had some hidden reason for the assassination. He noted what several other preachers had, which was the opinion that Lincoln was not converted to Christianity until after visiting Gettysburg.

Tyler, George P. *The Successful Life.* Brattleboro, Vt.: Vermont Record Office, 1865. This sermon was delivered on April 19 at the Center (Congregational) Church of Brattleboro. Using Lincoln at his example, Tyler spoke of the qualities that contribute to a successful life.

Tyng, Stephen H. "Sermon IV." *Our Martyr President.* 65–84. On April 20 this Episcopalian rector from New York City said that the Southern rebellion has been a war against God. God gave victory to the North. Tyng appealed for conciliation between the two sections of the nation.

Umsted, Justus T. *A Nation Humbled and Exalted.* West Chester, Pa.: Republican and Democrat Office, 1865. This sermon was delivered on June 1 at the Fagg's Manor Presbyterian Church in West Chester.

Vincent, Marvin R. *A Sermon on the Assassination of Abraham Lincoln.* Troy, N.Y.: A. W. Scribner, 1865. In this sermon delivered at the First Presbyterian Church of Troy on April 23, Vincent proclaimed that Lincoln's work was done. Reconstruction would be administered by another more fit for the task; Lincoln would have been too lenient toward traitors. "If it be that the South is avenged in his death, she will find it to be a vengeance that will recoil upon her own head; for in him she has lost her best friend, and however little we could spare him, she could afford it still less." Vincent pointed out that Northern skirts were not clear of the President's blood either.

Walden, Treadwell. *The National Sacrifice.* Philadelphia: Sherman and Co., 1865. This Episcopalian rector charged the South with a long list of abuses and atrocities.

———. *Two Addresses.* Philadelphia: Sherman and Co., 1865. These two sermons, both of which address themselves to the assassination, were delivered on April 16 and 19. In the sermon of the 19th, Walden stated: "Not only must the man be avenged, but the PRESIDENT. Avenge does not mean revenge. Avengement is justice done, the right vindicated."

Wallace, Charles Clark. *A Prince and a Great Man Fallen.* Placerville, Calif.: Tri-Weekly News, 1865. This Presbyterian minister declared in this sermon delivered at Placerville on April 19 that there was evidence that Lincoln was converted after visiting Gettysburg.

Watson, Benjamin. "National Humiliation." *Lincolniana.* 218–30. In this June 1 address at the Church of the Atonement (Episcopal) in Philadelphia, Watson declared that the assassination proved the strength of the republican form of government as contrasted to the "decadent European governments."

Webb, Edwin B. "Sermon." *Sermons Preached in Boston.* 145–60. At the Shawmut Congregational Church of Boston on April 16, Webb declared the lessons of the assassination are that we must submit to Providence and execute justice in the land. He challenged Andrew Johnson to "Make the halter certain to [those] who are guilty of perjury and treason . . . and we will stand behind you, Andrew Johnson."

Welles, Theodore Wyckoff. *Victory Turned to Mourning.* Jersey City, N.J.: Daily Times Office, 1865. This sermon was delivered on April 23 at the Reformed Dutch Church in Bayonne, N.J.

Wentworth, Erastus. "The Nation's Sorrow." *A Tribute of Respect by the Citizens of Troy.* 223–29. On April 23, at the State Street Methodist Episcopal Church in Troy, Wentworth spoke of the unity the assassination had accomplished. "His sudden and tragical death has inspired the nation with mutual forbearance, sympathy, unity, fraternity. . . . Opposing parties shake hands over the coffin of their common father, and agree to bury past animosities and to stand nobly by his successor in this hour of trial."

Wentworth, J. B. *A Discourse on the Death of President Lincoln.* Buffalo: Matthews and Warren, 1865. In this sermon delivered at St. Mark's Methodist Episcopal Church and repeated at the Lafayette Presbyterian Church on April 23, Wentworth outlined the benefits of the assassination. We have learned the evil nature of rebellion; he spoke at length of the savagery and atrocities of the slave society. A Union has been forged in opposing treason and sympathizing with the government; Copperheads must not be allowed into government. There had been a reawakening of a moral sense; we had been too ready to forgive and reconcile. Davis, Lee, Stephens, and the Copperheads were all deserving of harsh justice.

White, Erskine N. *The Personal Influence of Abraham Lincoln.* New York: John A. Gray and Green, 1865. This sermon was delivered at the Presbyterian Church of New Rochelle, New York, on June 1.

White, Pliny H. *A Sermon Occasioned by the Assassination of Abraham Lincoln.* Brattleboro, Vt.: Vermont Record Office, 1865. On April 23, this acting pastor of the Congregational Church of Battleboro declared that "mercy to the guilty is cruelty to the innocent." He called for death upon traitors and Rebels; if John C. Calhoun, and others like him, had been hanged, there would have been no secession. "Abraham Lincoln was the choice of the people, Andrew Johnson was the choice of God."

Williams, Robert H. *God's Chosen Ruler.* Frederick, Md.: Schley, Keefer and Co., 1865. This sermon was delivered on June 1 at the Presbyterian Church of Frederick.

———. *A Time To Weep.* Frederick, Md: Schley, Keefer and Co., 1865. This sermon was delivered on April 19 at the Presbyterian Church in Frederick. Williams attempted to discount any argument that the South had nothing to do with the assassination. "No one can deny that the murderer was prompted by the same spirit, which raised and held together the armies of the rebellion. . . . It was a sly, miserable emissary of the rebellion who did the guilty deed. It was a plotting, cunning wretch, deeply in sympathy with the rebellion, who sought the President's life."

Williams, William R. "Sermon I." *Our Martyr President.* 1–32. On April 19 the pastor of the Amity (Baptist) Church in New York City declared that though God at times seems to hide Himself, He continues to rule and work through unseemly events to bring about His purposes. He compared Lincoln to William of Orange and emphasized that the assassination had assured emancipation forever.

Wilson, William T. *The Death of President Lincoln.* Albany: Weed, Parsons and Co., 1865. This moderate sermon was delivered on April 19 at St. Peter's Episcopal Church in Albany. Wilson stated that the Confederates were desperate but gallant Rebels. No Southern leader could have incited Lincoln's assassination. The preacher cautioned against vengeance. Rage was cruel and impotent. The possibilities of murder lie within every heart. Lincoln would not show revenge.

Windsor, John H. *The Surety of the Upright.* Biddeford, Maine: Office of the Union and Journal, 1865. On June 1 at the First Parish Meeting House (Congregational) in Saco, Maine, the pastor declared that it was the duty of the American nation to show the civilized world that treason is a crime.

Windsor, William. *Justice and Mercy.* Davenport, Iowa: Gazette, 1865. This sermon was delivered on June 1 at the Methodist Episcopal Church in Davenport by the pastor of the Edwards Congregational Church.

Woodbury, Augustus. *A Sketch of the Character of Abraham Lincoln.* Providence: Sidney S. Rider, 1865. On June 1 at the Westminster (Unitarian) Church of Providence, Woodbury made a statement at variance with many, if not most, Northern clergymen. "I do not agree with those who complacently say, that we needed a sterner and stronger hand than his to perform the labor of reconstruction and the necessary acts of justice."

————. *The Son of God Calleth the Dead to Life.* Providence: Sidney S. Rider and Brother, 1865. This sermon, delivered in the Westminster Congregational Church of Providence (Unitarian) on April 16, is an example of a pastor using his prepared Easter sermon and inserting the assassination event into it. The sermon concluded with a call for a national resurrection.

Wortman, Denis. *A Discourse on the Death of Abraham Lincoln.* Albany: Weed, Parsons and Co., 1865. At the First Reformed Dutch Church of Schenectady on April 16, the pastor-elect said that "God . . . had a special work for our late President to do. That work is done. He has another work now perhaps, and for that other work appoints another man." And he called for stern justice upon the South: we "cannot be as lenient as we hoped to be."

Yard, Robert Boyd. *The Providential Significance of the Death of Abraham Lincoln.* Newark, N.J.: H. Harris, 1865. This sermon was delivered on June 1 at the Central Methodist Episcopal Church of Newark by the pastor of the Clinton Street Methodist Episcopal Church. It was mostly a sermon that eulogized Lincoln and directed bitter attacks on the South. The assassination was necessary in order to bring unity to the North.

Yourtee, Samuel L. *A Sermon.* Springfield, Ohio: News and Republic, 1865. This sermon was delivered on April 19 at the Central Methodist Episcopal Church of Springfield. Yourtee charged that the plot to kill Lincoln originated in the councils of the Knights of the Golden Circle.

ADDITIONAL REFERENCES

Albright, Raymond W. *Focus on Infinity.* New York: Macmillan, 1961.

Andrews, Rena Mazyck. "Archbishop Hughes and the Civil War." Master's thesis, University of Chicago, 1935.

Barnes, Albert. *The Church and Slavery.* Philadelphia: Parry and McMillan, 1857.

Barnes, Gilbert. *The Antislavery Impulse, 1830–1844.* Introduction by William G. McLoughlin. 1933. New York: Harcourt Brace and World, 1964.

Bartlett, Irving H. *The American Mind in the Mid-Nineteenth Century.* 2d ed. Arlington Heights, Ill.: Harlan Davidson, 1982.

Beecher, Henry Ward. *Freedom and War.* Boston: Ticknor and Fields, 1863.

————. *Norwood.* New York: Charles Scribner, 1868.

————. *Patriotic Addresses.* New York: Fords, Howard and Hulbert, 1891.

————. *Sermons.* 2 vols. New York: Harper and Bros., 1868.

Beringer, Richard E., Herman Hattaway, Archer Jones, and William N. Still, Jr. *Why the South Lost the Civil War.* Athens, Ga.: University of Georgia Press, 1986.

Browning, Orville Hickman. *The Diary of Orville Hickman Browning.* Edited by James G. Randall and Theodore Pease. Springfield, Ill.: Jefferson Printing and Stationery Co., 1933.

Brownlow, Paul C. "The Northern Protestant Pulpit and Andrew Johnson." *The Southern Speech Communication Journal* 39 (Spring 1974): 248–59.

Bushnell, Horace. *The Northern Iron.* Hartford, Conn.: Hunt and Son, 1854.

Canfield, Sherman. *The American Crisis.* Syracuse: Journal Book and Job Office, 1865.

Chapman, Stuart W. "The Protestant Campaign for the Union." Ph.D. diss., Yale University, 1939.

Chesebrough, David B. *"God Ordained This War:" Sermons on the Sectional Crisis, 1830–1865.* Columbia: University of South Carolina Press, 1991.

Chesebrough, David B., and Lawrence W. McBride. "Sermons as Historical Documents: Henry Ward Beecher and the Civil War." *The History Teacher* 23 (May 1990): 275–91.

Clark, Frederick G. *Gold in the Fire: Our National Position.* New York: John N. Duychinck, 1862.

Davis, Burke. *The Long Surrender.* New York: Vintage Books, 1989.

Dunham, Chester Forrester. *The Attitude of the Northern Clergy Toward the South 1860–1865.* Philadelphia: Porcupine Press, 1974.

Dwinell, Israel E. *Hope for our Country.* Salem, Mass.: Charles W. Swasey, 1862.

Fish, Henry Clay. *The Valley of Achor a Door of Hope; or, The Grand Issues of the War.* New York: Sheldon and Co., 1863.

Foster, Eden B. *Two Discourses.* Lowell, Mass.: J. J. Judkins, 1854.

Frederickson, George M. *The Inner Civil War: Northern Intellectuals and the Crisis of the Union.* New York: Harper and Row, 1965.

Fuller, Richard. *Address Before the American Colonization Society.* Baltimore: Office of the Trust Union, 1851.

Fuller, Richard, and Francis Wayland. Domestic Slavery Considered as a Scriptural Institution. New York: Lewis Colby, 1845.

Gladden, Washington. *Recollections.* Boston: Houghton Mifflin, 1909.

Haven, Gilbert. "Three Summers of War." *National Sermons.* Boston: Lee and Shepard, 1869.

Herndon, William H. *Herndon's Lincoln: The True Story of a Great Life.* 3 vols. Springfield, Ill.: The Herndon's Lincoln Publishing Co., 1921.

Hibben, Paxton. *Henry Ward Beecher: An American Portrait*. Foreword by Sinclair Lewis. 1942. New York: Beekman Publishers. 1974.

Holland, DeWitte, ed. *Sermons in American History*. Nashville: Abingdon Press, 1971.

Howard, Victor B. *Religion and the Radical Republican Movement, 1860–1870*. Lexington: University Press of Kentucky, 1990.

Jones, Edgar DeWitt. *Lincoln and the Preachers*. New York: Harper and Brothers, 1948.

Lanphear, O. T. *Peace by Power*. New Haven, Conn.: J. H. Benham, 1864.

Lewis, Lloyd. *Myths After Lincoln*. New York: Harcourt, Brace and Co., 1929.

McKivigan, John R. *The War Against Proslavery Religion: Abolitionism and the Northern Churches, 1830–1865*. Ithaca: Cornell University Press, 1984.

McLoughlin, William G. *The Meaning of Henry Ward Beecher*. New York: Alfred A. Knopf, 1970.

Moorhead, James H. *American Apocalypse: Yankee Protestants and the Civil War, 1860–1869*. New Haven Conn.: Yale University Press, 1978.

Oates, Stephen B. *With Malice Toward None: The Life of Abraham Lincoln*. New York: Harper and Row, 1977.

Parker, Theodore. *Centenary Edition to the Works of Theodore Parker*. 15 vols. Boston: American Unitarian Association, 1907.

Potts, William D. *Freemen's Guide to the Polls and A Solemn Appeal to American Patriots*. New York, 1864.

Randall, James Garfield. *Lincoln the President*. 4 vols. New York: Dodd, Mead and Co., 1952.

Rankin, Jeremiah E. *The Battle Not Man's, But God's*. Lowell, Mass.: Stone and Huse, 1863.

Records of the American Catholic Historical Society. Vol. 34. No. 4. 1865. Philadelphia.

Robinson, James T. *National Anniversary Address*. North Adams, Mass.: W. H. Phillips, 1865.

Silver, James W. *Confederate Morale and Church Propaganda*. New York: W. W. Norton, 1957.

Stewart, Charles J. "Lincoln's Assassination and the Protestant Clergy of the North." *Journal of the Illinois State Historical Society* 54 (Autumn 1961): 268–93.

———. "The Pulpit and the Assassination of Lincoln." *Quarterly Journal of Speech* 50 (Oct. 1964): 299–307.

———. "A Rhetorical Study of the Reaction of the Protestant Pulpit in the North to Lincoln's Assassination." Ph.D. diss. University of Illinois, 1963.

Strong, George Templeton. *The Diary of George Templeton Strong.* Edited by Allan Nevins and Milton Thomas. 4 vols. New York: McMillan, 1952.

Sunderland, Byron. *The Crisis of the Times.* Washington, D.C.: National Banner Press, 1863.

Sweet, William Warren. *The Methodist Episcopal Church and the Civil War.* Cincinnati: Methodist Book Concern, 1912.

Terrible Tragedy at Washington, The: Assassination of President Lincoln. Philadelphia: Barclay, 1865.

Thomas, Benjamin P. *Abraham Lincoln.* New York: Alfred A. Knopf, 1952.

Tocqueville, Alexis de. *Democracy in America.* Edited by Phillips Bradley. New York: Alfred A. Knopf, 1966.

Turner, Thomas Reed. *Beware the People Weeping: Public Opinion and the Assassination of Abraham Lincoln.* Baton Rouge: Louisiana State University Press, 1982.

Wilson, Charles Reagan. *Baptized in Blood: The Religion of the Lost Cause 1865–1920.* Athens: University of Georgia Press, 1980.

Index

"No Sorrow like Our Sorrow"
was composed in 10½-point Garamond number 3 leaded 1½ points
by BookMasters, Inc.;
the text was printed by sheetfed offset
on 60-pound acid-free Glatfelter Natural stock
with halftones printed on 70-pound enamel stock,
notch bound over binder's boards in Holliston Kingston Natural cloth,
and wrapped with dustjackets printed in two colors
on 100-pound enamel stock and film laminated
by Thomson-Shore, Inc.;
designed by Diana Gordy;
and published by
THE KENT STATE UNIVERSITY PRESS
Kent, Ohio 44242